American Public Memory
and the Holocaust

American Public Memory and the Holocaust

Performing Gender, Shifting Orientations

Lisa A. Costello

LEXINGTON BOOKS
Lanham • Boulder • New York •London

Published by Lexington Books
An imprint of The Rowman & Littlefield Publishing Group, Inc.
4501 Forbes Blvd., Ste. 200, Lanham, MD 20706
www.rowman.com

6 Tinworth Street, London SE11 5AL, United Kingdom

Copyright © 2020 The Rowman & Littlefield Publishing Group, Inc.

All rights reserved. No part of this book may be reproduced in any form or by any electronic or mechanical means, including information storage and retrieval systems, without written permission from the publisher, except by a reviewer who may quote passages in a review.

British Library Cataloguing in Publication Information Available

Library of Congress Control Number: 2019950376

ISBN: 978-1-7936-0015-8 (cloth : alk. paper)
ISBN: 978-1-7936-0017-2 (pbk. : alk. paper)
ISBN: 978-1-7936-0016-5 (electronic)

Contents

List of Figures   vii

Acknowledgments   ix

Introduction   1

1   Claude Lanzmann's *Shoah* and the Opening of Testimony Archives: Gender and Performance in Public Memory   23

2   *Schindler's List* and its "After-Affect": *Son of Saul*, *Spielberg's List*, and the USC Shoah Foundation Visual History Archive   51

3   Is It Happening Again? How Women's Deferred Memories Perform Holocaust Public Memory: Ruth Klüger and the Levys   87

4   "Next Generation" Texts: Reclaiming the Body; Reclaiming Auschwitz   121

5   Performing Gender in Local Holocaust Museums: Memorial Spaces and Community Places   151

Conclusion   185

References   193

Index   209

About the Author   219

List of Figures

Figure 1.1: Ruth Elias composite scene openings (USHMM website, *Shoah* Outtakes).   38

Figure 1.2: Screenshot of Filip Mueller in *Shoah* (Lanzmann).   42

Figure 2.1: Screenshot of Saul washing the boy's body tenderly in *Son of Saul* (Nemes).   74

Figure 4.1: Screenshot of Adolek posing in front of crematory ovens (Broder).   127

Figure 4.2: Screenshot of one of the opening shots from *Dancing in Auschwitz* (Korman).   130

Figure 4.3: Screenshot of Vera Rosenzweig: "It's cool" in *Numbered* (Doron and Sinai).   135

Figure 4.4: Screenshot of Helen Rabinowitz with her two tattoos in *Numbered* (Doron and Sinai).   137

Figure 4.5: Screenshot of Grandfather Abramo and grandson Ayal in *Numbered* (Doron and Sinai).   142

Figure 5.1: Dallas Holocaust Museum, outside view (Costello).   160

Figure 5.2: Holocaust Museum Houston, outside view (Costello).   160

Figure 5.3: Florida Holocaust Museum, outside view (Costello).   161

Figure 5.4: Los Angeles Museum of the Holocaust, outside view (Costello).   162

Figure 5.5: DHM and Anne Frank image in entry (Costello).   166

Figure 5.6: HMH and Anne Frank image (Costello).   167

Figure 5.7: LAMOTH and Anne Frank images (Costello).   168

Figure 5.8: FHM without Anne Frank image but with Anne Frank story (Costello).   169

Acknowledgments

This book is the culmination of several years of study. I am grateful to Georgia Southern University for Educational Leave and the College of Arts and Humanities' Seed Grant in Spring 2015, which allowed me to jump-start this research and visit many of the museums I include in my final chapter.

I am indebted to the United States Holocaust Memorial Museum and the Center for Advanced Holocaust Studies and the opportunities provided by the Silberman Fellowship in 2012. The interdisciplinary seminar on Teaching Gender and the Holocaust has been a guide for my own interdisciplinary work. I have appreciated the accommodations made for my visits by the busy staff at the Holocaust Museums in Dallas, Texas; Houston, Texas; Los Angeles, California; and St. Petersburg, Florida.

My mother has been a champion for my life as a writer and an academic and was patient with the winding paths that got me there. Thank you to my sister, Jeanne, and my dedicated writing group members, Dr. Doreen Piano and Dr. Laura Carroll, who read multiple revisions of these chapters and provided crucial insights.

I thank also my children for being part of the strong, smart "next generation" for whom I write and hope for the future.

I thank the editors, readers, and staff at Lexington Press for their vision for and commitment to this project.

I could never have accomplished any of this work without the support and love of my partner, Richard M. Houser, to whom I dedicate this text. You bring joy and optimism to the world every day, and your incisive readings and revisions of versions of this text over the years helped me bring it together, finally. You never lost hope in me. You never let us lose hope together.

Lastly, I thank all the survivors and their descendants over the last several decades, who have shared their stories. Your bravery and insistence that we remember, remind us that we are *all* responsible for making the world a better place. We had better get to it.

Introduction

After all these years of doing research on the Holocaust,[1] I still mistype the word—almost every time. Is this an unconscious reminder of what I undertake every time I sit in front of my computer to write, to interpret, and to inadvertently impose my invisible or implicit biases on an event that evades understanding even today? As an American woman of Polish and Irish descent, several times removed from my distant Jewish heritage, raised Ecumenical by my mother and Catholic by my father, I know that my positionality as an author writing about the Holocaust might seem inappropriate, and yet I am compelled by it. I have been compelled since that first historical fiction book set in World War Two that I read as a fourteen-year-old: *QBVII* by Leon Uris. Did I know the true history and what was missing from the text? I did not. What I did sense immediately, however, was that the subject I was reading about—the Nuremberg trials—was a big deal—a world-changing deal; and I had known nothing about it up until that point. I understood, with the muddy clarity of a rising teenager, there was a lot of history I was missing in my education; it was at this precise point that my journey of knowledge seeking about the Holocaust began in earnest. I do not believe that writing about a traumatic history requires being a full-fledged member of that group, but it certainly requires self-reflection and caution and thoughtfulness, which I have attempted to enact at every turn in this book, my labor of love and remembrance. As Toporek has asserted, "The Holocaust has profound and particular power for those of us who grew up in its shadow, but that is where its particularity ends. As much as it affects us as Jews, it is not a Jewish story; it is a human experience" (2014, 10). The Holocaust is important not just for Jewish people but for *all* people. It is a human experience. Audiences need to reorient themselves to the stories of others beyond the group with whom they most readily identify. Helping audiences understand how Americans come to and continually revisit the Holocaust in public memory and why is the work of *American Public Memory and the Holocaust: Performing Gender, Shifting Orientations*.

My work fills a gap in scholarship because it examines how gender is performed in public memory processes to reengage, shift, or "queer" audience orientations (I will explain how I am using this term in a moment). This book examines non-binary, dialogic, and contra-historical perspectives on the Holocaust that take up the Jewish perspective of both those who lived *through* the event and those who are living *with* the event through memory rather than through direct experience. These new perspectives perform gender and memory both by adding the missing voices of women and by challenging the binary construction of gender representations. New perspectives also come with the analysis of new forms such as digital archives, YouTube videos, hybrid memoirs, and museums and how they engage with the old forms. This juxtaposition of old and new revitalizes the memorial process to engage an intergenerational conversation. What I call the "performance of public memory" marks a *kairotic* force in Holocaust public memory production by making the processes visible now and for the future. This book can help us understand how memorial processes stay relevant—it involves a reorientation of the self in relation to others—which are affective connections in the present we sorely need.

American audiences are directed toward Holocaust memory artifacts that record and memorialize from particular, and now somewhat "familiar," perspectives (think about the name recognition of Anne Frank or Elie Wiesel or the United States Holocaust Memorial Museum). But what is happening now around public memory and the Holocaust is increasingly centered on a visual culture from a range of perspectives: primary memory witnesses, the second generation, third and fourth generation (or "next generation") texts,[2] and localized narratives rather than national. These newer artifacts include new forms, as I note above, and this book fills a special niche because these newer genres and perspectives have not been examined in terms of gender, public memory, and performance, nor have they been considered part of "traditionally" archival material. By investigating newer public memory processes as performative, rhetorical (*kairotic*), and gendered, they become more visible and allow audiences to shift their orientations to the past. This creates a strong "turn" toward a plurality of voices and resists public memory's claim to neutrality about gender and power relations, inviting broader audiences into these processes to enter into relationships that are affective.

Affect changes the orientations of audiences productively. Sara Ahmed suggests strange and familiar objects "move us 'toward' and 'away' from such objects" (2006, 2). Audiences experience orientation (the familiar), then disorientation (the unfamiliar), and finally reorientation so that they reposition themselves to open to new knowledge and memories about the Holocaust.[3] This becomes "queer orientations" that allow openings for dialogue as they also create affective, shared communities of witness (2015, 94). For Ahmed, the discussion of queering centers around sexuality and difference. My focus in this text is on gender representation and difference; thus, I will not use the term "queer" for clarity and propose instead that this same process—orientation, disorientation, and reorientation—can apply to gender difference and representations of non-binary characteristics. I will call this the "shifting" of orientations, and it also involves groups of people who connect as a result of this orientation process and its ability to open us to affect.

The process of orientations, as Ahmed describes it, involves communities of shared witness grappling with affect; in this book, we can apply that concept of shared witnessing to a variety of affects as I do with her concept of wonder, for example. Ahmed's point is that the "stickiness" of affect (92) is in relationship with the shared witnessing of the affect at hand (and it importantly does not require that people be in the same place at the same moment). Affect is the end result of engagement; it is not synonymous with emotion. Ahmed argues that "truths" are only realized through emotion and by what "moves" us, by how "sticky with affect" something is (2015, 11). I conflate Ahmed's sticky affect with her concept of orientations because, as she says, we can make "the concept itself the site of an encounter" (2006, 5). Affect, witnessing, and orientation are sites of encounter that involve relationships to others and to objects. Affect comes from the productive relations we have with others. We can work together to negotiate the meaning in public memory artifacts through affect and orientation: turning toward instead of away.

Public memory work around the Holocaust is about memorializing those gone, but it is also very much about making our world a better place now; this is how memory might perform. Cynics might say this is a false sense of hope or optimism, but this book's argument is that affect that sparks hope or wonder might result in turning toward instead of away from each other. It takes a lot of work to memorialize; audiences must be both outward and communal and inward and reflective. Will we choose to orient ourselves toward action and connection, or allow ourselves to turn away and forget? Before explaining the theoretical approach for this text, however, I must first address the challenges of representing the Holocaust.

THE LIMITS OF HOLOCAUST REPRESENTATION

Although Saul Friedlander called the Holocaust an event "at the limits" of representation (1992, 3), the institutionalization of this memory continues in a number of genres, from testimony and memoir to literature and film and in a number of fields including history, literature, gender studies, and visual rhetoric.[4] Much of this work comes from first-generation eyewitnesses, but increasingly as time passes, the memory work comes from second, third, and fourth generations. Marianne Hirsch and Leo Spitzer work with the material traces of memory as they apply to intergenerational memory transmission and the Holocaust. In their article on testimonial objects, they suggest that physical "remnants carry memory traces from the past, to be sure, but they also embody the very process of its transmission. Now, at a moment in Holocaust studies when, with the passing of the first generation, we increasingly have to rely on the testimonies and representations of members of the second and third generations" (2007, 354–355). Lawrence Langer agrees when he says, "as the event recedes in time, it grows more and more difficult to recapture the way it was for those who faced it: everything has come to depend on who tells the tale, and how" (2006, xi).

Discussion about the Holocaust, however, has not always been present in American society. We have a tendency to avoid traumatic memories that implicate us, thus it can disappear again, like many other memories of trauma in American history.[5] Prior to 1950, the term "Holocaust," simply did not exist (Douglass and Vogler 2003, 21). Historian Raul Hilberg's *The Destruction of the European Jews* went years without a publisher. "Auschwitz" was listed in the 1969 American Heritage Dictionary as the German word for "Oświęcim"; the entries for Majdanek or Treblinka as death camps are absent (21).

While there was an initial silence about the Holocaust following the Second World War, a resurgent interest about the Holocaust has emerged in the last thirty years, especially in the United States (Cole 2000; Finkelstein 2000; Novick 1999; Young 1988).[6] Such resurgent interest is attributed to a myriad of issues including: the persistence of Holocaust denial,[7] the preservation of the State of Israel's existence and sovereignty, the tendency toward historical amnesia that goes hand-in-hand with nationalism,[8] the growing generational and temporal gap between survivors and non-survivors, and finally the increasing loss of survivor populations who can speak about this event as eyewitnesses.[9] Evidence of this surge of interest is revealed in the appearance of new Holocaust memoirs, the recovery and translation of other memoirs and diaries, the building of museums and memorials, and the burgeoning scholarship on this topic.

Though by 2002 "studying the Holocaust [was] recommended or mandated in public schools in at least seventeen states, prominent in all entertainment media, [and] the theme of many museums" (Douglass and Vogler 2003, 21), this does not mean that memories of this history do not fade. Indeed many public memory scholars have focused on public memory as a vacillation between remembering and forgetting.[10] Thus, it is important to think about what makes this knowledge "stick."

Public memory focus on the Holocaust has often brought critique as well. Some claim that continual attention to the Holocaust veils the transmission of other important global traumas of the past and the present. Michael Rothberg's concept of "multidirectional memory" helps us understand why this, in fact, may *not* be the case:

> Far from blocking other historical memories from view in a competitive struggle for recognition, the emergence of Holocaust memory on a global scale has contributed to the articulation of other histories—some of them predating the Nazi genocide, such as slavery, and others taking place later, such as the Algerian War of Independence (1954–62) or the genocide in Bosnia during the 1990s. (2009, 6)

Indeed, the blocking of historical traumatic memory seems to be one of the issues associated with history in general. As I note in Chapter Three, the occlusion of memory is a reality: a percentage of people remember some history but largely without detail. In a 1993 poll, over 50% of high school students nationwide could not explain the term "Holocaust" (Powell 2000, 2).

Some readers additionally might say that we know enough about the Holocaust, even if it is not detailed, and that research on the Holocaust is only relevant if it can be applied to other, more recent genocidal activity and wars as in Rwanda, the Sudan, or Kosovo. This book's contribution, however, is not to use the Holocaust *only* as a way to understand other traumas. As Hirsch notes, if we, "think beyond 'relevance or appropriateness' as analytical categories" and think through gender difference, it "can mediate the ways in which certain images and certain narratives have been able to circulate in the culture of the postgeneration" (2012, 17–18). Looking at Holocaust memorialization as a series of public memory processes along a gender spectrum helps theorize how and why they evolve as gendered, material traces of memory that might disturb the perceived "universal" nature of such processes, especially for the postgeneration with whom it attempts to connect. I use Ahmed and Hirsch among others to theorize a gendered perspective on performative memory. "Feminist and queer readings," Hirsch states, can show us not only what is present or absent, but also "how those stories are told, and how those images are constructed" (18).

This book is designed to provide a map of remembrance and memorialization to see what the action of affect might look like when public memory becomes performative and when our relationship to it is shifted so that we turn toward difference without fear or revulsion or denial (see more on this below). As we become three or four generations removed from this event, what we realize is that much of the "bigger picture" of historical narrative comes from perpetrator documents, occasionally punctuated by stories of survival but not always by survivors. This book seeks to remind us that these stories continue to be told, and learning about Jewish survival from survivors *and their children*—and not their killers—is an important contribution to our knowledge about the Holocaust. It is "impossible to conflate different survivor stories into a universal Holocaust experience because no such experience exists" (Waxman 2004, 496), yet this is often precisely the pattern to which public memory reverts because it seems simpler. Traumatic experiences are complex, however; survivor generations know this from personal experience. Part of the difficulty of representing the Holocaust is that "the post-war role of the survivor as witness and concept of the Holocaust demands that they also represent" those victims who did not survive, knowing that they are unable to do so (496). Marianne Hirsch has used the term "postmemory" to describe second-generation survivor trauma, and many second, third, and fourth generation survivors are now creating memorial work around this event; they are the focus of this book. In her 2012 book, Hirsch uses "connective histories" to "think divergent histories alongside and in connection with each other" (21). I use the concept of connection to think about the ways audiences connect with the past and each other to perform memory as a relationship and a turn toward affect. As she suggests, it is time for multidirectional and connective approaches. I hope that my approach to memory as rhetorical and performative so that audience orientations can shift toward affective connections contributes to these crucial frameworks.

HOW TO "RE-SEE": MY THEORETICAL FRAME

Rhetoric

Public memory and rhetoric is a relatively new subfield that includes the seminal work, *Places of Public Memory: The Rhetoric of Museums and Memorials* (see Blair, Dickinson, and Ott 2010),[11] but this text explores only the "sites" of memory as public. Jessica Enoch has noted that women's absence in privileged public memory sites gives feminist rhetoricians the opportunity to investigate the intersection of gender and public memory (2013, 64). The significance of *American Public Memory and the Holocaust* is its interdisciplinary reach and its expansion of public memory studies. Hirsch has noted that: "Numerous testimony projects and oral history archives, the important role of photography and performance, the ever-growing culture of memorials, and the new interactive museology reflect the need for aesthetic and institutional structures that broaden and enlarge the traditional historical archive with a 'repertoire' of embodied knowledge that had been previously neglected by many traditional historians" (2012, 2). My book is a unique answer to Hirsch's call because it broadens the definition of public memory to include texts, videos, films, and museums that perform memory, subvert binary gender constructions, and reorient audiences to connect. There are presently no studies that examine the *progression* of Holocaust public memory as it relates to both broad forms (textual, visual, spatial) and gender, and how this progression is performatively constructed to shift audience orientations and forge personal connections.

The rhetorical construct of memory as collective and cultural has been applied in Holocaust Studies for decades, and there is a rich scholarly tradition from which I draw for this book as a Holocaust scholar (as I detail below). As a rhetorician by training, I also draw on theories of rhetoric; thus I name memory "public" rather than cultural to extend the notion of its rhetorical properties. Artifacts that reside in the public's memory are rhetorical because they allow evaluation and interpretation by focusing on contexts and competing perspectives (Blair, Dickinson, and Ott 2010, 2). These competing contexts and perspectives represent an evolution not just of processes of memory but also of the power structures that exert pressure on them. Public memory can be an extension of power structures and dominant narratives, but when survivors and their families become active agents in the creation of public memory, or share their unedited story with audiences, it also importantly "narrate[s] shared identities, constructing senses of communal belonging" (6) and this construction process is ongoing.[12] For the Holocaust narrative to be broadened in particular, the stories must be multiplied and the dialogic forum must be filled with readers and viewers open to not just hearing but listening.

Building on Felman and Laub's (1992) construction of testimony as speech acts, I use Debra Hawhee's modern conception (from ancient rhetoric and sophism[13]) of *kairotic* force and *phere* to broaden this relationship to discover how audience reception relates to memorial force. Hawhee presents a nuanced notion of *kairos* as a force of time that is sometimes in opposition to *chronos* (as chronological time) because it exerts pressure at unexpected moments. *Kairos* in Hawhee's conception is catalyzed by the movements between "discursive moment[s]" (such as the discursive moment that a film is released and discussed), when a rhetor addresses the reader or listener. This rhetorical process is important:

It is therefore the *turn* itself, not the logoi, the very act of being taken elsewhere that Gorgias[14] foregrounds and mimics when he directs those present to listen, *phere*. *Phere* comes from the verb *phero*, which means "to bear" or "to carry" but can also (at the same time) indicate a yielding or producing [...] The act of listening then becomes just that: a productive, active, transformative act for hearers and speakers. This moment of direct address then, emphasizes the transformative encounter produced through discourse. (Hawhee 2004, 77–78)

Kairos is not just a force that marks and disrupts the "neutral" public memory of the Holocaust, but it is also an aperture that creates a performative space where the, "rhetor opens [himself] to the immediate situation, allowing for more of an exchange" (71).

Gender

I also draw on theories of gender to make visible the highly constructed processes of public memory that claim to be "universal" or neutral. Holocaust Studies is dominated by historical and cultural studies perspectives that often marginalize gender or ignore it completely (see Hirsch 2012; Rosenfeld 2013). A seminar on teaching gender and the Holocaust at the USHMM in 2012 was the first time this program had addressed gender in its twenty-year history. Feminist readings of memory work have sought to "uncover and to restore experiences" lost to the universal in public memory (Hirsch 2012, 15). I certainly do that here in Chapters One and Three. But there is another way that feminist and gender analysis can add depth. If we see memory as "counterhistory" as Hirsch suggests, it can be a "means to account for the power structures animating forgetting, oblivion, and erasure and thus to engage in acts of repair and redress" (16). Analysis informed by feminist approaches helps illuminate how and why public memory around the Holocaust tends toward making gender invisible as a category and deconstructs that arbitrary hierarchy.

An examination of the Holocaust from rhetorical, gender, and performance perspectives is an important interdisciplinary contribution to several fields. It is important to think about how this multi-layered analysis and presentation of texts contributes to the canon of 21st-century memory practices. In addition to the problem of erasure, there is a culture around public memory that is both accessible and superficial. The ways in which we connect with each other seem at once both more frequent (digital) and increasingly meaningless. This book attempts to delve into this distressing paradox to ask: How do gender, performance, and rhetoric subvert these tendencies to create meaningful connections?

Recent books that address topics in Holocaust memorialization with several genres include: Lawrence Langer's *Using and Abusing the Holocaust* (2006) and James E. Young's *At Memory's Edge: After Images of the*

Holocaust in Contemporary Art and Architecture (2002). A few authors focus on one genre such as Rotem's *The Construct of Memory: Architectural Narratives of Holocaust Museums* (2013) and Oleksandr Kobrynskyy and Gerd Bayer's *Holocaust Cinema in the Twenty-First Century: Memory, Images, and the Ethics of Representation* (2015). Hirsch's *The Generation of Postmemory: Writing and Visual Culture After the Holocaust* addresses gender and the Holocaust in terms of feminist analysis (2012). Goldenberg and Shapiro's edited collection addresses the absence of gender in historical analyses (2013). Patraka's *Spectacular Suffering: Theater, Fascism, and the Holocaust* is the only text that links Holocaust and performance but does not examine the performative or rhetorical nature of discourse (1999). Michael Bernard-Donals is one of the few scholars working on post Holocaust memorialization from a rhetorical perspective and his *Forgetful Memory: Representations and Remembrance in the Wake of the Holocaust* (2010) is just one example. (Vivian does some work but is not focused on the Holocaust.) Hirsch and Bernard-Donals have many books in the field and generally present memory processes and the Holocaust in relation to a concept like "forgetfulness" or "postmemory." Some focus only on visual culture, and some only on textual. Alan Rosenfeld's book *The End of the Holocaust* (2013), suggests that a proliferation of Holocaust memory and artifacts makes remembrance superficial, and would probably suggest that my book is redundant. Yet his "history" of texts includes only one from a woman, or a girl, rather: Anne Frank. My book suggests the proliferation as necessary in order to add previously silenced perspectives or new generational perspectives with gender in mind, as feminist theories advance. My book extends the work on visual culture and the Holocaust accomplished in Hirsch's work with photographs and in Barbie Zelizer's 2001 edited collection, *Visual Culture and the Holocaust*, with newer media forms and a focus on the construction of gender and memory as rhetorical and performative.

The study of gender and the Holocaust is similar to other areas of feminist studies in which there are waves of discovery and analysis. According to Anna Hardman's study, the first wave of studies of women and the Holocaust focused on glorifying the particularity in coping strategies and relationships and biological differences affecting persecution. The second wave focused on affirming the differences.[15] The 1980s saw an increased market in women's Holocaust memoirs in the 1980s, and there "was a steady increase in historiographical and literary interpretations of women's experiences," which were realized in an influential anthology *Different Voices* in 1993 (1).[16]

Such collections and articles of primary source material represent the first stage of feminist scholarship: the recovery of texts.[17] The second stage of feminist scholarship involves the analysis of such texts. Texts that have broadened historical contexts through gendered research are works such as: *Gender and Destiny: Women Writers and the Holocaust* (1986),[18] *Women in the Holocaust* (1998),[19] *Double Jeopardy: Gender and the Holocaust* (1998),[20] *Women's Holocaust Writing: Memory and Imagination* (1999),[21] *Women and the Holocaust: Narrative and Representation* (1999),[22] *Shaping Losses: Cultural Memory and the Holocaust* (2001),[23] *The Social Inheritance of the Holocaust: Gender, Culture, and Memory* (2002), and *Experience and Expression: Women, the Nazis, and the Holocaust* (2003). The issue of discovery is important because it is not that women weren't writing; they simply were not published. The movement from discovery to analysis in Holocaust Studies echoes movement that occurred in feminist studies much earlier. Because of the resistance to studies of women and the Holocaust, this movement occurred in Holocaust Studies about twenty years later than in other fields.[24]

By the year 2000, "despite resistance," claims Hardman, there is an active subfield of "Women and the Holocaust" which reflects "a growing interdisciplinary field concerned with women's experiences"; the development of gender studies is an "interpretive shift" that redefines this area of research as Gender and the Holocaust (2000, 4). New studies incorporate studies of gender and the visual as in Barbie Zelizer's "Gender and Atrocity: Women in Holocaust Photographs" (2001).[25] Further studies in this area thus, continue to be crucial, with texts like *Sexual Violence Against Jewish Women During the Holocaust* (2010) and *Different Horrors, Same Hell* (2013) appearing just in the last seven years. Most of the work I mention above expands historical studies of gender and a continued focus on women.

This book contributes to this rich scholarship but fills a particular niche, not a historical study but a cultural a study of public memory processes: the ways in which our public memorial practices reify, disturb, or ignore gender especially in terms of binary representations that prioritize or valorize the male experience. Sara Ahmed, in the *Cultural Politics of Emotion* argues that emotion has been categorized on the gender binary as a "feminine" trait, associated with irrationality and weakness because it is immediate and "uncontrollable." The "politicisation" and binary categorization of emotion, however, are both highly constructed and socially mediated by the past. Projecting emotion only upon the body of the other (as woman or minority), thus, "not only works to exclude others from the realm of thought and rationality, but also works to conceal the emotional and embodied aspects of thought and reason" that are present in everyone (2015, 170).

Additionally Ahmed importantly explores gender and what is queer in terms of orientations. In *Queer Phenomenology*, she suggest that queering is about turning but it is also spatial as in our direction or where we stand in relation to others (2006, 19). Queering is also about how "we reside" in spaces and how we might "clear space that is familiar" in order to reorient. In her work, Ahmed discusses orientations specifically in terms of sexuality. In this book, I use her framework to apply to gender representations and difference. Both turning toward and turning away take time and effort. Public memory, if performed, seeks these thoughtful turns as well. When I speak of gender or non-binary in terms of orientations, it is about this turning and time. To "queer" for Ahmed is to turn toward differences in sexual orientation. For my analysis, I will use the term "shifting" to discuss the same process of turning toward and away, so that readers are clear that I want to examine how powerful it can be to present non-binary gender representations in Holocaust memorial artifacts, so that audiences can reorient to difference and turn toward the "other" instead of away. I am not trying to "queer" something that isn't. This book explores how gender binaries of masculine and feminine can be blurred in Holocaust public memory so that our "queer turn" can be toward each other and toward survivors in ways that productively destabilize public memory gender "norms." The identities of those involved are not conflated through performative connections (i.e., audiences do not "identify" with survivor experiences); rather, relationships are built through these turns toward the familiar and the unfamiliar and strengthened with affect and empathy.

The Performative

Memory and gender are constructed, deconstructed, and reconstructed in a hierarchy of power based in binaries that are particularly visible in the public sphere, and while this process has often applied to gender construction[26] it is also important in the construction of public memory processes. This echoes Anzaldua'a original conception of the *mestiza* consciousness that "[shifts] out of habitual formations" to create consciousness that "incudes rather than excludes" (1999, 101), a process that might disturb binaries and make them more ambiguous. In Holocaust public memory, the images we see—and pointedly do not see—often reinforce this gender binary, but public memory artifacts that de-neutralize such default narratives can be "constitutive" of new interpretations about gender (Enoch 2013, 63). The artifacts I examine present a non-binary construction of both/and that reorients audiences toward the survivors as whole individuals, which moves discourse performatively from "being" to *doing*.

The performance of memory links to rhetoric and gender because it also constitutes new interpretations and exists in shifting spaces and contexts.[27] Performance studies can also be seen as "a 'new discipline' that brings together ideas from areas such as sociology, queer theory, anthropology, and theatre" (Love 2007, 14). In this book, performance studies exists as a "new discipline" that will meld ideas from performance studies, rhetorical studies, Holocaust Studies, and gender studies. Though I focus on Ahmed's queer orientations as they relate to relationships, affect, and performance, theories of mestiza, and other queer theorists who challenge boundaries of all kinds inform this approach. Halberstam calls for academic "disciplinary transformation" (2011, 7) to blur boundaries and open new learning but also champions the concept of queer as "the potential to open up new life narratives and alternative relations to time and space"(2005, 2). Kosofsky Sedgwick's queer theory embraces non-dualism and like Ahmed explores affect as a "double movement" that seeks "sociability" (2003, 37). Many queer theorists explore queer in relation to performance and affect. This book seeks to make these connections as well, but like Ahmed, the focus is on performance as social in order to see audience reactions to gender representation and difference and the potential for deeper relationship with Holocaust public memory.

To render the public memory processes around gender and the Holocaust both visible and active, I use Pollock's sense of the performative: words and visual/spatial texts have the power to *do* something in the world (1998, 75). I will detail in the following chapters how Pollock's conceptions of evocative, subjective, citational, metonymic, and consequential performative writing "map" how newer forms of Holocaust public memory increase audience connections to create action in the world. Indeed, Love sees performance and rhetoric as forging a link that is "insistent on connection" (2018, par. 1).

Holocaust Studies

The body of scholarship on the Holocaust and memory artifacts is large, and I could not have arrived at my thesis without having engaged over the years with Holocaust scholars like Baer, Cole, Goldenberg, Grossman, Hartman, Hirsch, Horowitz, Langer, Novick, Rothberg, Tydor-Baumel, and many, many others. Memory and the Holocaust has been a topic of study for decades with explorations of, for instance, "working through" trauma and memory (Friedlander 1992; Caruth 1995) and the difficulty of representing atrocity. The concept of "public memory" takes rhetorical studies and applies it to this field. Public memory as rhetorical is well applied especially to public memory sites in the United States like the USHMM (which opened in 1993) or big films like *Schindler's List (*1994), which created a new awareness in the American "public," but also applies to those genres that are less public but nevertheless seek public action. This book extends this interest with newer forms and a look at gender performance and audience connection as social acts.

I begin this book by reminding readers about the importance of multiple perspectives. As Franklin notes, "something important is missing when a book about the Holocaust depicts its Jewish characters through the eyes of bystanders and perpetrators" (2018, par. 29). This book focuses on a range of forms and on a range of generational perspectives related to Jewish survivors. Readers also have been socialized to expect memorialization artifacts about the Holocaust to come in the form of diaries, memoirs, photos, or documentaries, forms in which gender is often absent or marginalized through strict binaries of masculine and feminine, so this book focuses on gender representations as potentially blurring these binaries but not claiming to become transgendered. The ability of public memory artifacts to perform and *do* rather than be, as well as the ways in which audiences can reorient themselves to form meaningful connections to the past and to others in the present are also the foci of this book, because if we learn and yet do nothing, we cannot effect positive change.

In Chapter One, I open the discussion of visual culture and public memory by discussing Claude Lanzmann's *Shoah* as an influential public memory artifact with *kairotic* force that changed the landscape of Holocaust memorialization and yet had both an absence of gender and strictly binary representations of gender. This artifact is then complicated with a discussion of the recently acquired *Shoah* outtakes at the USHMM and how these absent interviews perform as action—they create *kairotic* openings for engagement—to narrate more complex depictions of gender with which the public can interact through open access archives.

In Chapter Two, I explore the new Hungarian film *Son of Saul* by a fourth-generation survivor as a public memory "after-affect" of Steven Spielberg's *Schindler's List*, in which the orientation of audiences is challenged to become both objective and subjective so that they might shift their orientation to the past and to gender depictions around the Holocaust. This chapter will also explore how *Schindler's List* expanded its impact in the last twenty years with the post-film creation of the USC Visual History Archive that broadens audience participation through education for the future. Comparing these artifacts shows how the use of non-binary representation and performative elements allows audiences to feel "affect" and connection to others. This shift in orientation moves them from distance, to disorientation, to reorientation and relation.

In Chapter Three, I focus on the stories of the three women: Ruth Levy, her daughter Anne Levy, and Ruth Klüger. Because of the norming of gender that undervalues the stories of women, the writers in this chapter deferred telling their story because it seemed it would have no further effect. Contemporary history suddenly compels each to make their private story public.

Public memory around these stories becomes *kairotically* and performatively charged as these women deconstruct gender binaries to grapple with rising racism in the American South and burgeoning Neo-fascists in Germany. These authors want to provoke audiences to political action with performative texts. Public memory, specifically with regard to these deferred memories in auto/biographies by women, is constructed in relation to the work of others and in response to history as it happens now. The authors seek communal actions that forge lasting connections.

In Chapter Four, I discuss the second- and third-generation texts 2012 Israeli documentary *Numbered* and the 2009 Australian video *Dancing in Auschwitz* by Jane Korman as performances of memory that break with "traditional" memorialization forms to celebrate life not just mourn death. Rhetorical bodies become the *kairotic* memory site upon which second and third generations reclaim the trauma of Auschwitz and the Holocaust legacy, and they do so in ways that challenge gender "norms." This chapter explores the ways public memory evolves in dialogue with newer generations most extensively.

In Chapter Five, I explore the performance of memory and gender in local museums on the Holocaust around the country (includes museums in Dallas, Houston, St. Petersburg, and Los Angeles). Using the USHMM as an example of a nationalist narrative, this chapter focuses on how the local sites construct memory specific to place and community. The performance of memory in these spaces resists the tendency toward "universal" narrative, and constructs gender specific narratives that challenge the binary. This chapter analysis focuses on how affective connections are created and how queer orientations move audiences toward social responsibility to build public memory within the community.

STILL... A BOOK ABOUT HOLOCAUST PUBLIC MEMORY: WHY NOW?

Philadelphia, Pennsylvania 2017: Jewish cemeteries are desecrated.

Charlottesville, Virginia 2017: An alt-right demonstration ends in violence.

Pittsburgh, Pennsylvania 2018: a lone shooter attacks a synagogue.

Two years prior to these events in America, a story appeared in *The Atlantic*[28] in April 2015 about the rise of virulent antisemitism[29] in Europe, especially in France. Jews are afraid to go to synagogue, to kosher markets, and some are taking down the *mezuzah* on their apartment door frames to hide their religious identity because of attacks. The title of the article: "Is It Time for the Jews to Leave Europe?" might also have appeared in a 1935 newspaper in Germany. When the Nazi propaganda machine took over, they were able to decimate the independent press within months and antisemitic newspapers like Julius Streicher's *Der Sturmer* could be found on any street corner for public viewing. At its peak *Der Sturmer* reached 2,000,000 according to the USHMM ("Writing").

Is the recent rise of populist politics, xenophobia, and nationalism in the UK, the United States, the Netherlands, and France, a "rehearsal" of intolerances we never shed with the Internet as its new vehicle to mass and rapid distribution? The present "force" of such hate speech or *kairotic* moments of intolerance seem to reside in their persistent reiteration. The resurgence of modern antisemitism (and other intolerances) unfortunately is very real. A 2017 article in *The Guardian* notes that in the United Kingdom post-Brexit: "The CST, which monitors antisemitism and provides security to Jewish communities, recorded 1,309 incidents of anti-Jewish hate last year, compared with 960 in 2015, a rise of 36%. The previous record number of incidents was in 2014, when 1,182 were recorded" (Sherwood). The 2014 number was attributed to Israeli actions in Gaza, but in 2016 there was no like act attached to the spike. Péter Krekó wrote in 2014 that there is a "troubling rise in anti-Semitism" in Hungary (30). Research revealed that in 1994, the year that *Schindler's List* was released, 14% of respondents "found Jews repulsive." By 2008 that figure was 28% (2014, 31). This is a significant jump, and what is more troubling, younger Hungarians seem to have higher prejudice against Jews than any other demographic.

These incidents are not relegated just to Europe either. As we can see from the incidents I list above, a list that is not comprehensive, Holocaust denial persists worldwide and is burgeoning on the Internet, and antisemitic acts reoccur.[30] As a global society we have attempted to address this tendency to regress toward separation and intolerance. For example, the International Day of Holocaust Remembrance was solidified in 2005 during George W. Bush's second term in office and became a resolution at the United Nations. Resolution 60/7 (proposed by Israel)[31] established on 27 January (the date Auschwitz-Birkenau was liberated) as International Holocaust Remembrance Day. This resolution encourages honoring the memories of survivors, preserving sites, developing educational materials, as it also: "condemns all forms of intolerance" against communities based on ethnicity or religion (USHMM "International").

January 27, 2017, was the 72nd anniversary of liberation and this Day of Remembrance was marked two days later by the 45th American President with a speech that did not mention Jews or antisemitism at any point, a departure from the last sixteen years of speeches from both Republican and Democratic presidents (Satlin 2017). The President's speech, when he should "reassert our commitment to human rights" as stipulated by the joint U.N. Resolution, instead was doubly marked: he *did not* mention the victims and *did* institute "extreme vetting": 120-day bans on immigration into the United States from majority Muslim countries. The increase of intolerance in present American policies and the shift in public memory discourse at the American national level have been rapid.

Only a week earlier, on Saturday, 21 January 2017, the day after the United States Presidential inauguration, *The Guardian* newspaper posted an article called "A New Online Generation Takes up Holocaust Denial," Jamie Doward notes that:

> The release of [the film] *Denial*—which centres on the libel trial brought by Irving against the Holocaust scholar Deborah Lipstadt—follows the controversy that erupted when it emerged Google's algorithms were recommending antisemitic, white nationalist and Holocaust denier websites for searches of the question: "Did the Holocaust happen?" The film has already been attacked by the new generation of deniers on YouTube, Reddit and Twitter. (par. 7)

This flurry of antisemitic Internet activity came just weeks before *Denial*'s worldwide release. Are these coincidences? With the rise of "fake news" and the skyrocketing popularity of alt-right news sources like *Breitbart* and conspiracy websites proliferating, especially with young people, one could say "maybe." All of these facts indicate a rise of intolerance and violence against Jews, but these align with rising intolerance (and public violence) against Muslims, women, people of color, and LGBTQ+ populations in the United States and elsewhere.

The doubt I had about focusing this book on memory and memorializing the Holocaust, with a focus on the intergenerational experiences of Jewish survivors because it might occlude other prejudices has disappeared. Because Holocaust memory is multidirectional and connective as Hirsch and Rothberg have argued and performative and rhetorical as I argue, continued study is an important tool to remember the past and to analyze the present historical moment. It seems that never before has it been so crucial to revisit the Holocaust as genocide of mass proportions. In the face of rising antisemitism seventy years after the Holocaust, never before has it been so important to revisit that event through the lens of gender and survivor generations. We must disturb the notion that public memory and the Holocaust is universal or neutral, or that public memory about the Holocaust is unimportant to the present. The hatred of one group is never far removed from the hatred of many groups.

My focus is a call to continue to examine why hate persists. As Americans who value freedom and free speech, never before has it been so imperative to re-see the ways in which we memorialize a historical event such as this one, and the ways in which we approach traumatic memory and those who suffer with it—over time and across generations. Clearly, intolerance ignored doesn't just go away. Turning away from each other with division and hatred is not the answer. In this historical moment we must come to back to each other to embrace difference.

When public memory is rhetorical, gendered, and performative, it seeks a dialogic with audiences. This book does not track a chronological history of artifacts; rather, it illuminates the trajectory of Holocaust public memory artifacts that perform with significant *kairotic* force at particular historical moments that are punctuated by concerns about gender, identity, and the absence of affect and connection and that engage multiple generations. I have been engaged with Holocaust memory for two decades and I have walked this path often with my mother. We are Jewish-Polish descendants. We have walked the grounds of Auschwitz together. We share Holocaust memoirs and newspaper articles every few months. My mother was recently diagnosed with Alzheimer's. It is still early in the disease, but the knowledge that her memories will not only fade but also disappear will change who she is to herself. Yet her legacy will live on in me. Our conversations expand beyond us, and my future conversations will expand beyond me now—to my children and to my students. This book pushes audiences to do that same communal, intergenerational memory work that includes trust, relationship, and connection—a shift in orientation through performative dialogic. How do we, and will we, continue to talk about trauma and prejudice and genocide? The power to make positive change, especially around intolerance and prejudice, seems elusive these days. This book will help readers to discern how and why newer public memory texts of the Holocaust challenge this stasis, and how each of us could apply this to our own lives.

NOTES

1. The use of the term "Holocaust" instead of "Shoah" follows the usage of major scholars like Marianne Hirsch and Efraim Sicher, where "Holocaust" is used because it is more recognizable to audiences. There is still a debate, however, as to the term best used to refer to this historical event. According to Wiesel in *The Sea Is Never Full*, the usage of the word "Holocaust" for the first time is attributed to him—"the word '*ola*' translated as burnt offering or *Holocaust [. . .]* suggests total annihilation by fire and the mystical aspect of sacrifice" (1999, 18–19). He finds its overuse vulgar now. And Erzahi notes that its usage is "unfortunately, consistent with a prevailing

Christian reading of Jewish history (1980, 2). *Shoah*, the biblical term now used in Israel, means an accident or natural catastrophe striking a community; yet, according to Wiesel, clearly the same word should not be applied both to pogroms and Auschwitz. Yiddish speakers referred to "the war" or the *Churban*, which also signifies catastrophe and destruction and recalls the "ransacking of the first and second temples in Jerusalem" (Wiesel 1999, 19). Hirsch has noted the problematic use of all of these terms as well, and includes the term "genocide." Many object to the use of some or all of these terms. Like Hirsch, I use the term "Holocaust" in my project too because I am aware that my audience will be unfamiliar with the other terms. I also use this term because this is the term that the authors I examine in this project use to refer to this event.

2. Marianne Hirsch was the first to conceptualize the transference of trauma onto second-generation survivors. Her concept "post-memory" has influenced my work from the beginning. Her work as a Holocaust and feminist scholar has inspired me in these areas of scholarship. This term "next gen" is one I first heard at the Holocaust Museum Houston.

3. See Ahmed's *Queer Phenomenology*, pages 6–9, for an exposition of orientation.

4. For selected memoirs see Primo Levi (1961) and Elie Wiesel (1960) as well as Charlotte Delbo (collected in English 1995). Lawrence Langer's work on Holocaust testimony and the Holocaust in public memory are crucial to any discussion of the Holocaust and its memorialization (see for example 1991; 2006). The first comprehensive Holocaust histories were the labor of eminent historians like Raul Hilberg (1985; 1992), Lucy S. Davidowicz (1975) and Omer Bartov (1996; 2000). See Marlene E. Heinemann (1986) and Joan Ringelheim and Ester Katz's conference proceedings (1983) on women and the Holocaust as groundbreaking openings in the study of gender and the Holocaust as well as Judith Tydor Baumel's (1998). Barbie Zelizer's (2001) work on the visual aspects of representing atrocity. James Young is influential in the areas of multiple genres and also memorials (see for example 1993; 2008). Waxman's work addresses issues of representation (2004; 2006), as Bernard-Donals does with forgetful memory (2009).

5. Most notably the genocide of Native peoples in North America and the legacy of enslavement of African peoples and their descendants in America.

6. But Friedlander notes that this "silence did not exist within the survivor community," rather it was maintained in relation to the outside world—imposed by shame—to tell a story that must seem unbelievable ("Trauma, Transference, and 'Working Through' in Writing the History of the Shoah," 1992, 48.)

7. See Vick (2005) and Doward (2017). I will discuss denial in other sections in this book as well.

8. See Wajnyrb (2001, 79).

9. For Holocaust scholar Peter Novick, the American Jewish community led this surge in interest. He claims the dissemination of information is inevitable because of the influence of the Jewish community in media, but denies any allegiance with Jewish conspiracy theory (xv). The surge is intentional while the resulting dissemination is spontaneous. This is unlike Norman Finkelstein's view that such intention was a

means to support the State of Israel. Finkelstein notes the pro-Israel lobby after the 1967 Arab-Israeli war as part of his evidence (2000). Novick looks at domestic affairs as well as foreign—seeing an importance in "ethnic exceptionalism" and the "growing importance of the story of victimization" (1999, xv). Finkelstein's is a Zionist narrative, Novick's is an ethnic Jewish-American narrative. Tim Cole agrees with portions of these arguments but his main point is this: the United States (especially as seen in the Holocaust Museum) wants to sell, not a Jewish narrative, but a nationalistic one (2000).

10. See Bernard-Donals and Bradford Vivian.

11. See Blair, Enoch, Phillips, Vivian, and Zelizer.

12. See Akcan, Marcuse, and Wagner-Pacifici.

13. In this book and in Hawhee's work, sophism means the "general wisdom" and the "practical application of rhetoric to political and civic life" (see philosophybasics.com).

14. Gorgias was a Greek philosopher and rhetorician from Sicily who is thought to be the originator of "sophism," which is the practical application of rhetoric to political or civic life (see www.iep.utm.edu).

15. Gender differences in experiences of the Holocaust were the focus of research in the 1970s when Joan Ringelheim, Sybil Milton, and Myrna Goldenberg explored whether there was "anything distinctive about women's experiences" (Hardman 2000, 1).

16. Holocaust scholar Esther Fuchs notes that "questions about the invisibility of women in Holocaust Studies" began with two studies: *Different Voices: Women and the Holocaust* (1993) and *Making Stories, Making Selves: Feminist Reflections on the Holocaust* (1993) and the criticism of the lack of representation of and information about the female Holocaust experience began with Debra R. Kaufman, *Women in the Holocaust*, a special issue of *Contemporary Jewry*, volume 17 (1996). This is a great deal later than Hardman claims.

17. Other collections that appeared on gender that Hardman does not note but that Anna Reading does in a more comprehensive list include: Kaplan's work on Jewish feminists before World War II; Sybil Milton's chapter in Bridenthal, *When Biology Became Destiny: Women in Weimar and Nazi Germany* (1984), Konnilyn G. Feig's chapter on Ravensbrück in *Hitler's Death Camps: The Sanity of Madness* (1983); Claudia Koonz's chapter on Jewish victims in her book *Mothers in the Fatherland* (1987); Eibeshitz and Eilenberg in *Women and the Holocaust Vol. 2* (1994); Vera Laska, *Women in the Resistance and in the Holocaust; the Voices of Eyewitnesses* (1983); Gurewitsch in *Mothers, Sisters, Resisters: Oral Histories of Women Who Survived the Holocaust* (1998); Rittner and Roth in *Different Voices: Women and the Holocaust* (1993); and Michael Berenbaum's and John Roth's reprint of *Holocaust: Religious and Philosophical Reflections* (1989) (Reading 2002, 15, 38).

18. *Gender and Destiny; Women Writers and the Holocaust* (1986) by Marlene E. Heinemann is one of the earliest works on gender and the Holocaust, highlighting gender issues in the memoirs of women. Heinemann works with female-centered themes (menstruation, maternity, and sexual abuse), characterization (survivor, victim, hero), inmate relations (privileged and unprivileged, selfish and cooperative),

and authenticity. Heinemann, like Young, refers to the genre of autobiography as important for audiences to see the story as authentic.

19. Dalia Ofer's and Lenore Weitzmann's *Women in the Holocaust* in 1998 was the first "original scholarship" to receive "mainstream critical acclaim" according to Hardman (2000, 1).

20. Judith Tydor-Baumel works on gender in fictional and nonfictional representations using the feminist theoretical framework of identity as it is conceptualized by Chodorow and Gilligan. Tydor-Baumel utilizes gender studies, intertwined with examinations of Jewish history, the Second World War, and the Holocaust. She examines, for instance, how women assimilated into the "male sphere" of the battlefield (1998, xii), discusses gender and identity from before the war to the present (sometimes using a comparative method), and uses "gender" as describing "the relationship between the sexes" (xiii). While my project also focuses on texts over a long period of time—postwar to the present—it focuses more on the consequences of the *social construction* of gender and its representation in nonfiction discourses.

21. Lillian Kremer highlights gender roles and reactions to the Holocaust in mainly fictional representations of the Holocaust by authors who were there and authors without any firsthand experience. This is a comparative, gendered analysis of themes: pregnancy, survival techniques in the camps, resistance, separations, and techniques situated in time and place.

22. The articles in this multidisciplinary anthology address direct questions about memory, narration, and gender. The comparative is employed here to ask if women and men do these things differently. As noted above, this book seeks not to pinpoint differences in women's and men's writings about the Holocaust. Rather, I seek to find similarities and differences that can reveal gendered moments in this history that are individual and non-binary and depend on each unique social context.

23. *Shaping Losses* is a series of essays edited by Epstein and Lefkovitz that highlights gender from historical, theological, and literary perspectives, respectively. This anthology seeks to become a speech of silence, "the verbal analogue to the ghosts" and is concerned with how personal memory becomes cultural memory and the implications of such movements (2001, 7).

24. Holocaust scholars Elizabeth Baer and Myrna Goldenberg contend that the reaction to gender studies in Holocaust Studies follows the trajectory of gender studies in any field—scholars bristle at bringing women into discussions typically discussed, or universalized, from the male perspective (see their Introduction to *Experience and Expression: Women, the Nazis, and the Holocaust*, 2003).

25. Zelizer focuses on how gender is represented in photographs of the liberation of the camps. Zelizer's thesis is that constructed gender roles are falsely re-created in these photographs, taken by mainly male soldiers. Zelizer references Vera Brittain (1957), who asked: didn't women have their war as well? Zelizer would like to suggest they did, but that visual records do not accurately reveal this (2001, 268).

26. See Butler (1993), McKenzie (1998), and Phelan (1998).

27. See Austin (1975), Pollock (1998), DeCerteau (1984), and Love (2007).

28. See Jeffrey Goldberg (2010).

29. This spelling of the word aligns with the IHRA Alliance's April 2015 Memorandum: "the International Holocaust Remembrance Alliance (IHRA) would like to address the spelling of the term antisemitism, often rendered as 'anti-Semitism' and Microsoft's auto-correct feature. IHRA's concern is that the hyphenated spelling allows for the possibility of something called 'Semitism', which not only legitimizes a form of pseudo-scientific racial classification that was thoroughly discredited by association with Nazi ideology, but also divides the term, stripping it from its meaning of opposition and hatred toward Jews."

30. On 15 March 2017, the Fresh Air radio show on National Public Radio (NPR) broadcast author Daniel Torday reading an essay about desecrated Jewish cemeteries. He said for the first thirty-eight years of his life he had to travel to Europe if he wanted to witness, as a Jew, the desecration of Jewish cemeteries. As he worked on the cleanup of one cemetery that was vandalized in Philadelphia in 2017, much as others had been in St. Louis the same year, he said the violence of it struck him hard: it happened in Philadelphia to a cemetery over 100 years old. Before this moment, he had only seen desecrated cemeteries in Eastern Europe. Now he has seen them in 2017, in America, when down the road 100-year old Christian cemeteries are left untouched ("Searching" 2017). These occur as we experience shootings of black men and women by American law enforcement and LGBTQ folks are targeted and killed as in the Pulse nightclub shooting in Florida.

31. The proposing nation is not neutral, as their record of human rights abuses against Palestinians grows. There are also other genocides that have not been formally remembered in this way.

Chapter One

Claude Lanzmann's *Shoah* and the Opening of Testimony Archives

Gender and Performance in Public Memory

DEDICATED IN MEMORIUM:
CLAUDE LANZMANN: 27 NOVEMBER 1925–5 JULY 2018

Public memory is constructed: that is, it is always contested and in process depending on hegemonic forces that create but also erase or rewrite histories.[1] Repetition in public memory and in gender representation can confer authority and become "irrefutable and universal" as Butler suggests (1995, 205), but in such a "highly rhetorical process" (Phillips 2004, 2), many seek *not* to remember the past exactly as it was, but rather to: "formulate the past in ways that confirm or disturb ideas about the way things are or should be" such as with rigidly constructed gender roles and representations (Enoch 2013: 62).[2] Bodnar goes further to argue that "memorial culture" is not only a "restatement of reality in ideal" (a binary structure) but also a rejection of that reality in "complex and ambiguous forms" (a non-binary structure) (Haskins 2007, 403). Although American public memory around the Holocaust has become particularly visible, what we "see" around Holocaust public memory is what has "been allowed" to be made visible as an ideal. This ideal manifests as a desire to retain "universal" narratives that are simplified or unambiguous. An artifact like Anne Frank's diary continues to have value in the American present not only because it reflects this ideal.[3] It is a work accessible to children and taught widely; moreover, it engenders an idealized formation of the past that enshrines innocence and optimism as the best responses to extreme discrimination.[4] In contrast, the nine-hour documentary French film, *Shoah* directed by Claude Lanzmann, eschews the "ideal" and gains power through the complexity and ambiguity of survivor representation.

I first saw the film *Shoah*[5] in Los Angeles in 1995, the tenth anniversary screening. My best friend from Germany, whom I had met in Israel on a kibbutz the year before, was a film student, and she told me: "you need to see this film." She was right. I did need to see it. It was nine hours of absolute terror, a quiet terror, but terror nonetheless. The perpetrators' matter-of-fact retelling of heinous crimes was chilling. I cried in the silence when a survivor stood among his former neighbors, the exotic other, almost invisible and still without human value to them. Ten years later, I had become a scholar of such Holocaust artifacts, public memory, and gender, and with this theoretical background I saw the film more deeply. Through my studies, I came to understand that the intense emotions I felt watching the film the first time were elicited from me, manipulated out of me even; the scenes were not organic and were often staged by Lanzmann. While I might have felt a level of betrayal at this fact before becoming a scholar, armed with theory, I could see the film for what it was: a highly crafted archive of never-before-seen survivor testimonies. This had great value—this film was akin to an archive of new memories; it changed what we knew about the Holocaust from the perspective of survivors and this had enormous, positive impact on the revival of Holocaust memory.

I was still disturbed, however, by its distinctly gendered perspective. There is almost a complete absence of women's experiences depicted in the film. The film is presented as a repository of "neutral" survivor perspectives (a neutrality that is always already particularly masculine), and in so doing, served to reify existing gender binaries that excluded women altogether or subverted their experiences. I could see that clearly for myself, even before I became a scholar; women only appeared a few times in the film over the course of those nine long hours. As a scholar I learned just how crafted this gendered narrative really was. Whether Lanzmann consciously minimized the role of women in his film or unconsciously deferred to a binary system valuing the male voice more highly, the fact that these missing voices are typically overlooked as less important sheds light on how male-oriented institutionalized public memory exerts its power to become dominant (i.e., "universal"). Even though Lanzmann's film masters ambiguity and complexity in representation of the concept of "survivor," it fails at ambiguity and tends toward the simplified ideals in Anne Frank with overly binary representations of gender.

There are, however, newly released outtakes of footage from this film. In 2012, the United States Holocaust Memorial Museum (USHMM) released additional outtake footage from *Shoah* never before seen by the public. As a Silberman Fellow at the museum at that time, I studied the outtakes before general release. What I will discuss is how this new footage, when added to the edited film, *actually* achieves the complexity and ambiguity in Holocaust memory that Lanzmann wanted with its initial release, making it a "truer" artifact of non-binary gendered public memory of the Holocaust. In *Shoah*, it is precisely what is *not seen* that allows only the binary "norms" of gender to dominate what audiences see as the Holocaust ideal. When this film can include its outtakes footage, it is possible to break this binary system by including the more ambiguous gender representations Lanzmann left out. The "rhetorical process of gendering" in public memory relies on "discursive, material, and embodied articulations and performances that create and disturb gendered distinctions," says Enoch (2013, 68), and in these ways so-called "neutral" public memory narratives can be challenged. The newly acquired "outtakes" of this film, acquired by the USHMM in October 1996 and first made accessible to an online audience in July 2016, provide the necessary evidence for audiences to begin to deconstruct those gender "neutralities" around testimony and the Jewish survivor in *Shoah*. I am going to complicate Holocaust representation in this film by making it once again ambiguous; non-binary gender representations are a crucial aspect of the full film footage that reconstitute and reimagine public memory narratives and spaces.

THE *KAIROS* OF PUBLIC MEMORY: RHETORICAL, GENDERED, AND PERFORMATIVE

The Rhetoric and Gender of Public Memory

In order to see new constructions of ambiguity and complexity in survivor representation, we have to establish a theoretical lens. It will allow us to see things differently: how a comparison of released/known footage (*Shoah*) with unreleased/unknown footage (from the same era but only being revealed now) can make what is complex a "truer" complexity. I will focus on the performance rhetoric of memory (the relationship between memorial artifact and audience) and how that disturbs binary, gender representations in *Shoah*. Performative disturbances lead to the creation of *kairotic* moments, where the force of the moment overcomes the chronological timelines—they collapse the past into the present. The *kairos* created from the performance of audiences with the non-binary Holocaust representations found in digital archives disturbs the gendered distinctions that have limited our knowledge of the Jewish survivors and allows audiences to reorient themselves to this history—to bring a fuller picture into focus.

Within a historiographic context, we can learn a lot from looking at the "force" of repetition and the "chronology" of repetition from a performative and a rhetorical perspective. Both perspectives realize the liminal nature of time and experience, and "the impossibility of maintaining the distinction between temporal tenses, between an absolutely singular beginning and ending, between living and dying. What performance studies learns most deeply from performance is the generative force of those 'betweens'" (Phelan "Introduction" 8). Rhetorical time includes both "*chronos*," which "measures [the] duration" or chronology of time and "*kairos*," which "marks [the] force" of time, regardless of how long it lasts (Hawhee 66). Both fields find generative force in what happens in the "betweens" of past and present.

As I noted in the Introduction, I adopt a theoretical framework that posits memorialization as a rhetorical, public action that seeks an outcome (i.e., audience engagement). Artifacts that reside in the public's memory are rhetorical because they allow evaluation and interpretation by focusing on contexts and competing perspectives (Blair, Dickinson, and Ott 2010, 2). Marcuse has suggested that for public memory, the "intentions of those who established" memorials exert as much influence as the events themselves (2010, 155).[6] Blair, Phillips, Vivian, and Zelizer frame public memory as "a vernacular presentation of the past composed specifically for the purposes of the present" (Enoch 2013, 62). Reading sites in this way continues to be crucial to public memory because we know that making that past relevant to the present is the desired outcome, and by reading sites and artifacts rhetorically, we can discern those competing perspectives and expand them, especially around gender and the Holocaust.

To understand memorial making as a struggle for visibility and self-representation, especially in terms of gender, we must "understand it as a construction process wherein competing 'moral entrepreneurs' seek public arenas and support for their interpretations of the past" and the present (Wagner-Pacifici and Schwartz 1991, 382). Gender theory around performance (i.e., Butler) posits gender as constructed, deconstructed, and reconstructed in a hierarchy of power based in binaries, and this is particularly visible in the public sphere. In Holocaust memorialization, the images we see—and pointedly do not see—often reinforce this gender binary. In *Shoah* Claude Lanzmann, seeking to re-interpret the past, expands perspectives around survivors but limits them as well by *insisting* that these perspectives remain primarily male.

Though *Shoah* had elements of ambiguity, there was no way to challenge its strict binary in gender representation—until now. The digital archives at the USHMM acquired the *Shoah* interview "outtakes," over 220 hours of interview and site footage, which open up the memorialization in *Shoah* to more equal representations of the spectrum of *both* male *and* female survivor perspectives that can challenge a dominant or "universal" masculinist narrative. Gendering public memory can be "constitutive" of new interpretations about gender—a process that might disturb the binaries and make them more ambiguous (Enoch 2013, 63). This echoes Anzaldua'a original conception of the *mestiza* consciousness with its "tolerance for ambiguity" that "[shifts] out of habitual formations [...] characterized by movement away from set patterns and goals and toward a more whole perspective, one that incudes rather than excludes" (1999, 101). This enhances the notion of *kairos* and performance as the generative force of the "betweens." The concept of the "historical archive," previously limited to a chosen few, becomes suddenly and powerfully open and accessible to audiences and to their gender re-interpretations of that material. Audiences have the opportunity to engage in re-constructing those memories by listening to the survivors build their own stories without Lanzmann's final edits.[7] This active audience engagement, what I call the *performance of public memory*, marks a *kairotic* force in Holocaust memorialization; the past collapses into the present to become performance and a reorientation of self in relation to others.

Gender, Performance, and Orientation

The performance of gendered memory links to rhetoric because it values what words and images "do" and how they create action. For Striff, performances succeed when they draw in the crowds. In spaces like museums, which have thousands of visitors every year, a "crowd" is quantifiable on a daily basis. But any memorial "performance" including text, visuals, and space is "deeply concerned with audience response and participation" and seeks responses that move from a "passive decoding" to praxis: "a context in which meanings are not so much communicated as created, questioned, and negotiated" (Striff 2003, 8). Love sees performance and rhetoric as forging a link that is "insistent on connection" (Love 2018). In terms of Holocaust discourses, audience connection is integral to discovering how meaning can be made—how public memory is performative.

The performative, "constitutes a reality that is in some sense new" (Patraka 1999, 6), but when discussing memory and history, the reality is more so "recontextualized" and "displaced" rather than made new (Hirsch 2001, 218).[8] Patraka accounts for the performative and the "real" that is the history of the Holocaust by redefining a Holocaust performative as the "doing" and "the thing gone" (1999, 7). The performative thus, moves from "being something" to "how saying something can be doing something" (Parker and Kosofsky Sedgwick 1995, 16). Being something—the passive reception of personal stories and historical materials—can become doing something when the experience of reading and seeing Holocaust memorial artifacts creates new meaning. Thus, performing memory about the Holocaust becomes "writing as doing" and as the meaning made about the Holocaust through a dialogic process.

With regard to the self in relation to others, locationally or metaphorically, we are moved by where we turn within this dialogic. By using a non-binary lens to examine gender representation and the Holocaust, we can perform memory and shift our orientation to the past from "I or you" constructions to "us." This creates connections that forge new meanings about what we see. "Orientations," Ahmed argues, are about "how we begin; how we proceed from 'here,' which affects how what is 'there' appears, how it presents itself" (2006, 8). Orientation relies on the location and position of space and bodies, lines and directions, but none of these is a given. Some are just more familiar than others. Using Halberstam, Ahmed suggests that "the concept of 'orientation' allows us to expose how life gets directed in some ways rather than others" (21).

Public memory and gender representations are directed in the same way. The conscious shifting of orientation moves us through stages or locations that begin with orientation (where we are), become disorientation (where we have been), and then reorientations (where we might go or what we might become). When we perform Holocaust memory in order to shift orientations around gender representations, we begin with the familiar, the gender binary. We then move to the alienation from the horror and the loss of direction about what "is" or "should be." We then move to reorientation, which accepts "both/and" as a way to build connections on a spectrum. Our engagement with Holocaust public memory can resist compulsory gender representations by marking the absence of gender or re-marking binary, exclusively masculine spaces as non-binary and inclusive through this process. This applies as much to audiences as it does to subjects. With the opening of digital archives, audiences can turn toward alternative performances of memory and gender construction to complicate what has been heretofore been simplified into a "neutral" ideal.

As we gather information at faster and faster rates and it is shared instantaneously, however, the questions now arise: What do we do with it? Where does it go? What Haskins suggests about public memory online is that, "when technology offers the ability of instant recall, individual impulse to remember withers away," and she cautions that, "if archival preservation and retrieval are not balanced by mechanisms that stimulate participatory engagement, electronic memory may lead to self-congratulatory amnesia" (2007, 407). The performance of memory can counteract this amnesia by deconstructing binary gender representations and shifting the audience's orientation to Holocaust memory, as I will illustrate in my case study of the *Shoah* and the *Shoah* Outtakes.

As Haskins notes, 21st-century public memory work online brings with it increased access to technology but also the danger of public memory becoming meaningless in its lack of participatory engagement. As with the complexity I argue is the strength of *Shoah* and its subsequent outtakes, the complexity of memory artifacts layered one upon the other (as in this book) has the potential to touch audiences at several different points. An American middle school child might read about Anne Frank as part of her 7th grade standards, then while browsing on Instagram for news of her friends she might come across the Instagram posts "by a survivor" crafted and posted in 2019 (Liebermann). Perhaps this leads her to find out more about real survivors at the USHMM website. Perhaps. The *kairotic* impact of one artifact and its related artifacts is hard to measure, much as the level of audience engagement one artifact might engender is hard to predict, yet these repeated encounters, these performances, increase the "between" spaces that allow performative action, connections that might shift orientations.

BINARY GENDER ORIENTATION IN *SHOAH*

Shoah was an astounding film for its time. It is nine hours long and uses only testimony and footage of the abandoned concentration and death camp locations filmed in the present. No one had ever filmed the concentration camp sites in the present. No one had ever interviewed this many survivors or perpetrators on film. There was a *kairotic* force generated at the release of the film. It changed so much of what audiences thought they "knew" about the Holocaust, and opened up the dialogic space between rhetor and audience—the *phere* as "to bear" or carry as witness through listening—that allowed for new voices to be heard and new conversations to happen. When I saw it in Los Angeles ten years later (following the recent opening of the USHMM and *Schindler's List*), its screening was accompanied by scholars' talks after each evening and lists of resources being disseminated. These were all clearly radiating and related effects of its originary *kairotic* force.

For audiences in 1985, simply placing the survivors he interviews back into these death camp spaces bodily/physically in order to "re-construct" the memory, was *kairotic*. It shrunk the distance of time between past and present, while paradoxically showing how the landscape itself, growing over ashes and bodies, erases the event. He does not tell the story of the Holocaust as linear time; rather, he jumps from the past to the present by interweaving testimony about the past (told in the present) with the images of the geographical sites in the present. All of these aspects disturb audiences expecting a historical "story" from beginning to end. As a result, *Shoah* does not present the Holocaust as "*chronos*" which "measures [the] duration" or chronology of time (Hawhee 2004, 66), but rather as "*kairos*," which "marks force" (71).

Shoah became a memorial force as it disrupted public memory around the survivor in 1985 to positive effect.[9]

Though *Shoah* is categorized in the genre of documentary film, Lanzmann "insist[ed] that it is a work of art, an 'originary event' constructed with 'traces of traces'" (Liebman 2007, 4). Lanzmann seeks the traces that lead us to the sites of destruction because he was concerned with the ways in which the destruction of European Jewry would be portrayed culturally—our era's conception of public memory. Lanzmann's rhetorical method is to describe what "he cannot show," and challenges the viewer to construct what they cannot see but what they are hearing—it "encourage[s] us to try to construct a mental map (Camper 2007, 105). Most Americans had only seen footage from the camps, such as the bulldozing of corpses. With this new presentation of largely "unfamiliar details" and stories told sometimes for the first time (Liebman 12), Lanzmann sought to "wound the audience with brutal facts" and bring an immediacy to the film that would "impel intensely personal engagement" (9). Lanzmann felt the news reels made a gruesome spectacle that prevented audiences from doing the really *hard work* needed to get to this traumatic past: "listening, learning, and imaginative engagement" (Liebman 14).

The film opens with the sound of a train, before the audience sees anything else. A quote flashes on the screen, then we see a calm and peaceful river, and a boat. As the boat creeps into the camera frame, we hear singing. It is a child survivor, as we learn a little later, who has been asked back to this place by Lanzmann, to re-create his experience on this river as a boy in the concentration camp singing for Nazi soldiers. They loved his voice. Lanzmann also has this survivor later visit the town in Poland where he used to live, and he films Polish peasants, who talk about him as if he is not there. They do not welcome him home. These are the presences (singing voices of the powerless) and absences (human empathy, remorse for the past) that are immediately presented. They overlap with binary representations of gender in disturbing ways as the film goes on.

In *Shoah* Lanzmann attempts to disorient his viewers and create a discomfort for them that forces the memorial "work" he wanted to elicit, but without strong orientation to begin with, it sometimes fell short in terms of gender representation. If audiences are not familiar with the images Lanzmann is trying to replace with the reconstructed memories of survivors, there is no base from which they can relate. They relate only to the absence and presence of selected voices and bodies, ultimately "othering" the subjects of the film not given a voice. There is no shift in orientation toward those absent. Lanzmann, as director, controls the discourse of his interviewees and his audiences' reception. Although there are many opportunities to engage with the reconstruction of sites and experiences, these moments are selected and hierarchized by gender. While Lanzmann may have wanted to disturb the processes of memorialization and public memory, he was also strangely methodical in not disturbing the representation of gender as binary, especially for women. Almost all the interviewees in the film are men, and when women do appear Lanzmann has them reifying gender binaries that see females as passive in both act and speech, although Lanzmann appears to be presenting the different roles of "all" survivors. In terms of *kairos* it is not just a force that marks and disrupts but also an aperture: "the rhetor opens [himself] to the immediate situation, allowing for more of an exchange" (71). In this sense of *kairos*, real rhetorical force is lost in *Shoah* because the participants in the exchange are limited by the absence of gender complexity and the agency of whole voices. In my opening example, our first child survivor is given only a singing voice, as he was once forced to do by the Nazis. The absence of his real voice persists in every subsequent scene. I will first describe how women are portrayed in their brief excerpts in the film, and then move to discuss how the outtakes complicate representations of both women and men as opposing and hierarchal gender binaries.

Women appear in the film as translators for Lanzmann, as observers of others' stories, and as gender "foils," who underscore women's perspectives as petty. Polish peasant women, for example, are portrayed as only concerned with their men being attracted to beautiful Jewish women: "It's crazy how the Poles liked the little Jewesses!" they exclaim (Ash 2007, 141).[10] Relegating women's contributions in this film to assistants (to the director) and petty competitors for male attention during war reifies the perceived gender binary of men as leaders and women as followers. Women's roles in the film, "hiding, passivity, lament, invisibility," are "supported in the men's narratives about women," as Lanzmann constructs the narrative with gendered purpose. Any woman who shows resistance to these limited roles is shown as tormented and helpless and when she turns to some kind of action, it is usually futile (Hirsch and Spitzer 2007, 180). Lanzmann orients audiences not to the Holocaust as a whole, but situates viewers strictly to the binary of gender they "expect" then builds a series of personal narratives that support this.

The first Jewish female survivor who appears onscreen is Hanna Zaidl, who appears only in the background with her family, smoking and silent. Paula Biren, survivor of Lodz ghetto, appears next. She is interviewed only briefly and does not appear again (as other male survivors do) to describe her experience in the ghetto at length. In the outtakes, her actual interview is over *two hours long*, and she is calm, composed, and detailed in her information about experiences with Nuremberg Laws, in the Lodz ghetto, and in postwar Poland (much like many of the men who tell the same story). It seems that her testimony could have served as further evidence for the narrative of Polish antisemitism and bystander behavior that Lanzmann focuses on in the film, yet he presents only one minute of her story.

Inge Deutschkron is the only woman asked to relive her experience in the present, and it was in hiding. This hidden position, however, according to Hirsch and Spitzer:

> Emblematizes the position of women in the film as a whole. Unlike most of the male witnesses whose faces fill the screen for long periods of time, Inge Deutschkron is little more than a disembodied voice: her narrative is largely presented in voice-over as scenes of Berlin and departing trains occupy the space of the screen; her face and name appear only at the very end of her brief account. (2007, 179)

Another interview is with Ruth Elias. On Disc Four (Second Era: Part II), the final disc but prior to the Schneiders, Elias appears to describe some of the conditions in the Theresienstadt family camp.[11] She begins a story about resistance in Theresienstadt's family camp and the group's transport to Auschwitz that seems to lead to a description of the resistance activities in the camp. But Lanzmann picks up the story from this point in the film using only testimony from Rudolf Vrba and Filip Mueller. In the 1970s and 1980s, these narratives of Jewish resistance had not been extensively researched and were little known. There is no detailing of Elias's time in Auschwitz, her relationships, her witnessing of gassing, or anything with great detail, though it was certainly a unique experience (as I will discuss in her outtakes below). Her segments are provided in order to "set[s] the scene, provide[s] atmosphere, the affect, and not the facts or details," limiting the ways in which her complex experience could be portrayed (Hirsch and Spitzer 2007, 179). The audience is encouraged to see the representation of gender as a binary: women and men have "naturally" different ways to survive that adhere to the passive/active binary. With this binary, audiences seek orientations either toward or away from the subjects. Audiences are encouraged to see the active as admirable and turn toward that. The passive is considered weak and audiences turn away. Audiences are not allowed to see women's or men's representations that challenge this binary—and thus, they remain invisible.

The last two Jewish women onscreen, who precede the final description of the Warsaw Ghetto Uprising (Disc 4: Second Era: Part II), are Gertrude Schneider and her mother (who remains nameless in the film). They come onscreen to "sing a ghetto song." The mother cannot sing the entire piece, she ends up lamenting, and neither woman speaks. The orientation of these scenes continues to uphold a strict binary of female/passive and male/active. Any stickiness of affect in these scenes focuses all emotion, if men are present, onto the female bodies, suggesting as Ahmed does, that in a binary world reason and rationality are male and emotions and irrationality are female, denying the "emotional and embodied" experience of reason that is an aspect of *every*one (2015, 170). Audiences are asked to see those who sing and lament as only vessels through which others speak, which adheres to an outdated separation of mind and body as yet another binary. How then can audiences resist this insistently binary representation? We cannot, unless we are given an opening to do so. The digitized *Shoah* outtakes at the USHMM provide this opening.

KAIROTIC EFFECT: COMPLICATING GENDER ORIENTATION

Shoah was the first widely accessible documentary to use Holocaust testimony, and in order to build *Shoah*, Lanzmann created 350 hours of original site and interview footage. Yet in the final version, Lanzmann used only a portion of this footage and cut more than 90% of his interviews with females from the final film. Recognizing the value of these extended interviews, the USHMM purchased video reels of the outtakes from *Shoah* from Lanzmann on 1 October 1996. They now reside in the Steven Spielberg Film and Video Archive in the USHMM Collections and are jointly owned by the USHMM and Yad Vashem in Jerusalem. With the arrival of sophisticated digitization processes, many of these outtakes are now available on the museum website and extended versions can be accessed onsite.[12]

There are 220 hours of outtakes from *Shoah*, and they reveal that Lanzmann did not keep more complex portrayals of women out of the film because he did not have footage. He had the footage of women; he simply chose to leave it out. The outtakes reveal survivor experiences that add important gendered *pieces* of a memory narrative absent from Lanzmann's meticulously constructed work that is ostensibly about the Holocaust as a *whole*. The promise of these open archives is that memorial practices become more accessible and participatory; they become *kairotic* forces that open apertures for dialogue (Hawhee 2004, 71) and the performance of memory helps audiences connect to the past. Haskins agrees that online memorialization does have that potential:

> Instead of only official accounts disseminated by mainstream media and the government, all kinds of stories can now become part of an evolving patchwork of public memory. Formerly limited in time and space, ephemeral gestures can be preserved in still and moving images, ready to be viewed and replayed on demand. Previously banished to dark storage rooms, mementos left at memorial sites can be displayed for all to see. The boundaries between the official and the

vernacular, the public and the private, the permanent and the evanescent will cease to matter, for all stories and images will be equally fit to represent and comment on the past. (2007, 405)

Access to "all stories" that are available marks a disruption in present time, and certainly this availability poses its own danger to the integrity of factual history and testimony and its uses or abuses. But the disruption I discuss here, of Lanzmann's narrative in particular, results from access to larger storehouse of his own interview footage finally made available to the public (previously unknown and unreleased footage from the same era). The survivor interviewees, whose stories can finally be told "in their own words," become an action that re-orients audiences to an exchange in the present rich with affect. For instance, in the *Shoah* outtakes, Gertrude Schneider's interview is actually 2 hours and 18 minutes long (Film ID: 3221–3225), a great deal longer than the 1.5 minutes she appears on screen in the final film. The interview includes Schneider's mother but the outtakes also reveal that the interview includes Schneider's sister, who does not appear in the final cuts of *Shoah* (she and Gertrude were 11 and 13 at the time of the Holocaust). Their interview gives detailed information about the Riga ghetto. At the end of Clip 1 in the outtakes, Lanzmann asks about sex and abortion in the ghetto. At the beginning of Clip 2, Gertrude's sister says very frankly that pregnant women in the hospital ghetto were forced to have abortions, no matter how late in the pregnancy, even in the eighth month. She says also doctors in the ghetto were ordered to sterilize women. There was even a special room for these procedures, because there was "supposed to be no record." The three women also talk about one woman in the ghetto who had her child, named Moses Ben Ghetto, but he was discovered by the Nazis and killed. They recall the decrees that forbade sex in the ghetto and how "ridiculous" these were because they could not be enforced. Gertrude says she found these orders "interesting" evidence of the dehumanization process. They were meant to, "subdue any idea that one is human" (Clip 2).

This kind of concrete evidence of the dehumanization process regarding sex and abortion reveals very gender-focused practices by the Nazis, but Lanzmann does not include any of this information in the film. Further, Gertrude, her sister, and her mother all speak very clearly, calmly, and with detail throughout the interview. There is no point at which they break down. These behaviors are contrary to the binary gender representation of them as silent, lamenting, and passive women and present them as whole figure with emotions and behaviors that fall into categorizations of both "feminine" and "masculine." All three Schneider women recount horrific stories with very little emotion in these outtakes. Is this perhaps why Lanzmann does not include their pertinent information in the final film? These images conflict with his portrayal of a strict gender binary that has men who speak and women who are silent (or lamenting). The only portion of this interview he used in the film is the women singing, a scene which appears at the very end of *Shoah*. In the outtakes interview, however, only at the end of Clip 3 do the women begin to discuss singing (in the third hour of the interview). The three women describe talented singers who sang on the transports (one might assume to raise morale). At this point Gertrude says: "what was sad is that so many died and nobody cared."

Although in the final film Gertrude's mother remains voiceless, at this point in the outtakes, she says very forthrightly in agreement with Gertrude: "This was the greatest shame, that no one cared." Yet Lanzmann, even in the outtake interview, glosses over these observations of human behavior. These women pass judgment on silent bystanders to the Holocaust. Their words could create action in audiences by bringing their attention to what can happen when people do and say nothing. Yet, Lanzmann focuses only on their traditional gender representations: women must comfort, lament, or remain silent, and prompts them again to sing together. They do, but the mother interjects once more—refusing to be silent—to say that a man in Minsk was killed for helping Jews, but Lanzmann turns them away from the topic of rescuers to sing once more. The women do not choose to do so; Lanzmann prompts them. The fact that Lanzmann asks women, even commands them to "sing" is striking as a shocking gesture of mastery/domination. These gestures by Lanzmann are only revealed in the outtakes.

Although his editing of the film indicates a domination that silences women by making them absent in the final cut, these scenes in the outtakes are further evidence of a male dominance at work that limits the true and lasting *kairotic* force of the film in its original version. These women are repeatedly told how to behave and what to say, even when they resist. These brief clips of the women singing are the only portions of this lengthy interview that make the final cut. They sing the songs that were sung by others to comfort fellow prisoners. They are not allowed to comment on the ethics of society's behavior writ large. The idea that women were overly emotional and therefore "unreasonable" and unreliable is part of a false binary that not only excludes women from "the realm of thought and rationality," but also "works *to conceal* the emotional and embodied aspects of thought and reason" that are present *in everyone* [my emphasis] (Ahmed 2015, 170). The outtakes of the Schneider women disrupt that binary to suggest both reason and emotion reside in women. These three women demonstrate (in their own voices) agency, strength, and survival in the face of gendered torture around reproduction—key details that Lanzmann left on the cutting room floor. Audiences can perform memory by re-constructing those cut pieces into a whole representation that calls audiences to recognize the gendered nature of torture and the complex responses to that violence.

The outtakes reconstruct a gender representation that disrupts the binary of the feminine/passive and masculine/active as well by showing women in resistance and exercising agency in a time of crisis. The outtakes record almost fourteen hours of Jewish women's testimony, and yet they occupy less than thirty minutes of final film time. Ada Lichtman's interview, for instance, is three hours long (Film ID: 3270–3277). Her testimony was used to convict Adolf Eichmann in the 1965 Israeli trial, but her testimony does not appear in the film at all. She also reveals in her interview that Jewish women were "taken by the Germans for their personal use," which was not common knowledge at that time, all while she sews a doll—the job she had in the Sobibor death camp—cleaning and sewing victims' dolls for the children of the SS.[13]

Malka Goldberg's testimony, though only twelve minutes long and audio only (Film ID: 3869–3870), reveals that she was a part of the Warsaw Ghetto resistance and uprising, a culminating event in the final version of *Shoah*, to which her testimony could have added a new and gendered perspective. In the short interview, Goldberg tells Lanzmann that she was in the ghetto resistance, a revelation he glosses over like he does with the Schneiders, choosing to ask instead that she and her male companion sing a Yiddish resistance song. Women are constructed not as individuals with agency but as moral support for the group. Again, the outtakes from the film for Malka actively disrupt Lanzmann's binary gender narrative with new knowledge by presenting women in resistance with strong voices embracing a narrative both reasonable and emotional. Lanzmann is shown again and again commanding women to sing instead of listening to them speak.

Hearing testimony from female survivors through access to the digital outtakes, shifts the *orientation* of audiences to public memory about the Holocaust from the patriarchal "universal binary" of "who should and should not be remembered in the first place" (Enoch 2013, 64), to empower the individual audience member as "archive maker," who multiplies and genders those remembered into non-binary representations of both/and. Audiences are given the tools with which to resist an orientation that "others" the survivors, and instead have access to new images that make visible a complex gender representation in war and trauma. The opening that is created in this *kairotic* moment performs action by stimulating dialogue—not only about gender and Holocaust survival, but also about representation in public memory in general. If this many voices were absent from such a landmark film (that stood alone for several decades), what other voices might be absent from other narratives in public memory? The outtakes present complex retellings of personal narratives from female survivors that are emotional and unemotional, passive and active. As Ahmed suggests, emotion and reason are the purview of everyone, and when we can see both at once, the impact on audiences powerfully reorients them in the present toward the person who speaks from the past.[14]

REORIENTATION TOWARD CONNECTION IN *SHOAH*

As with *kairotic* effect, the non-binary construction of both/and reorients audiences toward the survivors. We are moved by where we turn; the act of listening in response to words that seek action performs that memory as a *kairotic* and emotional connection. Audience response to those survivors, and to the Holocaust itself, is related to our *affect* in relation to those memories. By reconstructing gender representation and the Holocaust as non-binary and ambiguous, we can shift our orientation to the past. Sara Ahmed states that this movement begins with orientations that become disorientations, and then reorientations as a way to build connections (Ahmed 2006, 6–9). Affect comes from such relations.

How can we know what this affect is or even that it occurs? I will first use an anecdotal example that describes my experience of reorientation, and then I will describe how we can theorize this *kairotic* movement further with regard to audiences. In 2012 when I spent time as a Silberman Fellow at the United States Holocaust Memorial Museum (USHMM),[15] attending a two-week workshop on Teaching Gender and the Holocaust, the list of readings included newly acquired archival items from the USHMM film archives: outtakes from the film *Shoah*. At this point, I had been studying and writing about the Holocaust for almost ten years. I thought I could not be shocked by anything I saw or heard, but I was very wrong. Ruth Elias's testimony was particularly difficult to watch.

In *Shoah*, Lanzmann only uses portions of Elias's interview to "set the scene" for Rudolf Vrba and Filip Mueller to describe their active resistance to the Nazis. What the outtakes actually reveal is that Elias herself had much detail to offer not only about women in resistance in Theresienstadt and Auschwitz, but also a chilling story of her resistance to the gendered torture of medical experimenters and to the fate planned for her by Dr. Mengele (Film ID: 3112–3118, Clips 1–7). In part six of the seven-part clips openly accessible on the USHMM website Elias describes the experiments that were performed on her on the order of Dr. Mengele. Though the idea of these experiments has become somewhat "familiar," the experimentation Elias endured is specifically gendered and unfamiliar. Experiments with childbirth and breastfeeding can only be performed on women to seek results about women. Much as Vrba and Mueller have described Jewish resistance (and Elias began to describe in Theresienstadt) on Disc Four of the film (Second Era: Part II), Elias's actions in the outtakes show the highest level of resistance. She actively refuses the fate dictated by Mengele for her and her daughter.

Elias was an inmate at the Auschwitz concentration and death camp, and she explained that she was experimented upon by the "notorious" Dr. Mengele (Elias, Clip 5). Although I knew his experiments were sadistic and inhumane, what he did to Ruth was more horrible than I had ever heard. Ruth got pregnant in the camp, and when she was discovered, she was brought to the medical unit. She describes in the video what happened once she gave birth. Dr. Mengele wanted to know how long a child could survive without being breast-fed. So, Ruth's breasts were bound, and she was made to lie next to her screaming infant as her daughter grew weaker and weaker, day after day. Watching this testimony, especially as a new mother, I cried until I was shaking. Six hours later, I was still crying in spells. I was shocked by what I saw and heard, but even more than that, I was shocked by the hours of powerful testimonies from women that Lanzmann had filmed and chose to *leave out* of his film. The opening of these outtakes from the archives radically shifted my viewpoint about gender and the Holocaust—unalterably.

Sara Ahmed argues that "truths" are only realized through emotion and by what "moves" us, by how "sticky with affect" something is (2015, 11). But affect is the end result of engagement and connection; it *is not* synonymous with emotion. Affect comes from a relationship with the past. When audiences "see" that past in public memory without "seeing" its false neutrality or degendered nature, they might think they "know" it, but it is incomplete, static knowledge. When audiences orient themselves to the past as dynamic public memory—as gendered, rhetorical, and performative—they can participate in bringing that history wholly to life in the present. In the uncut version of Elias's outtake audiences can perceive that she embodies both gender representations of strong and weak, emotional and rational (both/and

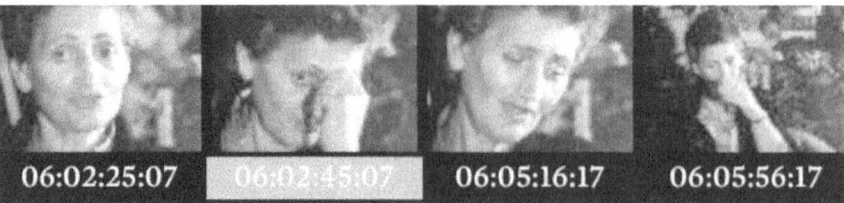

Figure 1.1: Ruth Elias composite scene openings (USHMM website, Shoah Outtakes*). Created by Claude Lanzmann during the filming of* Shoah. *Used by permission of the United States Holocaust Memorial Museum and Yad Vashem, the Holocaust Martyrs and Heroes' Remembrance Authority, Jerusalem.*

as non-binary and ambiguous), and they have the opportunity to re-construct her experience as a whole testimony that s*he* directs, allowing us to listen to her and with her. This powerful *kairotic* moment is a force in time—a past that breaks into the present—and opens an aperture for audiences to participate in that digital archive space. Elias's experience is not "othered" into an edited narrative that upholds a binary of male/female or rational/emotional. She is both.

After Elias described giving birth, she says the camp doctor (also a prisoner) told her Mengele's plans for both of them to die. If she injects the baby with a needle full of morphine, she argues, at least Ruth can live (Clip 6). Elias says she asked: "How can I be the murderer of my child?" The doctor replied, "You are young," she says, "and I must save you. Look at your child, how it looks" (Clip 6). Elias says she was persuaded and gave the child the injection. She cries as she recalls that it took the child one or two hours to die. Corpses were generally collected at the camp and placed in "heaps" in the middle of the camp. They took the child's corpse away early that morning and added it to the pile. When Mengele came back, he asked: "Where is the child?" "It died," says Elias. "I want to see the corpse," she says Mengele ordered, but he was unable to find the tiny body in the heap. She had stopped Mengele's plan to record research from her dead baby's body, but she says, "I was broken. I didn't care to stay or go." She is sent on the next transport to a Leipzig work camp, where she survived the war working together with groups of women to share food and aid each other's survival. Both strands of these narratives defy the "universal" narrative as gender neutral. Elias defied the Nazi's plans and, the camp doctor "saved her life," showing the courageous ability of women to make difficult life/death decisions (even infanticide), as well as the cooperative work that she engaged in with other women later in the work camp, which demonstrates the resilience of women surviving with strength and solidarity.[16] The testimony of Ruth Elias is an example of how audiences can reorient their perspective on the Holocaust survivor with affect—they create a relationship to the past by confronting the non-binary gender self-presentation of Elias. Audiences see her vacillate between emotional and unemotional retellings in this video outtake as she describes heretofore hidden truths about the gendered nature of torture.

There are gruesome details in all of these interviews with women that confront audiences with the baseness of brutality and murder—a complex message Lanzmann sought—yet neither this part of Elias's interview, nor any of the others, ever made it into the film. This interview would have confronted audiences who asked survivors about how they "managed to survive" when others had not (implying immoral choices in a landscape that actually had no morals).[17] It also could have disrupted the construction of torture as "genderless," because as later research showed, Nazi policies and torture targeted females and pregnancy in very specific ways.[18] Lastly, it would have disturbed the stereotypical, gendered narrative where males "actively" resist and females "passively" do not. Lanzmann's film reveals the rhetorics of public memory—gender is neutralized to serve a "universal" narrative or a binary where individuals do not have the chance to represent themselves beyond a narrow spectrum of gender expectations. The woman who testifies has less value for Lanzmann, but audiences can now *choose* to see women like Elias and hear her voice for themselves. They can reorient themselves to her "whole story" and turn toward her story in its depth. The unique experiences of the strong women noted here, now accessible to anyone with the Internet through these outtakes in the USHMM archive, contribute to the concept of the rhetorical, *kairotic* moment, the force in time that marks, that opens, and that extends gender in public memory. Audiences are given the opportunity to respond to the rhetor and resist the binary constructions of gender, re-orienting to build affective connections that perform action.

PERFORMING GENDERED MEMORY: WHO *IS* LISTENING?

The *kairotic* effect of an interactive dialogic that marks a cultural moment with force results from audience engagement with these outtakes to disrupt the binary of gender Lanzmann insists upon. The relationship is affective and dialogic. As Felman and Laub note, "by virtue of the fact that the testimony is *addressed* to others, the witness, from within the solitude of his own stance, is the vehicle of an occurrence, a reality, a stance or a dimension *beyond himself*" (1992, 3). This act of writing/representing experience is a social act that performs memory by demanding response, but this was not how it felt to survivors directly after the war.

The *Shoah* outtakes give audiences a window into why survivors took such a long time to tell their stories, especially women. Paula Biren says after the war she did want to talk, "but no one wanted to hear," so she "clammed up" (Film ID: 3108). Ruth Elias says in Clip 7 of the outtakes that "Nobody understood or wanted to understand what the survivors had been through at that time" (Film ID: 3118). Lanzmann gave audiences a chance to make Holocaust narratives speak into the contextual present in *Shoah*; audiences would have to work at truly listening.[19] But although Liebman claims that the "voices and bodies of those who had seen or themselves been through the worst, and yet were still capable of making their experiences come alive in the present, bear the principal burdens of conveying the truth of what happened" (2007, 14–15), that work is *not* the aperture to a dialogic as Hawhee argues it should be, because Lanzmann sought to elicit specific responses from the audience. These responses were based on not only limited gender representations, as I discussed above, but also on his elaborate re-staging of oral testimonies, that belie a "truth" about how these stories were told (to Lanzmann). Lanzmann's discussion of the ways in which he staged many of these scenes sheds some light on his use of affect to manipulate audience response toward a narrative about German atrocity and Polish complicity, rather than to expand the range of survivor experience (and the resulting audience connection it could engender).

In an interview, Lanzmann admitted that many of the scenes were staged. While filming in Poland, he found (by accident) a train conductor who worked the Treblinka death camp route during the war. Lanzmann described the man as "gentle." Lanzmann convinced him to go to the Treblinka station to reenact his role as the rail cars came through. During this reenactment, the conductor made a slitting throat gesture while looking at the imaginary boxcars coming through. "Compared to this image," Lanzmann claims, real "archival photographs become unbearable. This image has become what is true" (Chevrie and Le Roux 2007, 43). Lanzmann uses embodied reenactments in that present—as in the train conductor scene he describes—to map the past onto the present. Audiences are supposed to piece together these moments of the trains and the deportations from the past to map onto their present. This conflagration of time expresses a kind of force of memory but not one that is truly *kairotic* or performative.

Lanzmann wants the copy, his re-creation, to replace the original as what is "true." The "truth" the audience engages with, however, is one that is based on elicited affect not collaboratively experienced affect, as I described above with the fuller outtake testimonies of the memories of Elias, the Schneiders, and other women. Audiences participate to discern or observe but not to act. The dialogic exchange, the performance of memory—cannot occur because the words Lanzmann creates here are pieces of the truth, or in this case, a false truth that replaces the real event, segments that are commanded by Lanzmann in his "dominance" as director. This artistic subterfuge cannot forge an honest connection with audiences. They might become disoriented by a depiction, but they will never re-orient in a relationship to the past unless they can trust that it attempts to be faithful to those full memories.

Another example of Lanzmann's staging of events for a certain effect as master manipulator is in his interview with Filip Mueller, a survivor of the Sobibor death camp. Lanzmann directed the camera's focus on a close-up of Mueller's face as he speaks in great detail about the gruesome experience of being a *Sonderkommando*.[20] The telling is difficult, and the unrelenting close-up on Mueller's face makes the listening especially difficult for audiences. As

Mueller pauses at times to "collect" himself and control his emotional reactions to describing the burning of bodies and other atrocities, the audience is directed to wait with him and to feel uncomfortable as they watch him from a distance. The close-up does not bring audiences closer; the discomfort of his retelling casts Mueller as an "other" for audiences by disorienting them. There is no opening into which audiences can re-orient to Mueller by connecting to him, by seeing him as a whole person and a survivor. He is only portrayed as this broken man, attempting to wrestle with his experiences, which places him into the same category as the child and woman made to sing. He has no power.

In the outtakes, contrastingly, the audience hears more of Mueller's whole story without these staged moments of difficulty at the center. They are allowed to step away from the unrelenting gaze of the camera on Mueller's face and see him with Lanzmann sitting on a couch, experiencing the storytelling together, or stopping for a cut in the filming. They see Mueller as both emotional and rational not one binary or the other. They are allowed to see Mueller recalling that although he had very little power to change the imminent deaths of victims, he did have the power to tell their stories to the world as they wished them to be told.

For example, Mueller relates in his last scene in the *Shoah* film that a transport came in from Czechoslovakia, his home country. It was late in the war, and the people arriving knew where they were, unlike those on earlier transports. Mueller states that in order to get them to file toward the gas chamber

Figure 1.2: Screenshot of Filip Mueller in Shoah *(Lanzmann).*

in this case, the SS "violence used was extraordinary" (Disc Four, Second Era: Part II). They asked the victims to undress at the gas chamber, but only about one third complied, while the rest refused. They had to be beaten again and again to undress. As they were beaten, they began sing the Czech national anthem, recalls Mueller, and then the Haktiva. "That moved me terribly," he says and then breaks down crying.

At this point he says to Lanzmann, "Please stop." Lanzmann continues to film, not giving him a choice. Mueller continues: "That was happening to my countrymen and I realized my life was meaningless. Why go on living? For what? So, I went into the gas chamber with them. I resolved to die with them." A group of women came up to him and said, "So, you want to die? It's senseless. Your death won't give us back our lives. You must get out alive. You must bear witness to our suffering and to the injustice done to us" (Disc Four, Second Era: Part II). Up to this point, Mueller had felt not only helplessness, but also despair at finding any meaning in these deaths. The women give him back that meaning and purpose. They make their own death meaningful because he will bear witness to their suffering. Lanzmann begins to provide an opening for audiences to connect with Mueller in this human desire for hope.

The outtakes with Mueller, however, show the details that Lanzmann will not: the women Mueller refers to are not nameless (Box 3207, Clip 4). Mueller knows the woman to whom he speaks; he calls her Jana in the outtakes. He knows her betrothed; she gives him a necklace to give to that man. These are details about what was said between humans just before death. It recovers the humanity and the connections of the people who were dehumanized, and allows audiences to be affected by that connection and feel closer to the past. It gives a name to a woman burned to ashes and shows her courage; she was already thinking beyond her own experience about the historical record and her people in the broadest of ways. The outtake clip also gives audiences a chance to see Mueller decide what to share and when. It was important for him to remember this woman and this encounter. After this event, he says: "*Es war genug. Ich war voll*" (It was enough. I was done.) [my translation] (Clip 4).

The subjects of *Shoah* are unable to become active agents in the creation of public memory, or to share their unedited story with audiences, which as Blair, Dickinson, and Ott argue, "narrate[s] shared identities, constructing senses of communal belonging" (2010, 6). Lanzmann takes away that sense of belonging and connection because the agency in this film resides mostly with the director. With the opening of the USHMM archives with newly acquired outtakes from the film, however, audiences can access the testimony footage left out of the film and begin to collaboratively build a different patchwork of memory around the events detailed in *Shoah*, especially concerning gender. The non-binary representations build a fuller picture of survivors from the past in the present. These *kairotic* moments create space for a negotiation of intergenerational meaning-making. For new generations, who perform memory within new parameters of what memory and meaning-making can *do*, these are new paths that connect their present to the past.

What Ruth Elias says to an audience in 2018 about reproductive choice takes on different meaning than it did when she spoke to Lanzmann in the 1970s or when he released the film in 1985. It will be interesting to see how audiences engage with Elias in another decade. In the scenes with Mueller the gender binary is subverted in terms of masculinity when men break down; in these moments the performance of non-binary gender is complex; men embrace the spectrum of gender that includes strength, vulnerability, agency, and emotion, but Lanzmann staged many of these crying scenes with men to stand alone without the complexity of a range of emotions; perhaps he was striving for the maximum emotional disturbance for audiences rooted in the gender binary that asserts that men do not cry? What Lanzmann could not predict is that audiences in the 21st century might find this complexity inspiring. They might prefer to see the outtakes of the interviews more than the film itself because they can re-orient themselves to queer connections to the past. They do not have to remain distant and disoriented. With access to videos like Elias's and Mueller's perhaps that third generation of audiences will walk away with new conceptions of gender representations or gendered resistance (especially unarmed) and what it means to be a woman and a man in crisis.

The ability to engage with the testimonies from *Shoah,* without the heavy-handed mediation of Lanzmann, opens up the possibility of building a collaborative archive of memory that is interactive—it shifts audiences' orientation to the past and connects them through the performance of a dialogue. When audiences watch Ruth Elias talk about her experiences and then talk back to Lanzmann, audiences see an active memory narrative with which they can also engage. They can play Elias's testimony in order or play each clip at will. They can search the USHMM archive to find other materials related to Elias and her experiences, other testimonies, maps of sites, biographies of people like Mengele. The site itself promotes cross-referencing that performs memory. The audience listens to Elias unedited. They acknowledge that her interview is still guided by certain questions, as most Holocaust testimonies are, but the audience also has the option of seeking more information through links on the Elias page or with references cited at the bottom of the page.

But *will* audiences become active participants? This is perhaps the largest question that persists for memory scholars of the 21st century. What compels audiences, and how and why? Twenty-first-century audiences are becoming numb to trauma as civil wars rage worldwide and mass shootings and terrorist bombings increase. As I listened to several radio stories in May of 2019 about species extinction and another school shooting, the journalists asked their interviewees again and again how audiences might release that numbness to connect to the catastrophe. How does any artifact or site compel active remembrance? How do they produce relationship based in affect when we are so prone to numbness? The level of a memorial object's potential "interactivity" cannot define this. As Haskins suggests, the digital era encourages more access but: "one cannot ignore that today's memorializing occurs in a climate of rapid obsolescence and the disappearance of historical consciousness." Indeed, "much of computer-mediated communication serves commercial and entertainment purposes, and that interactivity can nurture narcissistic amnesia no less than communal exchange" (2007, 406). Framed in this way, the acquisition of knowledge—especially digital knowledge—has a passive quality. Audiences can absorb the knowledge and use it not to inquire or dialogue, but simply to reflect on themselves in an eternal present, outside of any culturally contextualized past or present.

As audiences grow increasingly distant in time from the Holocaust, the way that public memory is transmitted depends on the positionality and experience of the "entrepreneur" of public memory as well as the audience for that memorial act. One of the important mechanisms that stimulate participation in the construction of Holocaust public memory is precisely the fact that artifacts of memorialization do not exist in a temporal void of the eternal present. They are linked, sometimes intimately, often intergenerationally, to those artifacts or stories that have come before, and may come after. The "linkedness" forms a relationship that defies temporality. *Shoah* depended on the testimony work that David Boder performed in the 1940s.[21] It depended on the trust of the survivors Lanzmann interviewed. Its further relevance as a memorial act depends on audiences who watch the outtakes to understand the truly gendered nature of that public remembrance tomorrow and in a decade. Hawhee's *kairotic* force opens a space that audiences can step into to experience reorientation—a turning toward and connecting in a non-binary way. They can listen and respond, and are asked to consider stories and the ways these link with their own.

When audiences participate in this way, they perform memory—words can become action through communal memory work that includes trust, relationship, and connection—a shift in orientation that turns toward instead of away. Through interaction with the archive, audiences actively choose the information they need to increase their knowledge. The links to outside pages or to pages within the museum website are directed but not limiting. Whatever information a listener finds, there is always more information. The choice to learn more (or not to learn) is left up to that audience, which in some ways is dangerous territory. The value of the opened archive is its relationship to this artistic text *Shoah* and all the artifacts that memorialize the Holocaust, but the question will continue to be: *Will* audiences seek more information about something that makes them uncomfortable or that challenges the idea of the inherent "good" in humanity? Perhaps the master director Lanzmann himself might have the last word on what might be possible in the future in a posthumous statement about the importance of complex gender representations. Although he returned many times to the outtakes of *Shoah* himself to make related and shorter documentaries, one stands out in this analysis. *Les quatre soeurs* (*Shoah: Four Sisters*). In 2017, shortly after the USHMM released the outtakes to the online public, Lanzmann released this documentary that focuses only on the voices of women. He takes the interviews with Elias, Biren, and Lichtman, as well as Hanna Marton, and extends these into a four-hour documentary about the experiences of women in the Holocaust. Perhaps it will be this film that prods audiences to seek their own viewing of outtakes at the USHMM. Perhaps they will only see it on YouTube. Will it remain simply *chronos*, a point on a timeline, or will it become *kairos*, that force that can open dialogic witness? In either case, the new memory artifacts seek to open spaces that performatively bridge the "betweens" of past and present to connect people to the traumatic experiences of others.

CONCLUSION

Audiences play an important role in making the outtakes of *Shoah* in the USHMM archives performative memory work that recasts gender binaries to provide a fuller picture of survival. The outtakes, and the audiences who access them, have the potential to overcome Lanzmann's intent. Access to the outtakes of *Shoah* require only the Internet and the museum's website address.[22] Though my mother and I have read and seen so many Holocaust-related artifacts, she never saw the film *Shoah*. I think this nine-hour film was too much for her. When I told her about the outtakes, however, she went immediately and watched some of them online. She was moved by the unedited starkness of the language and emotions. Watching some made her want to watch more. The outtakes at the USHMM, though originally "authored" by Lanzmann, take on a life of their own when audiences are able to choose what to look at and when in the present. The outtakes actually overpower Lanzmann's work by de-gendering the film's masculine gaze.[23] Audiences do not have to hold on to the gaze in the same way as the film, and they also can shift their gaze, therefore lessening the limited gender representations of the subjects. The time period in which *Shoah* was created and released locate it on a spectrum of time; in the 1980s audiences did not have a nuanced understanding of the Holocaust and were just beginning to grasp the complexities of gender. But the modern, intergenerational experience is more fluid around these issues. This is the audience that is now engaging with Holocaust memory; thus, for this history and these memories to remain relevant in the present, it is important to understand how that memory work might be best performed to create action and response, which is the outcome that Striff and others have suggested memorial artifacts ultimately seek.

In the ever-present realm of social media, instant gratification, fake news, and extremist positioning, however, the concept of gender representation as non-binary and inclusive in Holocaust memorialization (or in any realm) might seem increasingly distant. Many 21st-century citizens come face-to-face with the foreclosure of the past as irrelevant to the present in the very visible representations of male-dominated right-wing populism in the United States and Europe, that encourages nationalism and scapegoating which targets Jews and minorities, and immigrants and Muslims. Perhaps audiences have become too familiar with a few stories about the Holocaust, convincing themselves that they know enough. The performance of memory for audiences now is not only necessary but also essential to the deconstruction of an exclusive, dominant narrative.

The consequences of not performing memory, of resisting a shift in our orientations toward others, are not only continued Holocaust denial,[24] racial and ethnic strife, hyper-nationalism,[25] and xenophobia worldwide, but also a regression to the ways in which we used to understand gender and human relations: as an unresolvable, combative binary. The Holocaust was a broad, gendered experience that exists, as traumatic experiences do, on a spectrum. Audiences are well served by confronting the complexity of memory, not by reducing it to a simplistic gender binary. Access to archives opens up the public memory space to non-binary representations of gender and experience to make it possible for audiences to perform memory with newly contextualized knowledge. General educators and Holocaust Education sites can help them find and engage with that knowledge (this is a larger discussion in Chapter Five). Audiences can resist regression to binary, universal memory narratives that only tell part of the whole story and turn toward the opening of *kairos* and the movement of orientations. They can perform these between spaces in the moments that they affectively connect.

NOTES

1. I am indebted to my reading group member, Dr. Piano, for the formulation of this sentence.
2. Bernard-Donals has also discussed public memory as a dialogic of remembering and forgetting (2009).
3. I refer to the well-known, published diary edited by her father. The unedited version of her diary has more ambiguity and complexity.
4. Even as it allows audiences to remain ignorant to the reality of her ultimate death in the Bergen-Belsen concentration camp.
5. Though it is categorized in the genre of documentary film, Lanzmann "insists that it is a work of art, an 'originary event' constructed with 'traces of traces'" (Liebman 2007, 4).
6. Akcan has noted that "the Washington Mall" reflects the fact that memorial making is one of "the most consumed mediums of self-representation and struggle for public visibility" (2010, 155).
7. This is of particular interest with regard to this influential film, but archives that hold Holocaust oral testimonies have become increasingly accessible. The USC Shoah Foundation Institute for Visual History and Education, started by Steven Spielberg after he released *Schindler's List*, is a good example of this.
8. Hirsch discusses this "recontextualization" in "Surviving Images" in reference only to *Maus*.
9. Public memory can also be disrupted in ways that are regressive. The Parliament in Poland passed a law in early 2018 that bans anyone from claiming that Poland was complicit in the war crimes of World War II before, during or after the Holocaust as a "collaborator." The revision of a nation's history and legal precedents for ideological purposes is gaining popularity in a country leaning increasingly nationalist and to the right. See Zerofsky's thorough article in *The New Yorker*, 30 July 2018, issue. Santora and Berendt covered the law and Israel's reaction to it in February 2018 in *The New York Times*.
10. This depiction of women as actively undermining other women because of their competition for the attention of men has become mythic in media for its consistent degradation of female intellect/ambition as well as its militant heteronormativity. Also, Ash is right to point out that although Lanzmann claimed "nothing essential in what regards the Poles is left out," his depiction of them in the film is as a callous people without compassion. What other research reveals, however, is that many details (as I am arguing about the missing gender piece of this film) are left out. Ash cites one text, Nechama Tec's *When Light Pierced Darkness*, which has over 500 case studies of Poles helping Jews (1987, 143).
11. Theresienstadt was the "model camp" that the Nazi leaders showed to international Red Cross representatives to prove that the Nazi treatment of prisoners was humane.
12. The USHMM archives, however accessible to the public, are still rigorously catalogued and protected. Users are prohibited from "mashing" up images in their own video montages, etc., which is why the museum has a strict user policy. All

users need permission to employ images from the site in public displays or on public sites. The access to this archival material, therefore, encourages accurate knowledge acquisition and sharing. The USHMM digital databases do privilege knowledge from their own site, but they also use extensive links to outside archives and historical repositories (for instance, information about the family memory books in Yiddish, *yizkor*, link to an outside archive that has digitized and translated many of these books). All stories, therefore, can become part of the "evolving patchwork of public memory" (Haskins 2007, 405).

13. This reenactment is part of how Lanzmann asked interviewees to "relive" their story of the past as they testified in the present.

14. Gender non-binary representation should include the complex, emotional stories of men as well, and the outtakes provide evidence of a bigger picture than the one Lanzmann originally constructed for men.

15. I thank the Silberman Foundation, the Center for Advanced Holocaust Studies, and the USHMM for this life-changing professional opportunity.

16. Other scholars have done excellent work on women and collaboration during the Holocaust. See, for example, Baer and Goldenberg's edited collection.

17. See Langer (2006) for more on "choiceless choices."

18. See, for instance, Gisela Bock's article: "Racism and Sexism in Nazi Germany: Motherhood, Compulsory Sterilization, and the State" (1983), which came out two years before *Shoah*, and the USHMM's extensively researched traveling exhibition: "Deadly Medicine: Creating the Master Race," an exhibit that still travels today, being shown in Tennessee in 2017, for example (ushmm.org). The exhibition also resulted in an edited collection (see Bachrach 2004).

19. Lanzmann, because he was already concerned with the ways in which the destruction of European Jewry would be portrayed culturally, saw his work as material traces that led directly back to the sites of destruction (the camps). He was disappointed with the timid production of the 1970s miniseries *The Holocaust* (Lanzmann 2007, 29–30). There was no grand narrative or a chronological explanation for how the Holocaust was "engineered," and to simplify that fact for audiences he saw as a degradation of the event. He did not see the simplification of gender in that way.

20. *Sonderkommandos* were assigned to burn the bodies that had been gassed. These were usually strong men, who were then killed after a few months to destroy the possibility of testimonial evidence of what they had seen. Mueller is one of the only survivors who served in this role and lived to tell about it.

21. Historical Commissions in Poland and the Soviet Union convened even before the war was over. These commissions recorded interviews with civilians and the military to make a record of the events that had transpired. These commissions continued after the war in Displaced Persons camps and elsewhere, and at Nuremberg, eyewitness testimony played a large role in convictions. Testimony from survivors was invited by Eisenhower and recorded as early as 1946 by people like psychologist David Boder. It was not until 1998 at the Illinois Institute of Technology, where he was a professor for 27 years—37 years after his death—that the institute library staff uncovered his 16-volume set of typescripts and transcribed and translated all the interviews into English to make them available for researchers in 2009. (Colotla

and Jurado 2014). Lanzmann would not have had access to all of Boder's tapes, but it was well known that Boder had done these postwar interviews and that other such interviews existed. For more on Boder see also Rosen (2009; 2012).

22. This access is a mediating difference between the audience and the artifacts of memory, unlike archives of the past. Now, one need not be an academic or a filmmaker to access the voices of the Holocaust past. This is true of this archive but also many others that have expanded exponentially in the last couple of decades. The USC Shoah Foundation Institute for Visual History and Education, started by Steven Spielberg after he released *Schindler's List*, is a good example of this. It contains over 52,000 oral testimonies, a portion of which are accessible to anyone on their website. Access to the full collection does require a membership (mostly held by universities).

23. See Mulvey (1975) for the first iteration of this concept.

24. Historical denial and ideological politics are the elements that led to the recurring rise of both neo-Nazism and its primary ideology: antisemitism (Goldberg 2015; Sherwood 2017). Denial of the Holocaust specifically has unfortunately persisted for decades. The best resource on Holocaust denial is Deborah Lipstadt's *Denying the Holocaust: The Growing Assault on Truth and Memory* (1994). She tracks a growing trend over two decades with the rise of antisemitic and neo-Nazi groups and politicians like David Duke. The story of Deborah Lipstadt and denier David Irving are detailed in the 2016 movie, *Denial.* So-called historians like Briton David Irving created "revisionist histories" that denied the Holocaust happened. Holocaust denial has been soaring in online spaces in the last two years especially. See, for example, an article in *The Guardian UK*, "New Online Generation Takes Up Holocaust Denial" 21 January 2017.

25. See endnote 9, for example, on resurging Polish nationalism.

Chapter Two

Schindler's List and Its "After-Affect"
Son of Saul, Spielberg's List, *and the USC Shoah Foundation Visual History Archive*

I first saw Steven Spielberg's *Schindler's List* the same year it was released in 1994. I had just returned from a long stay in Israel as a volunteer on a kibbutz, and my head was filled with the starkly colorful images of dusty buses laboring across the desert, machine gun–clad teenagers in uniform at my favorite falafel shop, and distinctive but coexisting religious sounds in the quarters of downtown Jerusalem. When I talked to survivors of the Holocaust on the kibbutz, they saw Israel as a haven from hatred and persecution, but they seemed rather blind to the reality that Israel's treatment of the Arabs and Palestinians in their midst might be understood as a similar kind of persecution.[1] Two years later, in 1996, I stood in the town square in Krakow, Poland, and later walked the nearby grounds of Auschwitz with my mother, the same locations where Spielberg had filmed, but unlike the film, these places evoked nothing heroic or mythic. I felt instead a deep sadness and mourning that was fueled by what seemed like an absence of knowledge and connection to this past demonstrated by the Polish natives around me. On the bus to the Auschwitz camp memorial, the bus driver continually referred to our destination as the city of Oświęcim, a way to return the German Auschwitz to its Polish language origin, to which I can relate, but he kept saying town and not camps, as if they could now be separated. My mother and I exchanged shocked glances but my grandmother seemed not to be listening. The distant relatives I met outside Krakow with my mother (and my grandmother and great-aunt) had the same amnesia-tinged memories of the war that my grandmother did in the United States. They were too busy farming or working to "pay attention" to politics. They don't remember the ostracizing prejudice, expulsion, or death of Jews in either of their contexts.[2]

WHAT "MOVES" US?

This experience comes to mind as I contemplate the tendency of a public's memory to oscillate between remembering and forgetting the Holocaust past in the present, and it does not have to do just with age or generation. Bernard-Donals explores the phenomena of forgetful memory and the Holocaust through the philosophical writings of Emmanuel Levinas and notes that: "if [...] Levinas's witness is someone who feels the weight of the event bodily and not just intellectually and existentially," we might find much in "what is said" (2009, 5). Feeling something in the body has to do with emotion—a powerful factor, but emotions (especially emotions like empathy or sadness) have also been maligned on the gender binary as emotions that make one vulnerable and therefore weak (unlike emotions like anger). Sara Ahmed, in the *Cultural Politics of Emotion* makes the point that emotion indeed has been categorized on the gender binary as a "feminine" trait, associated with irrationality and weakness because it is immediate and "uncontrollable" (2015, 170) as we saw to an extent in the discussion of the male witness in *Shoah* in Chapter One, although ironically everyone must know that a "masculine" emotion like anger has the very same characteristics. So why does the binary persist?

To fight the forgetfulness of memory, publics need to confront the complexity of memory by challenging simplistic representations of the gender binary. Audiences can resist universal and so-called neutral narratives that only tell part of the whole story by turning toward the opening of *kairos* and shifting their orientations to the so-called "other," whoever it might be in a historical moment. In *Shoah*, the resistance to a gender binary emerged in the outtakes, as survivors revealed the complexity of their gender roles and emotions along a spectrum (such as in resistance or through emotional displays)—a spectrum that Lanzmann resisted showing. In this chapter, I will show how *Schindler's List* opened a *kairotic* moment in American public memory but reinforced the binaries of gender representation. Like *Shoah*'s outtakes that dialogue with and complicate the original film, the two films I examine in this chapter, first briefly *Spielberg's List* and then more extensively *Son of Saul*, are in dialogue with *Schindler's List* responding to what I call its "*after-affect*." Emotionally *Schindler's List* was a powerhouse; this was part of the *kairotic* public memory moment. Many critics called its emotional effect superficial while fans embraced the powerful effect. This is the "after-affect" I mean to explore. What can these newer films reveal about the way we react to Holocaust films emotionally, and how might this build to a shifting of orientations to perform public memory and trauma so that we might be better able to connect with traumatic events and each other?

CONNECTION: STICKY WITH AFFECT

What repeats without reflection in public memory can be perceived automatically as something "true"; this is why historical fiction can become so problematic for audiences. As we move further away from the event though, these fictional and factual elements blur more and more. That blurring and ambiguity can lead to forgetful memory but can also put the bodily feeling Levinas noted into relief. Ahmed argues that truths are only realized through emotion and by what moves us, by how "sticky with affect" something is (2015, 11). Holocaust film is sometimes the "stickiest" with affect because it is based on audiences being moved by what they see; but "being moved" is passive and might easily lead to a binary categorization of "good" and "bad" without any of the ambiguity that exists in real life. With a complexity of gender representation in visual forms of Holocaust public memory instead, this audience experience, what I call here the "after-affect," can be a non-binary movement of working through a variety of ambiguous emotions: the holding of both repulsion and connection, for example. In Chapter One I discussed Lanzmann's "re-creation" as a resistance to trying to "return" to an event. There is an impossibility in return, which is the challenge of making memory and history matter in the present. Holocaust film as a genre has often relied on fiction and historical fact together, which both simultaneously reveal and obscure. This is one of the problems with fictional Holocaust representations.[3]

The release of *Schindler's List* was a *kairotic* moment in Holocaust public memory similar yet different than *Shoah*. The ways in which audiences responded emotionally to *Schindler's List* were similar to *Shoah* but multiplied by the millions of viewers it reached (unlike *Shoah*). *Schindler's List* was so popular, it became a reference point for American audiences to access anything related to the Holocaust (as I will discuss below). Remember that rhetorical time includes both "*chronos*," which "measures [the] duration" or chronology of time and "*kairos*," which "marks [the] force" of time, regardless of how long it lasts (Hawhee 66). Both fields find generative force in what happens in the "betweens" of past and present. Likewise, the performance of memory highlights the liminal nature of time and experience, and how generative it can be to explore the ambiguous space in between that emerges. What could happen in the space between *Shoah* and *Schindler's List*? How do we understand history more or less as a result of engaging with two very different kinds of fact and fiction, and those cinematic forms that follow?

Film is condensed and intense, which prevents it from working as a comprehensive history, but this is also one of the features that makes it widely accessible to audiences (most people can access films who might not have access to archives, libraries, or museums). Popular films are also more accessible than documentaries, especially in the time period I discuss here (before streaming). Part of *Schindler's* effect was that so many millions of people viewed it and were moved by it. For "affect to have an effect," says, Ahmed, there must be shared witnessing. The more people that can come together to experience and empathize with trauma *as witnesses* (which implies a responsibility beyond passive looking), the better they can connect to the other. The resulting public memory impact of this "community of shared witnesses"—what I call "after-affect"—can be enormous (Ahmed 2015, 94).

This after-affect tends to entrench itself in binary terms, however, especially in terms of gender representation and the perception of emotion, but that binary can also be broken to create openings (the performative and *kairotic* gaps) for productive audience response. Dichotomized audiences and critics hold views that seem irreconcilable, and yet there is an in-between, a non-binary gendered and emotional space that Ahmed says categorizes thought and rationality as embodied (as Levinas did): both rational and emotional. This inclusive space can be enacted through audience interactions with difficult films about the Holocaust (which many audiences will not seek out) but also by communal interactions with less difficult films like *Schindler's List*. As I mentioned in Chapter One too, there is an opportunity that comes from engagement with memorial artifacts that might lead to other engagements. The testimony archive resource that Spielberg was able to create because of *Schindler's List*, USC Shoah Foundation Visual History Archive, is one opportunity that leads directly from the film itself. I will first look at *Schindler's List* as an aesthetic artifact both praised and vilified and then analyze two newer films, *Spielberg's List* and *Son of Saul*, to see the ways in which gender representations may or may not have changed, and in what ways these newer films re-orient viewers to this history. Fictional representations of the Holocaust can be "stickier" with affect than other artifacts and filmic versions do so quickly and effectively to draw audiences into the story of a person or a family. The *effect*, or impact, of these films is closely related to *affect*, the ways in which audiences are moved to "see" the Holocaust (or not see it). I will then explore how this after-affect is multiplied with the USC Shoah Foundation Visual History Archive.

THE "RE-OPENING" OF PUBLIC MEMORY:
KAIROS AND *SCHINDLER'S LIST*

Part of the performance of public memory around the Holocaust requires discourse to become public and to seek an effect upon a listening audience;[4]

thus, these public memory artifacts can be classified as speech acts: performative acts that are "always spoken to others" (Ahmed 2006, 94) and that seek to share witnessing. I ended Chapter One with a discussion of listening and active audiences. The perception by survivors that there is someone who listens is crucial to their motivation to tell their story. In Chapter One, I cited the seminal work *Testimony* from psychoanalysts Felman and Laub that first discussed this in terms of a speech act. Mikhail Bahktin also explored the speech act in relation to dialogic communication as a linguist. Judith Butler insists that we likewise "act" in gender performance as "doing gender." Performance scholars like Della Pollock have defined the act of writing as "doing." Ahmed is a philosopher who broaches this topic through the lens of emotion and affect. The concept is similar; it is just that disciplinary boundaries shift and blur, to question what has been "standard." I purposely cross disciplines around this concept of performing public memory because boundaries, like binaries, can be arbitrary. What is important is that each discourse performatively seeks action in its audience.

Once the audience is listening to the speech act, they participate in "shared witnessing," or generative community building, which "is required for the affect to have an effect" (Ahmed 2015, 94), but the degree to which a public can access or participate varies. The almost simultaneous opening of *Schindler's List* (1994) and The United States Holocaust Memorial Museum (USHMM) (1993) created a significant *kairotic* moment in public memory that resulted in an aperture—an opening was created; Americans were made aware of the event on a mass visual and spatial scale.[5] Film can be one of the more accessible forms of public memory because it is widely distributed, and audiences also participate in communal viewing in large numbers.[6] In *Schindler's List* Spielberg's "documentary style" filming helped audiences feel like the past was bleeding into the present and "they were there." The movement of time for audiences made them feel closer to an event that was becoming distant in public memory when the film was released in 1994.

The concept of communal viewing suggests a theater and a film audience, which is part of what I mean here; but there is also the reality of 21st-century viewing practices that include home viewing through a streaming service like Netflix or watching on phones. Devices, as they have become more mobile are taken everywhere, accompany people where they go and often their viewing will be among a crowd (the viewer will eventually engage with those people around them—we hope—affected by knowledge they have just witnessed). But there is also the reality of solo viewing at home. Even in this case, the viewer connects with others through statistics like: "this # of people recently bought this film," or "viewers who watched *Schindler's List* also watched 'x.'" The 21st-century viewing community might not be physically there, but it is implied and can be digitally counted.

Thus, the opportunities for affective experiences and connections to occur through viewing are multiple. If emotions move us, these movements exist in time as moments, and they are often communal experiences. The performative nature of the *relationships* between speakers and listeners is crucial to understanding how public memory evolves, but the movements depend on force. As I explored in Chapter One, Hawhee nuances historical rhetoric to present a notion of *kairos* as a force catalyzed by the movements between "discursive moment[s]" (such as the discursive moment that a film is released and discussed), when a rhetor directly addresses the reader or listener to create an aperture:

> *Phere* comes from the verb *phero*, which means "to bear" or "to carry" but can also (at the same time) indicate a yielding or producing […] The act of listening then becomes just that: a productive, active, transformative act for hearers and speakers. This moment of direct address then, emphasizes the transformative encounter produced through discourse." (Hawhee 2004, 77–78)[7]

Hawhee claims the encounter produced through discourse is "carried" by listeners and becomes a transformative "act," much as performance can become action by doing. The concept of embodied listening as *phere*, as "to bear" is seen in Lanzmann's *Shoah*, where audiences were asked to work to make meaning. As it was the first major visual artifact that gave voice and vision to the experience of the Jewish survivor for large audiences,[8] it created a discursive moment, or opening, in public memory for audiences to imagine and feel the knowledge of shared memory and bear witness to that experience (the mind and the body)—viscerally. The viewing was never expected to be passive. Audiences must both "bear" or "carry" the memories presented, as they also must "yield" their preconceptions and "produce" an action in response as a dialogue.

The *kairotic* force in the movement of "discursive moments," however, "depends on openings as much as it depends on movements" (Hawhee 2004, 83), especially in the realm of public memory. A rhetor can open up to a listener and really ask something of them (or not),[9] but first there needs to be an opening to begin that conversation. Between the opening of public memory with *Shoah*, there was an almost 10-year period where the window on public memory and the Holocaust seemed to close with the rise of anti-memory phenomena like Holocaust denial, that had existed previously but seemed to increase in its proponents and its media publicity.[10]

Deborah Lipstadt, an American historian based at Emory University, addressed this disturbing phenomena in *Denying the Holocaust: The Growing*

Assault on Truth and Memory (1994), which tracked two decades of a growing number of deniers or so-called "revisionists." Sometimes moments like these produce a *kairotic* effect that is at first negative but opens a space for generative exploration into the spaces between past and present, calling on audiences to pay particular attention now—and respond to history in the present. The February 1994 release of Steven Spielberg's Hollywood film *Schindler's List* became one of these moments that responded to this rise in denial because it was successful and popular globally. The performative aspect of *Schindler's List* was that it garnered so much immediate attention that audiences, critics, and survivors responded and real actions resulted in the public realm to begin the conversations (such as the creation of Spielberg's testimony archive). The dialogue about the Holocaust that resulted was more multivalent than those around *Shoah* because it reached broader audiences that included scholars, critics, and the general public (whereas *Shoah*'s length alone prevented it from being as widely screened or viewed by general audiences). Jon Gross, a British critic for the *New York Review of Books* said Spielberg's film was a strong "new departure" in representing the event (1994, par. 4). Criticism also appeared, but it is significant to my argument that it mostly showed itself in academia rather than in popular media. *Schindler's List* sought affective response from audiences, and because it required less work and imagination on the part of the audience, it gained larger audiences than *Shoah*. The public loved this film.

Schindler's List was released in America in February 1994 and its impact was immediate. IMDb (an online film website) calls the film: "a testament for the good in all of us."[11] The film won seven Oscars and the American Film Institute ranks it as number three in the "100 most inspiring movies of all time" (IMDb). In December 1994 *The LA Times* called it "quietly devastating" (Turan 1993, par. 2). The year 2015 marked the 22nd anniversary of the film and in April of that year *The Boston Globe* called it *"still* the definitive Holocaust drama." The world of the Holocaust was one "where unimaginable humiliation was the stuff of routine, where people were murdered as an afterthought and everyone who saw it did no more than blink" (Matchan 2014, par. 1). The cultural impact of the film as a *kairotic* reference point for Americans comes, in part, from the timing of its release as I note above but also from the mythical origin story: a famous director goes against the grain of Hollywood to make a film without getting paid. He defies studio executives who told him to "just make a donation" instead of making a long, depressing film about the Holocaust (IMDb).

Yet numerous scholars found it rife with sexist and antisemitic stereotypes[12] and other filmmakers called it sentimental kitsch.[13] In terms of performance and the disruption of public memory, the film both "disturbed" memory by getting so many people, so immediately, to talk about the Holocaust when they had been silent but also "reified" many binary and gendered tropes about that memory. What was clear about the film (then and now) was its ability to open dialogue; it gave survivors a public opening into which to tell their stories (leading ultimately to the massive archive of oral testimony at USC), and it gave permission, said Stephen Smith, director of the USC Archive, "for people to speak about the Holocaust on a number of different levels" (2014, par. 5). American audiences needed a way to navigate this devastating historical event,[14] and *Schindler's List* provided the first widely accessible platform to do so. This film and its *kairotic* moment opened a path to other important public memory moments around the Holocaust that move audiences toward deeper connections to this history, but for public memory to become performative, it requires several "ways in" as I will iterate throughout this book, using the tentative "mapping" provided by the work of Della Pollock. First let's revisit audience orientation and the need to deconstruct binaries of remembering and forgetting through a closer look at *Schindler's List*'s gaps and the "after-affect" of its reach.

BREAKING THE BINARY: SHIFTING AUDIENCES' ORIENTATIONS

Though longer documentary films fall into a different genre, it is productive to rethink "orientations" as we did in Chapter One for the fictional films created for large viewing audiences, which is the focus of this chapter. In *Queer Phenomenology*, Sara Ahmed suggests that in phenomenology, we "'turn toward' objects" (2006, 25) instead of directing consciousness inward, allowing things to become "sticky" with affect. But what if this turning toward objects did not allow us to really see the "other" or the object? For fictional depictions, what is "true" is what audiences are directed to see. In *Schindler's List*, this is a rather straightforward process in which we see devastation and murder and are directed by the "documentary news style" to feel sad about the "fact" of murder and happy about the "fact" that some "victims" were saved with the help of their white, German savior.[15] The binary of good and evil is easy to discern (even if the protagonist we are supposed to cheer for is a Nazi—this is the ambiguous part of the story) and there is something to be happy about at the end of the story. Hollywood films are typically constructed in this way, and because audience expectations are met, they have larger audiences than documentaries.

This binary concept of good/evil echoes the dialectical tug-of-war that I mentioned at the beginning of this chapter between a public's desire to remember, countered by a strong desire to forget. The work around remembrance is hard, but instead of thinking in binary terms that reify memory as *either* remembering *or* forgetting, as male or female experience or generalizing the experience so much that the details of unique experiences are lost, there is the possibility that we can do much more to connect; but it requires audiences to work with the ambiguity of what cannot be seen or known.[16] Large audiences tend to avoid such ambiguities in film, and in real life.

On the 20-year anniversary of *Schindler's List*, Spielberg reflected on the documentary form as he recalled his use of the "documentary-style" 20 years earlier: "*Documentary filmmaking* is a mirror-image art form."[17] He described the filming technique he used to film *Schindler's List* as the "news camera approach," which he describes as:

> To effectively show the atrocities of the Holocaust and the difference that Oskar Schindler made in the lives of many survivors, I felt that I needed the camera to be embedded in the environment we were in—handheld at times, uncompromising in its presence, and omniscient in its impact. I needed it to be indistinguishable, unpredictable, and imperceptible to all of us on the set. To the best of my ability, I wanted to feel that *all of us were there* documenting the horrors of the Holocaust, not re-creating them [my emphasis]. ("Twenty" 2014, 3)

The blurring of the line between fact and fiction here seems to reveal "truth" because Spielberg sees his work as "documenting" not re-creating a story. And although *Schindler's List*'s after-affect seems to be generative and performative in that it creates action and reaction, to become performative and shift audience orientations—to push the interactive work needed to make public memory perform—a film should rely more on metonymy. Metonymic writing (or composition as in filmmaking) makes what is absent present through its attention to what is "gone" historically by presenting "partial or incomplete rendering" (Pollock 1998, 82–83).

Schindler's List makes absent history present by naming some of the people who died and the people who survived (especially when the real Schindler's list survivors place their stones on Schindler's grave at the close of the film). But the broad narrative, because it contains historical inaccuracies and reifies binary gender representations as it claims to tell a "whole" story (as *Shoah* did) fails to truly mark that absence.[18] Horowitz argues that though these filmic gestures to the past make clear that *Schindler's List* is part of a long tradition of Holocaust films, it also suggests itself as a "culmination" of these films, "that the present film functions as a master narrative for the murder of the Jews in Europe" (1997, 123). The metonymic performative marks both "the inadequacy and the impossibility of evocation" (84), which is the very evocation many image-based representations seek to achieve.

Schindler's List assumes the objectivity of documentary (which we know is partial anyway), and in convincing itself that this film depicts life "as if" the viewer were there, it becomes a spectacle, devoid of moral weight. If viewers watch from this perspective the viewpoint tends toward passivity, almost a voyeurism. Bystanders to the Holocaust watched without doing anything and replicating that for viewers leaves them falsely "innocent." [19]

Spielberg's technical artistry in the film genre allows audiences to be immersed in the experience of the film as a "masterpiece" without spending much time reflecting on details, or even being aware that the broad picture they see has been meticulously constructed for a certain emotional effect. Cole suggested that Holocaust memory in America started to suffer from commodification with the "simple lessons" offered by discourses such as *Schindler's List* (2000, 5). Cole calls such knowledge the "myth of the Holocaust" rather than the "historical event that has become known as the Holocaust" (xi); the event becomes a generalized story devoid of complexity and detail. The audience participates wholeheartedly in the camera's generalizing "gaze," without being asked to think about their positionality in any way, especially with regard to the binary representations of gender.

One trope that persists in film is the eroticized woman as a "side-bar" who neither plays a major role in the narrative drama, nor is given agency in that narrative. For example, Jewish women in this film are victimized or eroticized. In one scene, Amon Goeth, the commandant of Plaszcow, goes to the basement to visit his Jewish house servant, Helen Hirsch (an eventual "Schindler Jew"). Goeth is a violent man, and the scene suggests that a rape might be imminent, especially as it portrays her shivering in a wet shift that clearly reveals her body contours. Goeth does not assault her sexually, but the sexual tension of this scene is still present, broken only by his beating of her. Horowitz notes that male patriarchal viewpoints are uninterrogated and the film, especially in scenes like this one, and these viewpoints link the brutality toward women with the "construction of masculine identity and male bonding" (130). There are many scenes that simply reproduce such sexist imagery without critique, all in support of our hero's story. For Spielberg, the film was supposed to be an immersive narrative experience, but in falling for its own expressed "historical accuracy" and not interrogating overly gendered tropes, it fails to create performative action in audiences, relying too much on emotional distance.[20]

Patraka has noted that the Holocaust performative has a built in "accountability" where the postmodern sense of "play" discussed by scholars such as Butler is limited (1999, 8). According to Patraka, the two positions "[of reverentiality and play] comment upon each other: it is postmodernism that sees the deadness of that reverential gesture toward the Holocaust, but it is the Holocaust (and its goneness) that marks the point at which discursive play becomes a screen to keep the dead at a distance" (8). The consciously directed (but false) sense of objectivity in *Schindler's List* creates this kind of screen. The stylistic finesse of the cinematography lulls the audience into viewing power relationships in intimate close-ups (such as Amon Goetha and Helen Hirsch) and horror from a distance (such as the violent ghetto *Aktions* that rounded up Jews for deportation to camps watched through Schindler's eyes from a distance). The undetailed horror leaves more difficult emotions at a distance, a "spectacle" kept at arm's length. Viewers need not delve too deeply into the moral quagmire of the ghettoes, camps, or even the Holocaust itself.[21] *Schindler's List* is flawed by glossing over the details of trauma especially if this is the only artifact a person encounters about the Holocaust, but its popularity also made the creation of other artifacts possible, so that we might again see *and feel* the Holocaust in less "black/white" terms.[22] Each affective engagement with the Holocaust has the potential to become another engagement. Once the aperture is opened by a rhetor, there is generative space for response. A film that speaks directly to this "after-affect" is *Spielberg's List*, a documentary film by Omer Fast made about the real effect of the film in the Polish environs in which it was filmed.

PUBLIC MEMORY IN QUESTION: CHOOSING CONSTRUCTED FICTION VERSUS THE REAL

Precisely because of its popularity Horowitz said 20 years ago: "Spielberg's film may well be the one vehicle by which many Americans come to learn of the Holocaust" (1997, 128). Influential in some positive and negative ways, the film remains a *kairotic* punctuation that created an important opening for public memory. There are, however, "after-affects" that influence audiences' emotional responses on a much broader scale. Spielberg wanted audiences to "feel" like they were there, but sometimes fiction makes history feel real with disturbing implications, a process put into stark relief in a recent short documentary from Israeli Omer Fast called *Spielberg's List* (2003) which tracks this strong and disturbing "after-affect."

Fast travels to Poland to interview Poles who were extras on the film set of *Schindler's List* (many of whom also experienced the time period personally). Fast then contrasts these interviews with scenes from the film, and then with scenes of tourists visiting the sites of destruction. Some interviewees who experienced the Holocaust era admit that their experiences on the film set have blurred their memories of the real event. Many of the tourists Fast interviews also experience this blurring effect but with different purpose.

They want to "see" history, so they do not want to see the real Plaszcow camp or the Schindler factory, because these sites are in ruins. They prefer to see the intact buildings re-created on the film set of these locations. "The copy is preferred over the real version," says Modlinger, "just as Spielberg's film, at least for many, has become a 'better' point of access to the history of the Holocaust than the innumerable books and documentaries offered by historians" (2015, 168–169). This was also the argument that Lanzmann sometimes made when he claimed that his images made archival images obsolete. The argument Modlinger makes here aligns with the notion that public memory is constructed and reified through the performance (repetition) of one story that becomes "universalized" and applied to all histories, subsuming all individual subjectivity and gender (see the Introduction and Chapter One).

Schindler's List was sticky with affect for audiences worldwide—they connected with it, but in *Spielberg's List*, Fast shows us how "one story" repetition (even if it is fiction) can replace the "real" history not only for the tourist but also for those who lived through this experience. That real memories can be eroded by fiction suggests the tenuous nature of personal memory, which has important implications for public memory practices in the 21st century. Carr reminds us that:

> Just as our relationship to Holocaust history is changing [because we are losing survivors and are subjected to these decontextualized images] amid the encroaching presence of mediated imagery that can now stand in for that history and for the testimony of actual survivors, the imagery itself has become ossified and static enough to be appropriated for all manner of meanings and agendas. (2016, 3)

Especially in fictional depictions, we might wonder if public memory is constructed strictly on those ossified, fictionalized images, so static that they become stripped of meaning. I discussed this in terms of digital archives and online memory work in Chapter One. Haskins has questioned whether access to more information makes meaning or erases it. Rosenfeld seems to think the latter when he claims that the American landscape is so saturated with these artifacts that they have lost meaning; the implication is echoed by the title of his book: *The End of the Holocaust* (2013). Yet, there are openings for dialogue with the multiplication of artifacts as well. Fast's film directs audiences to contemplate the implications of this loss of meaning by highlighting its presence. In so doing, his film performs public memory metonymically. It shows how people "are filled with longing for a lost subject/object" (Pollock 1998, 84) and struggle with that longing in the face of the "impossibility of evocation" from the real. The tourists Fast shows long to connect to something about the history: they have traveled to the sites to engage with them but are flawed in their desire to only engage with something whole. The metonymic performative in memory work must be partial. Fast shows the flawed human desire for wholeness in order to reveal the partial reality.

The film metonymically marks the absent history in *Schindler's List* by revealing the presence of a "fake" history for the Poles in the film who have embraced Spielberg's version of their history over their own memories. Spielberg's film is beautiful and filled with binaries about gender and good and evil—easy to understand—while their own traumatic memories are likely difficult and ambiguous. The more accessible emotional connection that audiences seek—the "after-affect"—is tied to what seems the "most real." Spielberg's beautifully constructed sets allow audiences to feel "whole" in the face of this fractured and traumatic memory, yet they re-create a presence and fail to truly mark the absence. The ruins of real buildings over time are metaphors for the accretion of the human memory of these participants and the public memory of its memory tourists. Performative public memory artifacts like this film can recontextualize history and memory to mitigate these tendencies by making them visible.

The film *Son of Saul* (2015) also echoes this "after-affect" to perform memory. *Son of Saul* reclaims simplified representations of history and memory, representations that are binary and easy to digest, by shifting audiences' orientations to the survivor experience and to the things they think they "know" about a place like Auschwitz from films like *Schindler's List*. *Son of Saul* relies on 10 years of historical research to focus on one man's experience, but unlike *Schindler's List* where we see through the eyes of a German Nazi, the main character is a Jewish prisoner in Auschwitz, reorienting audiences to the survivor experience, as we saw in Chapter One in *Shoah*. *Son of Saul* re-orients audiences to respond or to shift away from the popular culture "version" of the Holocaust in *Schindler's List* and sets out to realign fictionalized Holocaust film with death, destruction, and the subjective experience of one man, who actively seeks redemption but is denied that consoling closure (as is the audience who watches); it shows us a different kind of hero's story.

SON OF SAUL: **PERFORMING PUBLIC MEMORY**

Son of Saul, directed by fourth-generation Hungarian survivor László Nemes, does not follow the Hollywood story line, nor does it give us much to be "happy" about. The film focuses in on the experience of one man, Saul, a Hungarian who works in Auschwitz as a *Sonderkommando*.[23] His motives and aspects are hard to discern, reinforced by filming only through his eyes and a shaky handheld camera. This might remind us of Spielberg's desire to make audiences feel "as if they were there," which becomes a spectacle devoid of moral weight. We can watch passively and inadvertently become bystanders, though our distance leaves us feeling "innocent." Yet, *Son of Saul* does not let the viewer remain passive, even though we are placed in the center of the experience by seeing everything through Saul's eyes. The film relies on performative metonymy by rendering nothing as "whole." We get partial viewpoints and splintered dialogue. There is no overarching narrative from which we can grasp a "truth." We know as little as Saul does, and this marks the absence of the trauma by making its presence so incomplete.

This camera angle depicts only the limited visual purview of Saul—objects appear, but we cannot assume that the character really "sees" what they are because the images are often blurred. The "manicured visual spaces of camps" that one sees in films like *Schindler's List*, are destabilized by the handheld, long-take shots in *Son of Saul* (Carr 2016, 2).[24] The result is physical and visual disorientation that shifts audiences' orientation to what they think might be a "typical" story about the Holocaust. Remember that in order to re-orient to the other (the final turning toward that results in affect and connection), Ahmed suggests disorientation first of all (2006, 24). Because Saul does not know where he stands or what he sees, neither does the viewer. Even if viewers try to turn toward the experience of Saul to connect, they are in many frames unable to identify specifically what they are seeing in this film. As orientations shift for the audience, this film also elicits the metonymic performative by making the Holocaust—its absent people and destroyed places—present (it is a film about the Holocaust) only to make them again absent (what audiences are actually "seeing" is obscured or hard to define). "Marking an absence," says Pollock, creates a "boundary space" where transformation can occur (1998, 85–86).

Director Nemes understands the importance of a boundary space and the opportunity for audience transformation as a result of engaging viscerally with depictions of traumatic experiences. *Kairotic* moments create apertures for "transformative encounters" says Hawhee, and Nemes says this about his intent with the film:

> The audience is not given any space to distance from Saul's reality or turn it into an abstraction of suffering, innocence, or goodness; the film doesn't depict the story of the Holocaust in generic ways that would encourage getting lost in a historical account. Rather, it allows viewers to *feel* its textures, and perceive the sights and sounds that make up individual experience. In this way, the film depicts what many critics have argued could not be depicted. (Balog 2016)

Critics argue that: "the personal [has power] to evoke deep emotion," but there is " also the danger that this evocation can lead to generalizations of feelings and obscure details of history. It is important to have all," says critic Damasio (2014, 18). As Barbie Zelizer pointed out in 1997, the "function of popular culture's representations—representations that appear every 'once in awhile'" (similar to my discussion of *kairotic* force) has been to "give pause to the ongoing record of historical events provided elsewhere" and should be to "shake up the public," not only about events themselves but to provoke publics to question the form those events take in the present (Modlinger 2015, 30).

Repetitive iconic imagery as in *Schindler's List* evokes response but does not allow for new knowledge to be constructed performatively with audiences, and in fact, much like the binary of emotion as separate from thought (in *Shoah*), this reliance on iconic imagery obscures the array of other real images and events and leads audiences to question nothing at all in the present. Focusing in on the camp, obscures the ghettoes, mass shootings, and the death marches, obscures the Holocaust as stages or the persecution of Jews as historical (rather than an anomaly), and obscures the individual choices that made the system of killing possible (Modlinger 166–167). What is seen depends on the director; the camera angle in film directs the audience's perspective. In an epic, the event is depicted as a whole with a desire to give audiences the sense of a broad view, but this sometimes sacrifices depth. In the Spielberg depiction of the concentration camp, for instance, we "see" Auschwitz in a long shot as the train heads to the camp. There are iconic images such as the train, the bystander child making the slitting throat motion, and the chimneys of the crematoria. These are a series of visuals that link the experiences of many people but do not go into depth with any of them. In *Son of Saul*, some details are obscured but not to generalize; they are designed to provoke the audience to be confused and afraid for this person and this story of which they know nothing but feel much (primarily fear and anxiety at first).

For Nemes, a focus on only Saul's perceived reality brings audiences deeply into that experience with all its ambiguity and unknowns, as it also encourages audiences to re-orient themselves to a deliberately constructed "other" in an affective relationship that relies on constant disorientation. We do not even get to know our character's name until the middle of the film. The feeling of being lost in that space of the unknown is metonymic—it is a boundary space. It is also emotional because there is little broader historical narrative to ground the viewer. What they can bring to the film about Holocaust history will allow them to connect, but they also connect to the fear and apprehension of Saul. In the first frame of the film, for example, he runs back and forth and breathes heavily, saying nothing but sensing everything. The performance of memory here is thus the movement between absence and presence, death and life, as well as the shifting of orientations—a disorientation to re-orient in affective connection.

PUBLIC MEMORY REORIENTED: "AFTER-AFFECT" AND *SON OF SAUL*

In almost all the reviews of *Son of Saul*, worldwide in 2015 and 2016, critics refer first to *Shoah* and then to *Schindler's List* as the benchmarks for Holocaust films to which *Son of Saul* can be compared.[25] That *Shoah* is a landmark artistic memorial work is generally not disputed, but many of the critics also include *Schindler's List* because of its global reach and its fictional elements (that make it similar to *Son of Saul*). This is why it was important to discuss the elements and influence of *Schindler's List* first in order to understand the different impact that *Son of Saul* has on audiences and on memorial culture; this is part of the "after-affect" of *Schindler's List* on other Holocaust artifacts. The reviews also have the same quality as those that came out in 1993 about *Schindler's List*. Either *Son of Saul* got it right or is an abomination of history and memory. The deconstruction of this binary can help us understand how *Son of Saul* can be about *both* death *and* survival, emotion and indifference, redemption and accountability. There is a connection in this film to feelings—a stickiness of affect orienting viewers toward both the subject matter of the film and pushing them to inwardly reflect on the self who is watching the film (instead of being passive bystanders).

Son of Saul "doesn't rely on conventional plotting" (Gire 2016, par. 5) like some say *Schindler's List* does. But even as I have argued that Spielberg's film opened the door to other paths of public memory, making Holocaust films has not gotten easier. Nemes's experience in getting *Son of Saul* to production is similar to Spielberg's, except that he did not have any funds of his own to use. Nemes faced a historical resistance in Hungary to films about the Holocaust.

Péter Krekó wrote that there is a "troubling rise in anti-Semitism" in Hungary (2014, 30). He suggests rather controversially that "it is not self-evident that remembrance as such will always have a beneficial effect" and while outright antisemitism is not prevalent there, "new forms" are on the rise. Two-thirds of Hungarians polled, for instance, feel that Jews try to "take advantage of having been victims of the Holocaust" (31). Research reveals that in 1993, the year that *Schindler's List* was released, 14% of respondents "found Jews repulsive." By 2008 that figure was 28% (31). This is a significant jump, and what is more troubling, younger Hungarians seem to have higher prejudice against Jews than any other demographic. Politicians there, Krekó says, play on this prejudice to get elected. This scenario sounds all too familiar in our American historical moment of 2017, and yet when these issues return, artists create in order to engage with audiences. They never speak into a void. There is a resilience to the persistent hope they, and we, must have in the power of education to combat these prejudices that raged in the past and that strive to rise again in the present.

Because he grew up in France, Nemes thought the project could work as a co-production with France and Hungary. He tried to get producers in France, Germany, Israel, and Austria to help finance it, but because the film's focus on death and perceived cynicism were considered too risky, no one would touch it. In the end, the Hungarian National Film Fund took on the costs, which is further evidence that a country's politics or prejudiced attitudes are often at great odds with its cultural and artistic milieu (Kilday 2015). Similar to Spielberg's film, this film was more popular with audiences than the producers imagined. When it was released in Hungary in 2015, it showed on 45 screens with 100,000 viewers. This is a record there for an independent film. After it won the American Academy Award for Best Foreign Film, it grossed over one million, which is the same average amount a Hollywood blockbuster achieves in Hungary (IMDb). That Hungary is experiencing this open reception makes *Son of Saul* as a Hungarian film even more powerful as a public memory artifact because the public, polled as highly antisemitic just one year prior to its release, is responding by seeing it by the thousands. Might it have the same effect in American public memory?

SON OF SAUL: ANOTHER *KAIROTIC* "SHAKE-UP" IN PUBLIC MEMORY?

Son of Saul is unusual for many reasons despite the familiarity of its origin story. Nemes imagined the film resonating worldwide; the fact that Hungarian audiences embraced it was perhaps unexpected given the historical and contemporary milieu. This is why Nemes wanted the film to premiere at an international film festival (it did—at Cannes). As a fourth-generation survivor, Nemes has always had a context for the Holocaust, having been introduced to the topic by his mother when he was five years old. He said about the genre of Holocaust film: "What disturbs me most in Holocaust films is that the events are always seen from a distance in space and time. You can feel a certain postwar separation; you're not really there and I wanted to capture the 'visceral level,'" a statement in which we can see echoes of Spielberg's spoken intent. Saul's story is invented but everything else was based on "10 years of rigorous research," Nemes says (DeBruge

2015, 65).²⁶ He used a real factory site outside of Budapest and did not build a set. The Nazi crematoria were set up like factories, and so he wanted it to be factory space.

The camera focus of the film is a narrow viewpoint, not an overarching, broad wide-angle, long shot that glosses over horrific details. What audiences see is up close and impossible to avoid. The film was shot in 28 days with only 85 shots for the whole film, and the camera never departs from the immediate point of view of its main character, Saul. These long, uninterrupted takes are unrelenting. The audience is supposed to be intimately involved in the viewpoint, while also being implicated in it. There is no respite for the viewer from what Saul sees or hears, and the viewing becomes a *kairotic* turn that directs those present to listen—*phere*, a dialogic where to listen is both to "bear" and to "yield" (Hawhee 77–78). This is the responsibility of the "shared community of witnesses."

Miriam Bratu-Hansen suggests that one of the weaknesses of *Schindler's List* is that it openly violates one of the major taboos around the Holocaust: representing images of the horror and not implicating the viewer enough. One of the problems with banning representation, however, is that it "reduces the dialectics of the problem of representing the unrepresentable to a binary opposition of showing or not showing, rather than casting it, as one might, as an issue of competing representations and competing modes of representation," which privilege the visual. "What gets left out" she says, is "the dimension of the other senses […] in particular […] the role of sound in the production of visuality" (1997, 85). Twenty years after she wrote this, *Son of Saul* has addressed this lack of sensory diversity. The sound recorders recorded eight languages for the background conversations, and these together with the vague sounds of fear and death (screaming or grunting, for example) are supposed to serve as a disturbing "acoustic counterpoint" to the narrow imagery (Kilday 2015). Nemes wanted to "make it impossible for the viewer to understand the camp as a single, coherent space, so it becomes a labyrinth" (DeBruge 2015, 65). The many rooms Saul enters and exits, without the viewer being able to identify any of them concretely (except the gas chamber), multiplies the labyrinth effect; this is highly disorienting for audiences. This effect is also performatively metonymic. What is shown is then un-shown. Nemes presents what is Saul's reality as opaque and hard to discern. His vision is literally blurred, "effectively making absent what mimetic/metaphoric uses of language [and in film images in this chapter] attempt to make present" (Pollock 1998, 83).²⁷ Every attempt at representation breaks down into something disorienting and indiscernible.

SHIFTING AUDIENCE ORIENTATION TO TURN TOWARD AFFECT

The Holocaust film genre spans from documentary style to more obviously fictive style.[28] One of the consequences of these repetitive images in Holocaust public memory, however, is that audiences might begin to take for granted that what they "see" (the spectacle) is the "truth," even if pieces of the story itself are fictional,[29] and any emotion they experience about the horror remains at surface level. Balog notes the historical trend that privileges the objective. She says:

> What Kierkegaard pointed out is a steady push in society toward more objectivity, and less engagement with subjectivity, with what is—sometimes derisively—called inwardness. There is less of a tendency for modern humans to live thoroughly immersed in life, experiencing it, and more of a tendency of being mostly distracted by its abstractions, by all the ways our culture conceptually frames our existence as individuals. (2016, par. 12)

Son of Saul's visual viewpoint is contrary to an objective (so-called neutral) point of view. Remember that Ahmed talked about queer orientation not only as feeling disoriented, but also as the feeling that one is turned outward but not seeing what is outside themselves. *Son of Saul* utilizes both a turning toward the unclear object as a disorienting element while also turning toward the inner self as the only available, true vantage point. In this way, the film is not objective or subjective but both. The human connection marks human significance. We are implicated as a participant in this film.

Son of Saul makes very pointed visual choices in order to heighten subjectivity and the experience of "deeply inward feelings." Not only is the camera's viewpoint restricted just to what the main character can see but even then, what is on the edge of his sight is purposely blurred. "No sooner have we glimpsed atrocity," says Romney, "than it is thrown out of focus, refused to us as an object of contemplation" (2015, 25). The film opens with a definition of *Sonderkommando,* and then moves to a landscape scene that is out of focus. The camera stays on this shot for some time and then one of the figures comes closer and closer, and finally the camera focuses in on one face. Audiences do not know who he is, where he is, or what he is doing. The camera follows his face and then from behind as we see him start to jog. "Let's go" says a man and slaps the back of his jacket, which is marked with a red X, marking his job as a *Sonderkommando* in the camp. This long take is shot with a handheld camera and follows the man as he looks ahead at the crowd in front of him, as he looks behind at the crowd behind him (we get blurred glimpses of the yellow star), and then as he helps them file into a room to get undressed and hang their clothing on hooks. His furtive looks in all directions reflect his growing anxiety that viewers can feel viscerally. He shuts the door and the camera fades to black.

In this long shot only two words are spoken to him, and the only other sounds were shouting and crying in the background. Inside the building people are whispering and crying. The next shot is at Saul's head level again but from behind, and someone like him says to the people undressing, "they need good workers"; "remember your hook number," which describes how the *Sonderkommando*, in addition to the horror of witnessing death and disposing of corpses, also had to lie to their countrymen and -women so that they would stay calm during the undressing process before gassing. The reality of the horror and emotional scope of their day-to-day job is heightened, and yet the audience sees only Saul's face, absolutely expressionless, as he goes through the motions of these activities. As the naked people file into another room, Saul stands to the side, lightly touching their naked shoulders as they file in. This is one of only two tender gestures of touch shown in the film, but Saul's face remains emotionless.

The audience (even if they know nothing about the Holocaust, though they probably do) has the chilling sense from this light touch from Saul that something fatal is about to happen. It is as if he says good-bye. As he and other workers start to go through the clothing, they hear the screams of those same people dying from Zyklon B gas. We have only been allowed to see what Saul sees and hears. This sound-only piece was chosen purposely *not* to visually represent the horror of gassing (as other films have been critiqued for doing); many critics, nevertheless, found this manufactured sound just as trivializing and horrific.[30]

Yet, many films about the Holocaust have been judged by their over-reliance on the visual to the exclusion of the other senses. The scene I just described is based almost entirely on sound and the blurred vision of Saul as he constantly looks forward, and to the side, and behind him. This makes the story fragmented and performatively tells a story about what we do not see by giving us what we feel and hear. Metonymic writing "invokes the presence of what isn't, ironically, by elaborating what it is" (Pollock 1998, 85). This scene invokes what is by focusing on what is not there: a coherent narrative and clear images. The audience is disoriented by what he cannot see, and at the same time, hurtles along with him toward an end point—they must. The disorientation of Saul might stand for the disorientation of those getting off the train, for the *Sonderkommandos*, and for the audience experiencing the scene with little established historical context. Nemes says that immersion leaves room for a viewer's imagination. The surroundings were purposely vague, because when you are immersed in a situation, "you don't have the distance or the perspective" (Murphy 2016).

Nemes said that the handheld camera work was planned "for years" with his cinematographer. They wanted to stay with what the protagonist was experiencing. In the camps, he says, "you don't have the luxury to see […] the main character is not looking and we are not looking as well" (Murphy 2016). The audience is not allowed to become distant. The visceral connection between viewer and the subject is maintained at all times. The camera stubbornly stays on Saul's face or his back, which forces us to look only at what he sees or does not see, and then to reflect on his facial expressions to understand how he might be feeling. Saul has less than 20 lines of the dialogue in the whole film, and there is no voice-over. The camera forces us to see and to discern feeling without anything being explained; the choice is not ours. We are not allowed turn away.

Son of Saul refuses to "soften the audience's encounter with the camps—by offering false hope and redemption" (Wachsmann 2016, 20). Some say there is no sanctification of victims, only degradation and despair, as there were also no heroes. The film is literally "unbearable," says Wachsmann. "But we should bear it, we have to bear it, if we want to get closer to understanding the 'reality beyond belief' that was Auschwitz" (20). This reminds us of *phere*: "to listen" and "to bear" requires a turning toward and also a yielding. Saul is shown as emotionless or indifferent, and though many have said this is one result of being surrounded by atrocity every day (one becomes numb), some have also noted the "moral complicity" of the *Sonderkommandos*, the viewpoint with which audiences must participate. But we need not yield to standing in judgment of those who were forced into Langer's "choiceless choices." As survivors of the *Sonderkommando* have noted (such as Filip Mueller in Chapter One), the imperative to live in order to bear witness was an important reason for continuing the work instead of seeking immediate death. "It's a strange strategy to put the blame onto the victims," Nemes has said in response to those who describe Saul as complicit: "In this film we wanted to give back dignity to the dead and the dying" (Taylor 2015).

The affect present here, however, is a combination of despair and redemption, of degradation and sanctification. It does not have to be a binary either/or. The road to dignity in Saul's case begins when Saul witnesses the sole survivor of one gassing, a young boy. Because his survival strength was so unusual, a Nazi doctor wants to do an autopsy immediately and suffocates this boy. The film hints that this boy is Saul's son although that "fact" is left unclear. After witnessing this boy's death, Saul seeks (against all reasonable thought) to bury his body. Saul's decision to do so directs the rest of the film toward a disjointed series of scenes that have emotional purpose: the audience should be confronted with emotions and orient themselves toward Saul, but the narrative is so disjointed and Saul's task so "unreasonable" that the emotions audiences feel might also be ambiguous. The mind and body must be reconciled to "not knowing" or "not understanding," which is often the end result of any encounter with the Holocaust, if its memorial activity really performs and asks the audience to work.

DECONSTRUCTING BINARY REPRESENTATIONS: MASCULINE GENDER NORMS AS "UNIVERSAL"

Claude Lanzmann, "famous for his disapproval of dramatic representations of the Holocaust on screen," approved of *Son of Saul*, calling it the "anti-*Schindler's List*." He expressed particular admiration for "the film's focus: rather than presuming to evoke the Holocaust as such, László Nemes concentrates on the experience of one man" (Romney 2015, 24). For both Lanzmann and Nemes, that individual experience, elevated as "the one" on which to focus, is again the experience of a male—"universalized" to be applied to all. Elizabeth Baer, in the forward to Lucille Eichengreen's second book, *Haunted Memories: Portraits of Women in the Holocaust* (2011), says books by and about women's experiences specifically can, "disrupt the master narrative" of the Holocaust that assumes "women's experiences can be generalized from the male's" (8).[31] Yet binary representation continued in *Shoah*, and *Schindler's List*. While *Son of Saul* does not stray very far from those binaries (women are not main characters), in a few key scenes, *Son of Saul* challenges some gendered representations, much as the outtakes did for *Shoah* in Chapter One, by depicting representations of non-binary constructions of experience and emotion for men.

The path from indifference to connection for Saul becomes one of the primary themes of the film, and this juxtaposition with the continued, historical actions around Saul (actions from which he is still largely detached) deconstructs the binary and creates a disorienting balancing act of both survival and death and resistance and indifference, but not in the way audiences are used to thinking about them. The film only covers a period of two days. The two days, significantly, are the days preceding the historic *Sonderkommando* uprising in Auschwitz on 7 October 1944. The preparatory activities for this rebellion are going on at the same time that Saul has turned toward his desire to bury a boy's body, a boy he claims is his son.

As the film proceeds, we see that burying the boy will be a monumental task that includes stealing the body, finding a place to bury it, finding a rabbi to say the prayer over the body,[32] and then burying it.[33] Liebman says that many of the *Sonderkommando* were Orthodox Jews, and would have understood this desire to bury the boy, so in spite of the story's improbability, it still has great "emotional resonance" (Liebman 2015, 2). Grissemann gives Nemes credit for upending visual tropes and stereotypes in the film because he says: "[Nemes] disputes the idea of passive victimhood by casually restaging the inmates' revolt that took place in Auschwitz on October 7, 1944," in the background (2015, 29). But what takes up the most space in the film is a focus on another kind of resistance (of a religious and personal kind) that might allow many audiences to turn toward this character with affective connection.

Nemes seems to present both without judging one as better than the other, and this is unusual. Armed resistance is typically both armed and masculine—respected for those reasons (we saw how this played out in *Shoah*; though women resisted they did not get to tell that story). Grief, on the other hand, especially for a child, often centers on the mother, who might be depicted as "overly" emotional, out of control, or overtaken, a passive state suggested by the term "grief-*stricken*." Saul, in his participation in both the armed rebellion preparation and the mourning of a child, embodies both of these gendered spaces in the film (instead of just one). The sustained non-binary presentation of resistance becomes both the push toward the rebellion, which most audiences could recognize and support, contrasting with an obsession with grief, a form of resistance audiences recognize less and often do not understand.

As the men and women in the camp prepare for the rebellion (in which prisoners will blow up the crematoria), the men in his barrack recruit Saul as an agent. He is asked to pick up a package of gunpowder from a woman in *Kanada* (the place where they sorted items confiscated from the dead). Ella is the one figure in the film whose name has a historical basis. She was tortured and killed for her participation in the rebellion, but her inclusion here reminds us (unlike in *Shoah*) that women were integral to the rebellions and that resistance involved both men and women. And although *Son of Saul* is mostly devoid of women, except for the blurred images of naked bodies at the frame's margins, this scene also undercuts the trope of the eroticized woman we saw in *Schindler's List*.

On the way back to his barrack Saul is caught up in a chaotic scene where a new transport has arrived and various people are shouting that the crematoria are full. The new arrivals are forced to run toward what the *Sonderkommando* call the "pits": huge pits where Jews were shot and their corpses burned en masse. As he is running toward these pits, Saul sees one of the men from the transport and through a disjointed lack of communication believes him to be a rabbi. As he struggles through the chaos of this death and murder to save this man for his boy's burial, he loses the gunpowder package. He succeeds in his own goal, but fails the larger resistance. The visuals in the background are of horror, fire, and people being burned alive, but the camera stays on Saul as he brings the rabbi back to the barrack with him, saving this life, while we have just witnessed the killing of hundreds of others. The saving of one life (which echoes the tag line for promotions for *Schindler's List*) is done for selfish reasons, but there is also the reality that saving any life in that setting is miraculous. The juxtaposition of one man at odds with the collective, undercuts the cooperation, bravery, and ingenuity that was required to accomplish the bombing of the crematoria,[34] yet the film continues these parallel tales without judging one as necessarily better than the other. The non-binary presentation resists hierarchizing.

When Saul finally arrives back in the barrack, he moves toward the place in the barrack where he has hidden the boy's body. From the time that Saul has stolen the body and carried it to various places with the intent of burying it (though he gets continually interrupted), he always handles the boy's body tenderly. As Saul and his rabbi (we never know if this man actually is a rabbi or not) sit behind a curtain, Saul says to him: "That's the boy. I hid him. You'll tell me what to do." There is a close-up here on Saul's face. It is the first time we see him smile, just slightly. He begins to wash the boy's body with a rag, and the tenderness with which he does this is one of the most moving scenes in the film. But like many such scenes, Saul is not permitted to linger and neither is the audience. Emotion has been exposed but is quickly forced into another setting, broken by forces outside the individual. Although we know the boy is dead, the body is not depicted as degraded in any way. Saul's love for him is clear in the way that he gently washes each arm and

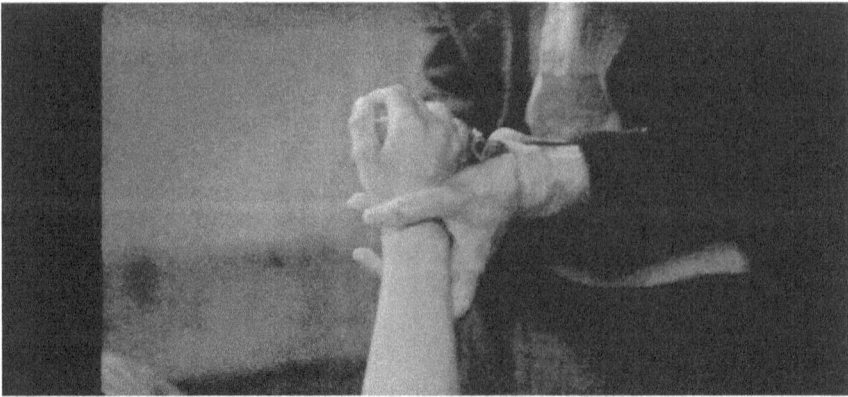

Figure 2.1: Screenshot of Saul washing the boy's body tenderly in Son of Saul *(Nemes).*

lays it gently down again. But this is the only time that he gets to make those intimate connections that grief demands.

He is interrupted by one of the men, Abraham, who berates him for his failure to procure the gunpowder. He asks: "You picked a rabbi from the dead? You lost the bundle? Son of a bitch." He then questions if the boy is Saul's son at all, then says: "The man can stay. You get rid of the body." The next scene shows Saul gently trimming the rabbi's beard by candlelight. He continues to be connected to this boy and this man, despite the admonitions of the other men. Scenes like this remind the audience that indifference is not a given in the face of atrocity. It is, in fact, possible to know and feel something is right and important to do, even when others say it is not. Outside, the other men involved in the rebellion are also disgusted with Saul. They look at him and the new rabbi: "We'll die because of you two. We're already dead." The resistance to indifference is important for Saul, but surrounded by the death of hundreds of others, and the potential danger he has caused them by both his action and inaction, the value of that resistance is called into question. Because the film continues to portray these two paths as parallel progressions of action, however, the survival of humanity and emotion exists beside death in this film—it does not "triumph over it."

Hansen says the trope about "passing through Auschwitz" to life (typical of Holocaust films like *Schindler's List*), "mark[s] a shift in the public commemoration of the Shoah" concerned with, "the survival of individuals, rather than the fact of death, the death of an entire people" (Hansen 1997, 82). *Son of Saul* refuses this binary. Instead it depicts both survival and death, performing memory as metonymic by making both resistance and destruction unrelentingly present and at other times absent. The *Sonderkommandos* after the uprising manage to escape across the river, but as we know from history, they do not survive. The last scene shows the men hiding in a shed to catch a breath before running on. The escapees seek to meet up with the partisans they know are in that forest. Saul sees a young boy standing in the doorway staring. None of the other men see him. Saul says nothing but slowly begins to smile, when he has heretofore been largely expressionless. The boy he sees (who in reality gives them up to Nazi soldiers)[35] stands for the boy he has connected to. He has achieved the ability to feel something again. He has connected to the murdered boy through his commitment to preventing the degradation of his body. The final scene shows the forest as we hear the Nazi gunfire.

The film ends in death because Nemes says that the film is not about survival. "It is about the reality of death. Survival is a lie; it was the exception. [Saul] is a character representing something universal" (Liebman 2015, 3). But the reality of experience is that it is *not* universal; each human experiences even death uniquely. Death in the camps was "omnipresent"; it "is everywhere and every death is the same," he says, but I disagree. The *Nazis* wanted every death to be the same. If one is dehumanized then each body becomes the same and nothing. *Son of Saul* makes sure to include that dehumanizing language in the first scenes of the film. Every person in and around the gas chambers refers to the dead bodies as "*Stuecke*" ("pieces" in German). Nemes wanted to depict death as everywhere, but he also wanted to have Saul's focus on one death and the burial of that boy's body to become a way for him to find his humanity again. I would argue that this is the unintended focus and strength of the film. Despite death being everywhere, every death does not have to be the same. Audiences connect to the intimacy of this representation even if they do not understand it. They are disoriented in order to re-orient to others and connection. This film ends in death but it does not deny emotional redemption (a form of survival) for Saul even if that redemption is flawed. This devastating but ambiguous co-existence is part of all of human experience.

PERFORMING MEMORY TO CREATE ACTION IN THE 21ST CENTURY

Nemes's motivation to do the film comes from the fact that the Nazis murdered his mother's grandparents, and she shared this story with him when he was five years old. He says now that, as a fourth generation survivor his motivation is increased because: "With each generation," he explains, "the Holocaust slips farther away from us, losing meaning and emotion. Time just does that. I thought that we needed to be reminded in as visceral and immersive a way as possible" (Haun 2015, 24). Modlinger suggests that representation and reproduction for Holocaust memory have a particularly complex relationship, especially in terms of truth and fiction: "the 21st century in Holocaust cinema sees not so much a changing relationship between history and memory as much as a change in, 'the public'" and the "changing role of memory and imagination itself," as well as shifts in the way information is "offered and consumed" (2015, 162). Audiences come to film with new ways of seeing information. Do they question its veracity? Do they seek more information because so much more is available? Or do they experience information apathy, seeking what is easy rather difficult? *Son of Saul* is difficult for audiences because it "depicts a loss in subjectivity both at the larger societal level, as well as the level of the individual," says Balog (2016, par. 17). Modern audiences are obsessed with their own subjectivity but have trouble connecting to the subjectivity of others. What happens when that ability to define the self is taken away? Many populations in America know what this experience feels like. Balog calls Nemes's technique a "double engagement of subjectivity" that makes the film "effective" because audiences do not get let "off the hook." They have to participate in those losses.

The after-affect of *Schindler's List* in American 21st-century public memory is not limited only to films like *Son of Saul* or *Spielberg's List*.[36] This after-affect is present in other memory artifacts related to this film, specifically the visual archive at USC that Spielberg started post filming. While a film's reception and interpretation can change also over time but not its content, with the archive, an audience's interaction is just one piece of the evolving process that involves curating and adding material and access points. Remember that Modlinger suggested that 21st-century information is offered to and consumed by audiences in ways that are in a continual process of change. The way we approach information is different than it was in 1994, or even last year. I discussed that some critics felt Spielberg saw his film as a master narrative. I argue, however, that with time, that interpretation might be productively revisited. *Schindler's List* (in ways that other films do not), also speaks forward into the future through the creation of the Shoah Visual History Foundation (which became the USC Visual History Archive) as a direct result of the filming. Spielberg realized, as he was making it, that his film would become part of a longer dialogic of public memory.

The Visual History Archive now houses over 55,000 personal survivor testimonies from men and women, Jewish, LGBT, and Roma survivors, perpetrators, collaborators, and liberators. The range of voices is enormous, and the archive is able to expand audience perspectives on both the specific gender and cultural aspects of experience. Spielberg reflected on the 20th anniversary of *Schindler's List* that:

> while the story of Oskar Schindler and the people he rescued may serve as a microcosm for the events surrounding the mass murder of 6 million Jews, it was important to me, as a filmmaker and a Jew, that we do our best to properly recall the ultimate consequences of the Holocaust and the role of the war itself in these considerable crimes against humanity. That is something that could not be done in its entirety during the making of *Schindler's List*. In fact, it required me to take my "news camera" approach and apply it to the creation of the Shoah Foundation. ("Twenty" 2014, 3)

In the 23 years since the film's release, the opening and expansion of the USC Visual History Archive performs memory in a very special way that mitigates some of the negative effects of the film's representations to create positive *e*ffects and *a*ffects in the realm of education. Spielberg's creation of the Shoah Foundation to record Holocaust testimonies blurs the concept of the film as a "culminating" point. It performs instead as Hawhee's "aperture," aptly evoking a camera lens, which opens to other paths and other voices, instigating dialogue and extending an ongoing conversation about Holocaust memory into the present. The release of major films, as I have discussed above, function as *kariotic* forces that exert pressure from the past onto a historical moment in the present, but how long does that pressure last? How soon do audiences remember only to forget?

If we consider the ways in which public memory narratives about the Holocaust are presented, from films, to books, to museums, to archives with better digitation technologies and better online and interactive platforms, we see that public memory around the Holocaust relies *more* on media rather than less.[37] This means that access to public memory artifacts like primary documents (diaries, military documents, etc.) increases but the ways in which publics interact with those changes.

According to the website, most of the 55,000 testimonies housed there were recorded between 1994 and 1999, and they include testimonies in "41 languages, [and from] 62 countries (USC)." Several years after the creation of the Visual History Archive, Lanzmann expressed skepticism. *The New York Times* quoted him as saying of the Shoah Foundation's then 52,000 testimonies of Holocaust survivors and witnesses: "Who will see this?" (Smith 2014, 33). Yet this archive, like the one in Chapter One is becoming increasingly accessible with time. The USC Archive was planned from the beginning as an educational tool that would be social and communal. That means its effect creates *affect* by purposefully interacting with the society around it to form relationships. It is searchable by any user, as it is also offered as part of an educational package that promotes survivor testimony as an important way for audiences to connect with this history.[38]

The entire archive is entirely accessible today because, even though to see every testimony "would take 12 years of 24-hour viewing to watch from beginning to end," it "has a built-in search engine that enables users to pinpoint moments of interest to the minute" (USC "About").[39] In terms of access, the whole archive is available at 79 universities and institutions worldwide, and the online version with 1,866 testimonies can be found simply on the USC Archive website, accessible to anyone with the Internet (USC). Who will see this, asks Lanzmann? Anyone, potentially, who knows about it; as I noted in Chapter One, some of this relies on educators and Holocaust Education sites to help people make those connections. Access to at least a portion for anyone with web access makes it an artifact that promotes interaction and connection for the user, who creates a shared community of witnesses.[40]

The archive also looks outward to the future when it states its mission and purpose: "To overcome prejudice, intolerance, and hatred—and the suffering they cause—through the educational use of the Institute's Visual History Archive." Educational use is a primary function of the archive. The indexing system that the archive has patented "allows students, teachers, professors, researchers and others around the world to retrieve entire testimonies or search for specific sections within testimonies through a set of more than 64,800 keywords and phrases, 1.86 million names, and 718,000 images" (USC "Home"). The use is not proscribed. Eyewitness testimony can be used to present multiple perspectives: "each collection adds context for the other" and also multiple usage methods to "provid[e] multiple pathways for students, educators and scholars to learn from the eyewitnesses of history across time, locations, cultures and socio-political circumstances" (USC "Home"). The information is designed to be a network, not enclosed or isolated but linked to itself, as it also links to the world outside and the array of other historical and memory artifacts around this event.[41]

The platform for the archive was groundbreaking when it began and has continued to grow and evolve to expand access. There are professional development programs for teachers and innovative assignments for students to learn skills like editing and archiving.[42] The archive has partnered with the Anti Defamation League (ADL) to produce an educational packet called *Echoes and Reflections*.[43] This is a clear *e*ffect of the archive's content, organization, and outreach. But what about the affect? What is the "after-*a*ffect" of one film on one archive that changes the ways in which audiences come to history? They certainly are not allowed to be distant and passive viewers, as they were with *Schindler's List*, or even a more engaged viewer as with *Son of Saul*. The *after-affect* comes with the reach and impact of the interaction of audiences with history on a daily basis. Repetition in this way can have a performatively positive effect.

CONCLUSION

Films can have amazing impact—*kairotic* forces that raise awareness—but their reach is still limited. Spielberg ends *Schindler's List* with a sentimental scene where the factory survivors make Schindler a ring that bears the inscription: "Whoever saves one life saves the world entire." Itshak Stern says to Schindler: "There will be generations because of what you did." Though some have denigrated this ending as "happy," the meaning is not unimportant. The black and white film fades into color with the real survivors placing stones on Schindler's grave. One subtitle stands out: "There are fewer than 4,000 Jews left alive in Poland today […] There are more than 6,000 descendants of the Schindler Jews," and the last frame shows one rose with the words: "In memory of the more than 6 million Jews murdered." This ending juxtaposes survival with death. Alan Mintz, in his analysis of popular films and Holocaust memory, says that: "Focusing on [only] destruction is not what Jewish life is about" (2001, 161). The transmission of intergenerational Jewish memory relies on Holocaust artifacts like these films but also a myriad of other tools including education about the entire Jewish history, destruction, and survival.

Physical, online archives like this one are important tools that perform memory around the Holocaust. A sixth grader can view the same testimony in Poland, the United States, and Argentina. Now they can also ask survivors questions and have an even greater level of interaction. A new technology allows the archive to film survivors with several cameras so that they can create the sense of a conversation, which is especially helpful for children's education.[44] These kinds of cross-cultural links were impossible 20 years ago.

The archive as an educational (and research) tool is about relationships. The *affect* is the connection between two human beings—one person telling a story and one person listening. Each individual is vulnerable to emotion, and that vulnerability does not reside in a binary of weak and strong. To be vulnerable is to be open and hopeful—that hope can be empowering. Spielberg understood that by making *Schindler's List* sentimental it would create affect in audiences (but in too many ways superficial), but that hope has radiated outward through the archive. Multiplying the listening relationship thousands of times creates a large, spatial effect and affect. It enacts Ahmed's community of witnesses. Spielberg said about those who testified on camera:

> I'd like to think the same is true of the women and men who came forward to give testimony and the interviewers, videographers, and staffers themselves—that we are making ourselves vulnerable to one another in the name of tolerance education. The survivors and witnesses of the Holocaust did not avert their eyes because they knew that one day they could show us the importance of bearing witness. Here we are—20 years after the start of the Shoah Foundation—doing more than I could have ever imagined with that simple notion of documentation, that concept of examining the historical record for the purposes of remembering it and reflecting upon it so that with a camera and a clear mission of genocide prevention, we are both teaching tolerance and inspiring the otherwise indifferent. ("Twenty" 2014, 3)

The archive has expanded since 1999 to collect testimonies from four other genocides: "The Armenian Genocide (1915–1923), The Nanjing Massacre (1937), The Genocide Against the Tutsi in Rwanda (1994), and the Guatemalan Genocide (1978–1996)" (USC). The focus has not remained on the Holocaust as an "exceptional"[45] or isolated event.[46] When Claude Lanzmann later reviewed the Visual History Archive and the USC Shoah Foundation's current work, he said, "It is perfect work [...] very important work. Many people and places in the world are viewing this, and there [will] be no end" (Smith 2014, 33). Interpretations change, content changes, form changes. But history remains, as does our emotional connection to that history, if we make ourselves vulnerable enough to learn. All American audiences need education about a history that is both destructive *and* hopeful, as they also need to see that the Holocaust is important history not "just for Jews." Audiences need to be disoriented in order to be implicated—to feel responsibility. If to feel is to become vulnerable, then to be vulnerable is to be strong enough to connect emotionally with others and perform memory with real-world outcomes.

NOTES

1. The Palestinian question persists with authors and activists such as Angela Davis and Alice Walker among others, weighing in on injustice. The sense of belonging one group seeks or achieves is often at the expense of others, from whom they turn away or may even oppress or injure. It has happened so many times, so violently, in the United States as well.

2. For the Poles, I mean they often "don't remember" the Jews being discriminated against or being expelled between 1939 and 1945. Likewise, my second-generation Polish grandmother, raising a family in the 1940s does not remember prejudice or racism against blacks in the Ohio Valley and has no memory of the EO 9066 and the expulsion of Japanese citizens from their homes in the West.

3. This has not prevented the marriage of effective and moving history and fiction in Holocaust depictions (see, for example, Ida Fink's *Scrap of Time* [1989] and Cynthia Oznick's *The Shawl*, 1990).

4. I continue to use this term "public memory" around the Holocaust to discuss how memory is built collectively in the American social archive. Memorial artifacts continue to appear and create an ongoing relationship, both among themselves (as citational references) and with audiences. Memory, testimony, and witness happened as the Holocaust was happening (diaries) and directly after the war (in Yiddish memorial texts shared only among family members and other survivors). The lack of "public" for these artifacts in the beginning does not reduce their value. My work focuses on the trajectory of how memorial artifacts began to interact with a listening public and how that transformed the public's relationship with the Holocaust as a historical and memory event.

5. I examine the USHMM and local Holocaust museums in Chapter Five.

6. As noted on page 55, the concept of communal viewing suggests a theater and a film audience, which is part of what I mean here; but there is also the real viewing practices of many viewers today (many of them "next generation") that include home viewing through streaming on Netflix or watching on phones.

7. See note 14 on page 19.

8. Though I noted that its weakness was that the survivor was often depicted as a victim and the perspectives as gender neutral, they deeply privilege the masculine.

9. Recall Felman and Laub's work *Testimony* from Chapter One.

10. See Chapter One for my first mention of this. So-called historians like Briton David Irving created "revisionist histories" that denied the Holocaust happened. The best resource on Holocaust denial is Deborah Lipstadt's *Denying the Holocaust: The Growing Assault on Truth and Memory* (1994). She tracks a growing trend over two decades with the rise of antisemitic and neo-Nazi groups, politicians like David Duke (see my Chapter Three), and academic works that distort facts.

11. This quote appears on just about every website that offers or discusses this film. Some wide-ranging examples include: www.movietoekn.net, the Europe Zone on www.amazon.co.uk, and www.1africa.tv. Accessed 29 June 2017.

12. See Horowitz, for example, on sexist tropes (1997, 128–130) and also Wachsmann on stereotypes in general in this film (2016).

13. Survivors who had already told their stories have spoken out against the film in some cases. Hungarian Imre Kertesz called the film kitsch because it was "falsified." He said: "'It is said that Spielberg has in fact done a great service considering that his film lured millions into movie theaters'" including many who would never have engaged with the Holocaust before, but why should, "'I be pleased when more and more people see these experiences' when they are so 'falsified?'" (Modlinger 2015, 173). The depiction of the ghetto in Krakow, for example, was not historically accurate. Interestingly, Kertesz, Elie Wiesel, and even Claude Lanzmann spoke favorably twenty years later about *Son of Saul,* the film I explore later in this chapter.

14. Ben Kingsley kept a photo of Anne Frank in his pocket during filming. He says his connection to her, "started during 'Schindler's List.' And I had no idea that I'd be offered the beautiful opportunity to play Otto. I had a picture of Anne Frank in my coat pocket, and I would say to this picture of this beautiful girl before takes: I'm doing this for you. My simple, direct line from me to her" (Simon 2011). Kingsley epitomizes the idea of the performance of memory that is at once rhetorical, performative, and temporal. By reflecting on her as he worked, he embodied the spirit of communal memory where voices performatively "cross the grave" to speak into the present.

15. As the protagonist and a German non-Jew (aligned with perpetrators), Schindler is constructed as a Christian "savior." This construction stands in binary opposition to the Jews, who are shown as passive victims receiving "redemption" (Horowitz 1997, 128–130). Cole agrees that *Schindler's List* perpetuates the stereotype of the passive Jewish victim (2000, ix).

16. There is much scholarship on the difficulty of representation and the Holocaust, which I have noted in my Introduction.

17. He adds that: "More than most other art forms, it asks us to examine reality, to evaluate our own behavior relative to the subject matter, and to consider what the particular historical account means to our life today, what it has perhaps meant to our ancestors, and what, in these examinations, it might mean in years to come" ("Twenty" 2014, 3). What Spielberg describes here is actually a much more

subjective approach to documentary filmmaking. The examination of our own behavior is not the result of watching this film.

18. What we "see" is limited by the choices of what to show and how to show it. Miriam Bratu Hansen cites Gertrud Koch to suggest that Spielberg's tendency to "subsume" the films he cites is rather "authoritarian." He uses images and tropes from other Holocaust films to pretend that his story is being told "for the first time" (1997, 82). But we still do not get to see a spectrum of Jewish experience, because Spielberg uses familiar film techniques that provide superficial (and sometimes false) representations.

19. Also the perspective of being behind the camera, watching from a distance, has a voyeuristic quality to it as well and, implicates the viewer as a bystander simply watching fates unfold—fates and events that are, like *Shoah*'s, staged, but much more elaborately and with much less self-reflection. As Sara Horowitz pointed out soon after the film's release: "Ultimately, of course, verisimilitude—no matter how successful—is not reality but artifice posing as reality. When this 'as if' posture goes on uninterrupted by a self-conscious moment, the film presses its claim for historical truth simply by virtue of being film. Especially with films representing the Shoah, this unproblematized transparency—an illusion created by elaborate staging has dangerous undertones. Staged, that is, falsified, film images played an important role in facilitating and justifying the Nazi genocide in German newsreels" (1997, 122–123).

20. Some critics found this distance to be a strength. Citing the use of real locations and the use of black and white as a "distancing element," *LA Times* critic Turan argued that Spielberg "understands how important it is to show casualness of the nightmare." Turan wrote further that: "to approach the Holocaust from a dramatic point of view, detachment and self-control almost to the point of coldness are essential," and he aligns the film with other landmark Holocaust films that create "detachment" like *Shoah* and *Night and Fog* (1993).

21. The quagmires could even be seen as being shortchanged by simplified metaphors like the "red coat."

22. I use this binary purposefully, as those who may not have seen the film may not know it is filmed entirely in black and white except for the "red coat" coloration of a little girl, the sighting of which is shown to be instrumental to Schindler's moral "turning point" in the film.

23. The film begins with a definition of this word so that audiences are clear about this job. *Sonderkommandos* were chosen by the Nazis to work in the gassing areas and crematoria. They were tasked with leading Jews to the gas chambers, convincing them to undress, and going through their clothing for valuables. They had to clean up the chamber, bring the corpses to the crematoria to burn, and dispose of the ashes. *Sonderkommandos* were given privileges like more food and larger quarters because of the physical nature of their jobs. Some critics (even critiquing this film) have called them "morally complicit," but to choose not to die and bear witness to the world was a moral choice of sorts, but this misses how little we understand about the camps: "one of the problems with listening or watching survivor testimonies is that we bring to the confrontation a mindset that has been nurtured by premises irrelevant to the stories we are about to hear" (Greene and Kumar 2011, xii) because we belong to a "privileged

world of moral choice" (xii). Filip Mueller says as much in *Shoah* (see Chapter One) and Primo Levi noted this in his memoir, calling it the "grey zone."

24. Alter notes that *Son of Saul* has been "condemned and praised" for presenting the horrors of the German death camps "around the blurry edges of the frame, rather than in plain sight." It adds to the film's message about "the things we can't or choose not to see (not to mention the desensitization that might accompany being around atrocity on a daily basis)," but he says too: "a strong case can be made that the stark realities of the Holocaust are too important to obscure" (Alter 2015, 93). The debate around these depictions, even though they are fictionalized, is similar to that of *Schindler's List*. The public conversation has been opened.

25. *Artforum*, a famous French film journal called Nemes's style "showboating," and the *New York Times* critic Mahola Dargis called it "radically dehistoricized [and] intellectually repellent" (Liebman 2015, 1–2). Zacharek admires how the film treats suffering "as a living, breathing entity," not as a tool to "punish" the audience (2016).

26. The event in *Son of Saul* was also depicted in the film *The Grey Zone* (2001), and both films were based on the same documentary materials: "the Hungarian doctor Miklos Nyiszli's eyewitness account of his work in the crematorium's autopsy rooms and the extraordinary testimonies buried in anticipation of their own liquidation by several members of *the Sonderkommando*" (Liebman 2015, 2). This burying was only mentioned in one passing line between Abraham and Saul in the film. Saul threatens to expose where his writings are buried if he takes the boy's body. This exchange demonstrates their equal commitment to a cause.

27. The reasons for this were very clear to Nemes and the crew. Nemes says: "When you hear 'Holocaust film,' you immediately see what that is, and we wanted to make another kind of movie," he said, referring to the sentimental themes and recurring images that have threatened to turn the genre into a cliché. "We wanted to make a visceral kind of film" (Taylor 2015). The term "visceral" comes up for the director but is also used in several reviews of the film, often in contrast to the critique of *Schindler's List* as sentimental.

28. See Horowitz for a good synopsis of major Holocaust films since the 1950s.

29. I do not use the term "truth" here lightly. Truth is based on factual evidence, but with the rise of concepts like "alternative facts" or "fake news," it is hard for publics to discern fact from fiction in modern news, which has historically been evidence-based information. This makes films like *Schindler's List* and *Son of Saul* even more fraught with obstacles in the present because they mix fact and evidence with fictional elements. The critical-thinking faculties of audiences might continue to be compromised and prevent them from watching with this critical lens.

30. Grissemann calls the sound "an obscenity." He asks how one makes sounds off screen to mimic death by gassing. The film, he claims, is an "exploitation film not despite but *because of* its technical skill and resolute cunning" (2015, 29). *Schindler's List* was critiqued for its depiction of gas chambers as well: "While Spielberg repeatedly explains that he filmed *Schindler's List* to affirm his Jewish heritage and the historical truth of the Holocaust, the film's treatment of the phenomenon of the gas chambers seemingly confirms not the testimony of Holocaust survivors but the claims of Holocaust deniers that the Nazi genocide never occurred" (Horowitz, 128).

31. I will explore this more deeply with women's auto/biography in Chapter Three.

32. Saul shows his lack of religious orthodoxy because he does not know that the burial does not require a rabbi (See Liebman 2015).

33. In the stages of Jewish mourning: "The first, most intense period of mourning is the period between the death and the burial. This period, called *aninut*, is characterized by a numbing, paralyzing grief. During this period, the first degree relatives' all-consuming concerns are the funeral and burial arrangements." The ways in which the Holocaust desecrated Jewish spaces, holy texts, rituals, and bodies—ending with murder was all-consuming for the Nazis. Burning bodies was the antithesis of Jewish burial practices; thus, Saul's obsession with the burial of the boy, though improbable in this setting as Liebman notes, revealed a strong inward connection to his spiritual self (which to this point in the film appeared irrevocably destroyed) (Chabad 1993; 2017).

34. These same men also took clandestine pictures of the camps and wrote and hid diaries destined for the outside world to bear witness.

35. There is an ambiguity here between the "value" of personal versus collective goals in this scene.

36. The reference to Schindler and the List appears in the titles of several women's memoirs that were published several years later. These belated narratives, as I suggest in Chapter Three, were not written or published until after the audiences were perceived to be listening. Laura Hillman, one survivor in Orange County, who I interviewed in 2004, wrote a book called *I Will Plant You a Lilac Tree*. This title reflected a promise made by her future husband in Auschwitz if they survived together. When Simon and Schuster picked up the book for publication as part of their adolescent reading collection (2005), they added this byline: *Memoir of a Schindler's List Survivor*. Roma Ligocka, the girl in the red coat pictured in the film wrote her memoir belatedly as well, and the memoir was called: *The Girl in the Red Coat*.

37. I worked with the USHMM on piloting a digital database that was built as a teaching resource (2014–2017) that used these improved digitization processes and platforms.

38. Museums realized the potential for survivor testimonies to allow special connections to history for audiences as well. As I will outline in Chapter Five, survivor testimony plays a large role in all the museums I visited.

39. "Developing such a robust search mechanism required innovation, and the USC Shoah Foundation currently holds 11 patents on digital collection management technologies" (USC "About").

40. One of the archive's educational platforms, IWitness, "is the Institute's signature educational website for teachers and their students. The free site has been used by students and educators in all 50 states and over 80 countries including Poland, Czech Republic, Ukraine, Hungary, Australia and France" (USC "Home"). The number of people who will see these testimonies expands exponentially with the expansion of the archive's access and outreach.

41. The mission of the archive indeed has four "strategic priorities": education, research, access, and global outreach (USC "Home").

42. The USHMM and other Holocaust museums have been doing this important education and outreach work as well, and in some cases for longer, as I will explore in Chapter Five.

43. I used this packet when I led a summer teacher-training workshop in 2014. It is a thorough and in-depth resource made available to teachers in rural and underserved areas for free.

44. "USC Shoah Foundation has also partnered with USC Institute for Creative Technologies and Conscience Display to conceive and design a cutting-edge technology called 'New Dimensions in Testimony,' which enables people to interact with a projected image of a real Holocaust survivor, who responds to questions asked in real time. With this endeavor, a handful of Holocaust survivors who have already sat before a camera for USC Shoah Foundation's Visual History Archive are giving testimony again. This time, however, they sit before 50 cameras arranged in a rig to capture a three-dimensional recording of them telling their stories in a new way, by answering questions that people are most likely to ask. Funding for New Dimensions in Testimony was provided in part by Pears Foundation and Louis. F. Smith" (USC "About").

45. Though Holocaust denial remains an exceptional phenomenon directed only at the Jewish genocide and no other.

46. As we will see in Chapter Five, Holocaust museums have moved in this direction as well.

Chapter Three

Is It Happening Again? How Women's Deferred Memories Perform Holocaust Public Memory

Ruth Klüger and the Levys

In Chapters One and Two, I discussed the performative and the ways in which discourse can create action in audiences, as well as how the binary and gendered nature of discourse is limiting. In testimony, as we saw in Chapter One, there is no rehearsal and no revision, but in Lanzmann's *Shoah*, extensive editing achieves an artistic vision of "re-created" places of atrocity that claim gender neutrality. New access to the film's outtakes at the USHMM have given audiences the opportunity to engage with narratives of women and men that challenge such binary gender constructions and their supposed neutrality. Chapter Two examined the after-affect of *Schindler's List*, *Son of Saul*, and the USC Visual History Archive as they performatively bring audiences metonymically into connection with the artifacts and survivor stories and the impact of re-orienting audiences to shift their knowledge of this history by turning toward the survivor perspective with intensity and connection.

As I sat down to revise this chapter in 2018, so much had changed. I read my original descriptions of David Duke, the white supremacist politician that Anne Levy had confronted 25 years ago, as a "spectre" of the past banished by the important work of second- and third-generation Jewish survivors and other political activists.[1] Yet, I was wrong; he is alive and well, campaigning for and now ardently supporting President Trump. The complacency of second- and third-generation post-Holocaust Germans and Americans, who Ruth Klüger calls out in her auto/biography (below), a group mildly jolted 15 years ago, seems, with another generation, to have returned to a quiet apathy or a willfully ignorant bystander stance in the face of a new intolerance and bigotry. With these political revelations in my own world, this chapter takes on increasing significance. These women saw a need to speak into their socio-historic context to create change, and so in retelling their stories, I too speak into my own socio-historic context to try to re-create change through their eloquent voices. They saw hope for a better future; do we? My mother and I read texts about the Holocaust together and though we talk about them, we do not always have the same outlook. I am a consummate pessimist, but short term. My mother is a consummate optimist, but as she ages this is also short term, perhaps because she is losing her memory but also because she has seen too much of human nature. Still, she is a tireless optimist about the benefit of education: words *can* make things better. This is why these women wrote. This is why she keeps telling me to write—so I do.

Writing memory in the form of memoir or auto/biography,[2] as the writers in this chapter do, allows for both a strong narrative arc as well as reflection, revision, and editing (like our authors in Chapters One and Two); in memoir and auto/biography, however, though the aesthetic choices can be made reflectively and with intention, these stories are not creative non-fiction as with *Schindler's List* or *Son of Saul*, nor are they a collage of voices, scenes, and interviews as in *Shoah*. They are first person narratives of one person's story. As contributions to public memory, many historians have judged the authenticity or value of such narratives based on their proximity in time to the event. Recollections made closer to the event, they argue, such as diaries or testimonies given during 1945–1948, will have more detail and be less "filtered."[3] Yet even testimonies are considered "suspect" (like Hilberg says in *Shoah*) "partly because they are not written and partly because they usually are offered many years after the event and thus are based on the faculty of memory, which many consider untrustworthy" (Greene and Kumar 2011, xvii). Is written, first person testimony in the form of a memoir or auto/biography also suspect because of its distance from the event?

"Recent neurological research" about imprinting suggests that this claim of memory "fading" with time might be a fallacy (xvii). Even if memories are repressed, it is argued that the imprint of trauma is real and vivid. Part of my argument for auto/biography in this chapter is that these narratives are vivid, accurate, and detailed and also that there is the phenomenon of "deferred" memory. This means that the traumatic memory has resided at the forefront for the survivor; the memories are not repressed or unavailable, rather the survivor *chooses* not to share their story because of their performance of strictly constructed binary gender roles. Women simply do not tell important stories—men do.

In this chapter, I focus on three women. Ruth Klüger wrote her memoir, *Still Alive: A Holocaust Girlhood Remembered*, in the late 1990s in response to the rise of Holocaust museum and memorial culture in Germany and America, as well as to the continued invisibility of gender in Holocaust narratives. She wrote a second version in English in 2001 to address American audiences specifically. In contrast, Anne Levy and her mother Ruth Levy shared their deferred narratives in the 1960s and the late 1980s because they were compelled by the rise of neo-Nazi ideology in the American South. Both Levy stories are compiled in *Troubled Memory: Anne Levy, The Holocaust, and David Duke's Louisiana*, a Holocaust auto/biography written with Lawrence Powell that appeared around the same time as Klüger's American version in 2000. Each work employs specific performative techniques that *kairotically* open the conversation around public memory, gender, and the Holocaust. In Chapter One I explored the performative as a generative force of "betweens" of past and present. In Chapter Two I explored the performative metonymic: partial renderings as a way to mark what is absent in the present. In this chapter I explore several performative techniques at once to highlight the special ways that written text performs to engage audiences in challenging socio-historic contexts. I use three of Pollock's other performative techniques as "a way of describing what good writing *does*" and to map the movements of these artifacts within the public memory conversation from the past into the present (1998, 75).

I have been discussing the "stickiness" affect in Chapters One and Two to explore what "moves us" to turn toward others, but in this chapter affect and connection are not necessarily what these authors seek in audiences. The performative approaches that these women employ to engage audiences are quite distinct because they want them to listen and then to act. They call upon audiences to see that something is very wrong in the present, and it is *their* responsibility to change it. Exploring the performative technique these authors use might give us insights into how we might respond to our own challenging socio-historic contexts in the present.

We have discussed some of Pollock's methods to "map" performance in the previous chapters. The authors in this chapter want to provoke audiences out of apathy and into action; performing memory is an effective way to push that "turn" toward the experience of the other. Ruth Levy's writing is performatively evocative, which confounds "normative" binaries. Ruth Klüger's is performatively citational, which repeats what has been seen before but with a difference (in this case gendered difference), and Anne Levy's displays performative subjectivity, which is the demonstration of multiple subjectivities. With these techniques, their writing *does* something because memory work is built collaboratively, which means that it begins with one voice but requires all the participants to be co-constructors of meaning.

As communal social acts, public memory specifically in the examples in this chapter (deferred memories in auto/biographies) is constructed *in relation* to the work of others and *in response* to history as it happens. It requires that audiences shift their orientations so they are able to turn toward these stories instead of away to create a shared community of witnesses. Recall that in Ahmed's "community of witnesses" knowledge is attained as a group, as a public. As to that "public," no speaker speaks into a void; all speech depends upon what came before it and what will come after it, as I suggested in Chapter Two with the idea of "after-affect."[4] This community requires that the survivor tell and that the audience listen. The *phere* of *kairos* means that audiences must both listen and "bear" witness while also yielding. For the women writing in this chapter, we will discover that an audience willing to listen to traumatic memories is certainly not a given in the American landscape especially when it comes to women's stories, but these authors persist in telling their story in the present to instigate political action.

DEFERRING MEMORY NARRATIVES

In discussing the public memory work around the Holocaust, Sara Horowitz describes "belated narrative" (2013),[5] in which women who have firsthand testimony refrain from publicizing that testimony because of the specifically gendered nature of their trauma. Traumatic memory around motherhood, abortion, and rape and the Holocaust involve events that have been socially constructed as taboo, and this creates shame in survivors and delays their telling. There is excellent scholarship in this area in both primary texts and secondary texts.[6] This is certainly at play for some of the experiences of the women I discuss in this chapter as well, but there is another gendered aspect of belated memory that I call "*deferred memory*," in which the delayed retelling of memory is a result of the performance of socially and rigidly constructed gender roles of both authors and their audiences that relates to taboo but has more to do with feeling and being unheard.[7] The writers in this chapter deferred telling their story because they felt the Holocaust story "had been told," mostly by men, and their story would have no further effect. Yet, for each of the writers in this chapter, her present socio-historical context compelled her to write her story for audiences in the present as a communal act: in dialogue with the work of others and in response to history as it was happening to create action.

AUTO/BIOGRAPHY AND PERFORMATIVE PUBLIC MEMORY

As I noted in Chapters One and Two, public memory is a dynamic, dialogic process of both remembering and forgetting. Jessica Enoch extends the notion of public memory as dynamic work that "confirms or disturbs" and is "constitutive," in that it shapes "identities, communities, and interpretations, especially about gender" (2013, 63). This is especially important when we think about the "traditionally" gendered spheres of public and private, and how they become reconstituted with each generation. As I examined in Chapter Two, the binary of emotion and gender representation persists. In this chapter the binary insists what is "feminized" be private and personal. It is "typically" less valued by the community at large. In the examples in this chapter, memories that have been *deferred* because they are deemed "less valuable" in the public realm are recovered and shared by authors for a concrete purpose in the present. These authors purposefully break the binary of gender to tell their stories because they *do* matter. Their writing can *do* something in the world. In the case of *Still Alive* and *Troubled Memory*, there is a performative[8] dialogic enacted between survivors and second and third generations in response to historical events in the present—events that cast a dark shadow on the idea of "never again."[9] Ruth Levy's writing is performatively evocative, writing that "confounds normative distinctions between critical and creative (hard and soft, true and false, masculine and feminine), allying itself with the logics of possibility rather than of validity"[10] (Pollock 1998, 81). This allies itself with breaking the binary, which Ruth Levy does writing as a woman in the 1960s American South.

Ruth Klüger's writing is performatively citational. She disrupts the gender binary by writing her story, but she also utilizes direct address to confront readers. Citational performative writing reveals "the fragility of identity, history, and culture constituted in rites of textual recurrence." Because identity cannot escape its construction, performative elements can exert "counterpressure" where the repetition is a "repetition with a *difference*" (Pollock 1998, 92). Klüger is in dialogue with her audience. She repeats aspects of the Holocaust "story" like Auschwitz or *Selektions*, but with a *difference*. She exerts counterpressure by insisting audiences look at the gender gap in history as it applies to the facts of that history and to their own lives in the present. Identity is constructed, so it is important to think about how gender constructs the self.

Anne Levy's story displays performative subjectivity. The performative subjective is, "the performed relation between or among subjects, the dynamic engagement of a contingent and contiguous (rather than continuous) relation between the writer and his/her subject(s), subject-selves, and/or reader(s). This brings the writer and reader in critical intimacy, and the relationship as shifting and contextual (Pollock 1998, 86). For Anne Levy this was true as she engaged with audiences in different eras and for different purposes.

While the telling of such stories is not always straightforward, fortunately, the construction of public memory is an ongoing process, and the performative allows a mapping of techniques in these Holocaust public memory artifacts to see *how* each of them brings audiences to connection and action. These movements can shift audiences' orientations toward the authors instead of turning away. Public memory is not just about the witnesses, historians, post event testimonies, or publics—it involves all of these in active relation. If public memory is to enact its work performatively, it should provoke audiences to constantly contemplate the past in new contexts, challenging them to improve their present. It is precisely the belief that the past can do nothing to change the present or the future that produces apathy. We see this today with millions of voters who do not bother to vote in elections or people who will not read the news because it is too negative. The women in this chapter, who chose to write their stories of the Holocaust so many decades after the event, know the danger of such apathy. When memories recede and publics become forgetful about traumatic pasts, the markers that might alert us to rising antisemitism, discrimination, and racism (though they might be dressed in different contexts) are easily overlooked. These women lived with the Holocaust every day, but did not feel strongly enough that their stories mattered to the world until a particularly *kairotic* moment occurred in their own present.

HOLOCAUST MEMOIR AND AUTO/BIOGRAPHY: WHO *IS* LISTENING?

In the years following the war, oral testimony was taken[11] and memoirs were written, but many of these remained hidden from public view. After the *yizkor* in the early years when only a few memoirs were being published,[12] most narratives were almost exclusively male-authored. Survivor Primo Levi's memoir was written right after the war ended, and he sought a publisher for years before it was published in 1947. Elie Wiesel's *Night* was published in 1960. Charlotte Delbo, an exception, wrote her memoir in the 1970s in French, but it was not translated into English until 1995.

This initial period of publication of a few memoirs in the 1940s and 1950s was followed by a period of quiet. The war had ended and the camps had been liberated. Survivors stayed for years in Displaced Person (DP) Camps,[13] yet survivors who emigrated to the United States largely stayed silent about their experiences. In 1950s America there was no word "Holocaust." Few stories beyond Elie Wiesel's or Primo Levi's were widely publicized.[14] "Nobody was listening to us back then," says Shep Zitler, a survivor colleague of Anne Levy's in New Orleans (Powell 2000, 414).[15] The Holocaust imagery that was publicized of the Holocaust had been graphic and disturbing. Some in the general public were asking questions about how people could have survived, and what they might have "done" to survive, because the atrocity perpetrated was so beyond the realm of knowledge at that time; no one knew what the camps had been like. Thus, many who had survived spoke only of these events with other survivors. Back then no one had discussed at length that those who judged the survivors did so wrongly, because they (as non-survivors) belonged to a "privileged world of moral choice" (Greene and Kumar 2011, xii), and such a world did not exist in the camps.

Sidra Erzahi sees that small, initial period of publication period as only "a small ripple in the public consciousness" (1980, 21). There was no resulting wider dialogue about the topic following these publications, and without the presence of a perceived listening audience,[16] many survivors were not inclined to share their stories with the world; the memories were too traumatic. Anne Levy remembers that survivors did not tell their stories because they "were afraid of being judged" and Shep adds: "Non-survivors didn't understand" because "it was beyond belief" (Powell 2000, 414). The contemporary world would use a moral compass constructed from outside the gates of concentration camps and ghettoes. So survivors kept their silence, sharing only with friends and family. The survivors in New Orleans, according to survivor Ralph Rosenblatt, were both "too busy" to think about the past, but were also actively "trying to forget" (414). With traumatic memory, however, it was hard to keep those memories at bay. Child survivor Ruth Klüger admits: "Running away is what I am best at [...] but you may find yourself running in circles" (2001, 205).[17]

Many writers, like Ruth Levy (Anne's mother), used the memoir format to describe these experiences. Memoir is episodic, meaning that it focuses on several episodes within one large event (or a series of events). It tends to focus on a unifying thread and is not always chronological. Holocaust memoirs generally follow a similar trajectory: writers focus on events before the war/leading up to the war, during the war (the Holocaust) and after the war (liberation). Elie Wiesel's book, *Night*, might be the most well-known memoir that follows this structure. Although it is often assumed to be a single memoir and taught as a stand-alone text, it is part of a trilogy.[18] While Wiesel broke his story into three parts, most of the authors in this chapter chose to communicate their stories in the longer auto/biography form.

Auto/biography differs from memoir in that it attempts to depict a whole life. It is more chronological, and it follows a protagonist, who has an important impact on the world. To take on the work of auto/biography assumes a certain sense of a larger self and larger purpose. From a feminist perspective then, it is not surprising that the auto/biography genre was primarily a white, male-dominated format for centuries (such as Augustine's *Confessions* or Benjamin Franklin). Within this historical tradition, therefore, female auto/

biographers (and those of color) are seen as interlopers. In order to enter into this realm of auto/biography, a woman must break out of the binary of "traditional" gender construction that renders her words or actions as less important than a man's.[19]

If we reflect on the male-as-universal paradigm for "classic" auto/biography, deferred public retellings of women's autobiographical Holocaust experiences "fits" in this rigidly constructed gender context.[20] Feminist auto/biography theory posits that subjectivity is "produced in discourse and/or performance" through the *act of writing* autobiography (Cosslett et al. 2000, 10). Lucille Eichengreen, who wrote *Haunted Memories: Portraits of Women in the Holocaust* tells readers that she waited "because it was too painful to go back. It still is" (2011, 2). Elisabeth Baer says Eichengreen also waited for several other reasons that apply to all female authors: (1) biographies of women of the Holocaust were not "popular" 50 years ago. "Only men were considered credible witnesses," (2) publishers did not see these as big "money makers" (2003, 8),[21] and (3) Baer says that Eichengreen's books "disrupt the master narrative" of the Holocaust that assumes "women's experiences can be generalized from the male's" (8).

KAIROS: WHEN TO TELL? WHAT TO TELL?

When survivors eventually do write about their experiences, Sidra Erzahi outlines five primary motives: a desire for revenge, the need to bear witness, to commemorate the dead, to absolve the self of passivity or complicity, and to warn humanity (1980, 21). The need to bear witness has been noted as the most compelling motive.[22] For many Jewish writers, bearing witness in general has its origin in the Talmud, where "once an unjust event is known, it must by law be reported" (Young 1988, 18). Because many survivors discuss feeling as if they had died with their comrades in the camps, *writing* about their experiences becomes an act of bearing witness to what they saw and experienced, and an act of bearing witness to what their lost comrades experienced. The other motives are also at play for many writers, but for the women in this chapter (and for many who deferred their telling), I argue that bearing witness was not a primary motive at this late date—but warning humanity is. This warning is the action they seek audiences to heed. As I will outline below, each of the narratives have particularly performative qualities that allow their writing to *do* something—to warn; their realization that their contextual public does not know about the Holocaust, and thus, a similar experience could be happening again compel their voices to become part of public memory at a precisely *kairotic* moment, allowing an aperture to open up for dialogue.

Public memory is meant to be active and communal, as these authors argue implicitly in their works of deferred memory. Earlier memoirists like Levi or Wiesel wanted to clarify the facts around the Holocaust directly after the traumatic event, but they also sought to convince others to talk about the Holocaust. Wiesel's choices reflect his desire to "truth tell" and also reflect the unique social/historical context in which his memoir appeared.[23] I have argued that the desire to bear witness and to "warn humanity" begins in first-generation survivors, particularly those who have deferred telling their stories for personal reasons. When they finally write, it is into a *kairotic* moment; their memories enter into a socio-historical context that has the possibility of shifting orientations by appealing to affect. The authors in this chapter speak directly to audiences about these common denominators of shared memory, because they have witnessed a fading of public memory—forgetfulness—around the Holocaust. These authors' gestures reach back to the past while holding an open door for the present, so that the "neutral" and de-gendered narrative can be contested. Because their stories have been deferred, the writers in this chapter take for granted that certain "truths" about the Holocaust are now historically self-evident, as a result of decades of meticulous historical work and hundreds of memoirs and auto/biographies. They write less to "prove" information than to reiterate the meaning and import of that information as educational and potentially transformative knowledge in the present, especially because they see an erosion of shared public memory about the Holocaust. Wineburg et al. discuss this fading of public memory using the term "occlusion," the antithesis to collective memory:

> Occlusion [...] speaks to that which is no longer "common knowledge," no longer easily retrieved or taken for granted. The connotations that attend this term—partiality, opacity, blockage—ask us to think about the stories, images and cultural codes that have become muted in the transmission from one generation to the next. Archived in the documentary record and present in lived memory, such stories are at risk of being lost in the everyday processes of how societies remember and transmit their past to a new generation. (2007, 66)

These educational researchers have argued that: "Common beliefs demand common denominators" (66). I suggest that next generation survivors like Anne Levy[24] seek to remind audiences what those common denominators might be in order to prevent occlusion and to make a strong statement into their present socio-historic context. But what is most important is that these authors take that process a step further by performing writing that does something. This writing does not seek only common belief; it seeks negotiation and difficult disorientations in order to connect real people to real survivor lives, not only the memories of destruction and death.

I will use a third woman's memoir as an initial example of this phenomenon. I have discussed Wiesel's memoir, *Night*, previously, and it is one of the most well known and most frequently taught memoirs in the United States. In *Night* he uses the word "Auschwitz" to describe a place that for the character has no meaning beyond initial dread. Because Wiesel's memoir was published in 1960, part of his task is to describe for audiences what life was like in a place like Auschwitz, a hellish location with which audiences were not yet familiar. In the opening Prologue of Laura Hillman's memoir, *I Will Plant You a Lilac Tree: Memoir of a Schindler's List Survivor*,[25] in contrast, she begins with an excerpt about going to "Auschwitz." There is no explanation of the term; she simply writes: "It is Auschwitz" (2005, 1), assuming that audiences know what this place is. Hillman assumes that most American readers will know already that Auschwitz is an awful place.

Hillman's choices about which events to represent also reflect the unique social/historical context into which she writes her memoir. When I spoke with Hillman, she related that she wrote not only to bear witness to and memorialize her husband and other victims, but also to teach and warn young people (2004). Her experiences as an educator in Southern California revealed that young American students did not know very much about this event in detail. Like Klüger, Hillman writes for an American audience that is one, two, or even three generations removed from the event. They may be familiar with the Holocaust in general, but not in much detail.[26] Hillman, therefore, spends a considerable amount of time on the events leading up to the Holocaust, focusing a third of the book on the gradual buildup of the Nazi regime in Germany, especially the ways in which she was legally excluded from places and activities (like theaters and school), experiences that young readers in America could relate to with relatives who experienced Jim Crow laws or homophobia, for example. The second third details her experiences in a variety of lesser-known concentration camps (many in Germany), and the last third with her arrival in Auschwitz and her experience with Oskar Schindler in Poland—a comprehensive timeline about the German-Jewish experience that many American readers may not know.

The other women in this chapter also performatively recontextualize Holocaust history and memory by connecting with what audiences might know (as Hillman does) to shift their orientation toward the experiences of others and build the community of witnesses. Additionally Della Pollock's notion of the performative as "writing that does something" is an important frame for the writing of these women. Often the "doing" of writing is theoretical as in the conception of a "speech act,"[27] but speaking out can also lead to action "on the ground" that has *kairotic* force. The act of listening in response to words that seek action (the warning that these authors want to send the world) performs memory as a powerful *kairotic* and emotional appeal that has the power to shift audience orientations to difference. As I argue throughout this book, Holocaust public memory artifacts perform with significant force at particular historical moments that are punctuated by concerns about gender, identity, and the absence of affect and connection. Hawhee's conceptualization of rhetorical *kairos* is not just a force that marks and disrupts the "neutral" public memory of the Holocaust, but it is also an aperture that creates a performative space: "the rhetor opens [himself] to the immediate situation, allowing for more of an exchange" (2004, 71). Rhetorical force comes when the participants engage in a dialogic about Holocaust experience and gender complexity; when they are presented with constructions of gender that challenge gender binary, each new the Holocaust "story" frames the past through a new lens, reorienting audiences toward survivors as whole individuals.

So if many survivors resisted telling their stories to bear witness, what compelled them to eventually change their minds? In 1961 the televised trial of Adolph Eichmann and the 1979 American television miniseries "Holocaust" opened the American public to the event we now called "the Holocaust." Shoshana Felman and Dori Laub have explored, through psychoanalytic and speech act theory, how the "readiness" of an audience to listen allows survivors to tell their stories. When there was no one to listen, the traumatic re-telling of survival stories seemed to have little public purpose, so when the audience becomes receptive, more stories can be told (see Chapter One). With these public narratives and legal proceedings, there was a greater public receptivity; it seemed audiences were ready to start listening. But even with the increase in public awareness and reception of narratives about the Holocaust, those narratives remained primarily male-authored. With deferred memory, women, and the Holocaust, not only does there have to be the sense that there is a willing and listening audience, but there also needs to be a political/historical event that compels the telling of that story for the first time. Ruth Levy's decision to write her history in the 1960s is a good example of such a *kairotic* moment and attempt to connect.[28]

RUTH LEVY: *KAIROS*, ORIENTATION, AND THE PERFORMATIVE EVOCATIVE

In the case of Ruth Levy, special historical circumstances in the 1960s South compelled her to tell her story. Despite resistance from her husband and the community, Levy, a first-generation survivor of the Holocaust, dictated her memoir to a young seminarian, which seemed random to her friends because she hardly knew him, but in reality he was the right choice because as her daughter Anne notes: "to become a priest, you have to be sympathetic and people oriented and *willing to listen*." [my emphasis] (Powell 2000, 431). In her New Orleans survivor community, Ruth Levy upended most of her generation's constructions of gender roles by telling her story to someone other than the survivor community. While she perceived that many did not agree that it was "her place" to tell, she had discovered that a listening audience existed (the priest)—*at the same time* that racists were reviving their anti-black activity in the South (her new home).[29]

Almost simultaneously with events publicizing the Holocaust like the Eichmann trial noted above, there was a neo-Nazi movement led by George Lincoln Rockwell that was gaining steam over and above the already strong presence of the Ku Klux Klan (KKK) in the South. The rise of this movement, replete with the symbols and language of Nazi Germany, caused both great fear and great anger in the survivor community in New Orleans, in a way that the Jim Crow segregation had not. The images of swastikas and antisemitic language reminded survivors on the sidelines that one of the reasons they had survived was to bear witness to those who had not.[30] It also reminded them that the Holocaust only became possible because so many people did nothing in response. Bystanders who were silent or turned away from the realities of disappearing neighbors and random police raids on certain neighborhoods, were one of the reasons the Nazi program could be so "successful."[31]

Rockwell was gaining fame and followers in the South. He did a lot of publicity stunts, one called the "hate ride" to undercut the "freedom riders" who were traveling north to south during the civil rights actions.[32] On May 20, 1961, Rockwell and other extremists informed the New Orleans Police Department (NOPD) that they were planning to picket the opening of *Exodus* and the National Association for the Advancement of Colored People (NAACP) office in New Orleans. This event was timed to match headlines elsewhere in the South. In Alabama, Klansmen had attacked an "integrated group" of Freedom Riders at the Greyhound bus station in Montgomery. This group of buses was slated to move to New Orleans next. The beatings got nationwide coverage, and Rockwell wanted to time his "ride" to coincide with the arrival of the other buses (Powell 2000, 407).[33] New Orleans was experiencing raucous opposition to desegregation efforts, but many Holocaust survivors and local teenagers wanted to show their opposition to the hate ride as publically as possible, and they "mobbed" the Rockwell picketers, seeking not physical or violent retribution, but rather the "emotional satisfaction" of speaking up and acting in public in a country where they had a legal right to do so (408). The protestors were eventually charged with "criminal mischief" in 1961, charges that were then overturned in 1962 (422).

With both the Eichmann trial and the Rockwell experience in the early 1960s, Ruth Levy felt compelled to make her private story public: "'When I hear today that people like Hitler, start following the same program, it makes me sick just to think of it' she told Powell, and that was why she had decided originally to get the Skorecki family history on paper with the help of a young neighborhood lawyer and seminarian, Harry Hull, in the 1960s. Anne says about her mother, "All her life she was afraid to let somebody know too much. She was always on guard. You just don't say too much, was her philosophy, and the mindset goes back to our experiences with the Holocaust" (431). Yet Ruth was realizing that stories like hers were becoming unknown to younger generations, who did not even know what the Holocaust was. The absence of this knowledge must again be made present. Evocative performative writing "operates metaphorically to render absence present" by connecting the reader to what is other (not present) in the text "by re-marking" it (Pollock 1998, 80). Unlike the performative metonymic in Chapter Two that seeks to make absence present through partial renderings, the performative evocative seeks to mark absence in the present by re-marking a thing familiar. Deferred memory narratives perform this re-marking by telling stories similar to those told before but to different audiences and in different contexts. According to Pollock, the evocative does not aim to report about a "verifiable event" but strives to "create what is self-evidently a *version* of what was" (80), but evocative, performative Holocaust writing *does* aim to report (to some degree) on a verifiable event. It marks the Holocaust as a representation: real events and absences that cannot be recovered yet must be marked in order to be felt and seen.

Yet it seemed that for many American audiences absence was desirable. They were not ready to hear survivor stories. Many survivors were unsure about telling stories about which they felt guilt or shame to anyone. Powell, as the collaborative biographer of this mother/daughter auto/biography says that: "Ruth was clearly uncertain how Hull [her transcriber] and future readers would react to her wartime conduct" (2000, 432). Ruth Levy tells the story of a grandfather asphyxiating his own grandson so that a group of people would not be discovered in hiding, but she does not talk about what those people did afterward, and cannot admit that the boy even died (172). Powell claims this is survivor guilt "throw[ing] up roadblocks to the return of memory," such that the details of these stories are absent (172). When Ruth describes having to part with her two children (she sent them away from the ghetto to save them), she describes it as a "hard decision" that was probably harder than "she was willing to admit to herself let alone admit to strangers later on," says Powell (197). The guilt comes from being judged poorly in a gendered way as a "mother."

Ruth's story seeks to mark the absent event that is the "Holocaust" with performative evocation in the present that challenges binary gender roles as it also aligns the Holocaust past with the racist present for audiences. The focus on herself and also her daughters and their children makes the trajectory of the tale intergenerational and seeks response by asking audiences to turn toward both of these events. Her story becomes the stories of all those relatives she lost, as well as all the people who survived, including her children. Ruth's auto/biography of the Skoreckis can be built collaboratively with her audience. They must shift their orientation to the Holocaust as an event with victims but also with survivors—generations of survivors—her children. Audiences become disoriented to the death around the Holocaust so that they might reorient to the living generations of this event. The affect that might result from this engagement could also find them realizing that *their* actions right *now* can stop the George Rockwells of the world, as those who were bystanders during the Holocaust did not. There is an active interpretation that occurs between her words and the world at large. As we will see in the last section of this chapter, this transfers literally to Ruth's daughter Anne, when she finally decides to tell her own story.

Ruth Levy told her story because she felt that there was someone listening, but her storytelling is a gesture more than a public action since not many copies were published. Her ability to re-orient larger audiences, therefore, and bring them into a community of witnesses—to shift their orientation to the experience of the other—was limited by her reach, but this does not make the performative nature of her writing less powerful. Several decades later in a different historical moment and a different geographical location, Austrian child survivor Ruth Klüger gained much more reach with her texts and performs writing in a different manner and a different context.

RUTH KLÜGER: KAIROS, ORIENTATION, AND THE PERFORMATIVE CITATIONAL

For Ruth Klüger, a child survivor born in Vienna, Austria, who emigrated to the United States after the war, the fall of the Berlin Wall in 1989 was the *kairotic* moment that resonated in both her German/Austrian historical context as well as her American one. Klüger published one auto/biography in German in 1992, *Weiter Leben*, that received wide attention, and spoke directly to German-speaking audiences. She published another in English in 2001, *Still Alive: A Holocaust Girlhood Remembered,* that spoke directly to English-speaking American audiences. Within this historical moment of about a decade, a *kairotic* and rhetorical aperture was opened, which allowed both these audiences and the author to open a dialogue.[34] Klüger uses the performative citational to directly address audiences to make this dialogue explicit. Citational performative writing reveals "the fragility of identity, history, and culture constituted in rites of textual recurrence," and in the case of Klüger, textual recurrences were the public memory practices arising in her country of origin. Because her identity cannot escape its construction, performative elements exert "counterpressure" where the repetition is a "repetition with a *difference*" (Pollock 1998, 92), and in her text Klüger applies this counterpressure through direct audience address. Whatever they think they know (how they orient themselves to Holocaust history) must be interrogated and made disorienting. Klüger confronts her readers with the fact that she knows they might resist listening to her. She knows they need to be pushed away from their apathy.

Specific events compelled Ruth Klüger to tell her story. First, she describes the troubling interactions she had with those around her in both the United States (where she had emigrated) and Germany (where she visited).[35] It was the rise of memorial and museum culture of the death camps in Europe and the absence of gender in Holocaust narratives, however, that compelled her most of all. These public memory narratives involved competing "moral entreprenuers"[36] who sought to control the narratives, yet they continued to ignore gender as constitutive of identity and experience. By insisting her audiences become participants with her in performatively constructing her auto/biography, Klüger subverts the social construction of gender roles that insists that war stories "belong to men." Klüger wants audiences to add to their own historical knowledge but she acknowledges that this work may be too disorienting, eerily prescient of what Ahmed would note about queer orientation almost two decades later. Klüger seemed to know already that she must disorient audiences in order to reorient them. Only then could they turn toward her story and toward connection.

Klüger uses herself as an example of how memory work can be disorienting, and with this self-reflective turn, she shifts the orientation of audiences as a way to be in dialogue with them. She knows the work is hard. She does it too—this is why she expects it also of them. In her struggle to find out more about her father (in life and death) Klüger notes how she feels "it's an ongoing story," then relates an incident, which proves "how ongoing these stories, these deaths, really are" (2001, 39). Klüger had imagined her father on one transport that ended in the gas chambers. She has tried to reconcile stories about people fighting their way to the top for air with her gentle, non-confrontational father. A French historian e-mails her after reading her book in French and says that her father's transport was number 73 out of 79 and it was 900 men who "didn't go to Auschwitz, but to Lithuania and Estonia, and who knows how they were murdered" (40). Her imagined memories now come into conflict with what is established as "true" by historians, and she has to realign that knowledge. This information should make her relieved, and yet pain comes with reconciling this new "imagined" memory. Her memorialization of her father, her memories of him, "her mental furniture," must be rearranged in her mind: "It feels as if I am running through my house in the dark, bumping into things. How *did* he die then? I know so little about who he was, and now I don't even know this final, inalterable fact" (40).

For Klüger, memory is like a neatly ordered room in which you feel familiar. There may be dark corners, but you know how to avoid them, and the furniture there is used and worn—you will not bump into anything in the night. You have oriented yourself; but when information comes along which alters those memories, the neatly ordered furniture must be rearranged. The disorientation is always a painful task, but one that must be done. She insists on doing it and expects her audience to do the same, even though she knows they will resist. The tendency to turn away results in isolation for the narrator and the audience. By describing to audiences her own difficulty with reconciling competing memories, Klüger opens up a space for audiences to connect with her story. She gives them the chance to re-orient themselves to new ways of considering memory work as in process. This is also the force of *kairos*. Each time Klüger encounters new information, there is disorientation until she reconciles it with previous information. Having an arranged room is familiar but asking questions about history will alter this, creating discomfort and disorientation for audiences. Klüger models shifts in orientation for audiences as she asks precise questions even though she knows most people "want to be left in peace" (17).

While Klüger uses her own example to allow audiences to connect with her fragile and shifting identity in relation to memory, she also uses the performative citational to elicit communal action as well. Recall that citational performative writing reveals "the fragility of identity, history, and culture constituted in rites of textual recurrence"; Klüger's story as a public memory artifact is a work in progress, as all of our identities and communal histories are. Performative elements can exert "counterpressure" where the repetition is a "repetition with a *difference*" (Pollock 1998, 92), so as Klüger talks directly to audiences about what they "know," she is also repeating in order to add what they do not know and probably don't want to consider.

In one example, Klüger talks about the *Selektions* at Auschwitz. She expects her audience to know something about this. She says she survived a second selection at Auschwitz, sneaking into another line after being condemned to death in the first. Klüger describes the line moving toward an

SS man, who, "Judging from photos, [he] may have been the infamous Dr. Mengele" (referencing her own ongoing research into her own history to supplement her memory) (2001, 107). As she comes to the front of the line, the clerk, a woman of about 20, asks her age; 13, Klüger replies. "Fixing me intently, she whispered, 'Tell him you are fifteen'" (107). As Klüger arrives at the front of the line, she relates what transpires:

> "She seems small," the master over life and death remarked. He sounded almost friendly, as if evaluating cows and calves.
> "But she is strong," the woman said, "look at the muscles in her legs. She can work."
> She didn't know me, so why did she do it? He agreed—"why not?" She made note of my number, and I had won an extension on my life. (108)

After relating this story, Klüger addresses the audience directly: "But don't just look at the scene. Focus on it, zero in on it, and consider what happened. There were two of them: the man who had power he could exert on a random object [. . .] And she is the other. I think his action was arbitrary, hers voluntary" (108). Klüger writes: "Her [the guard's] decision broke the chain of knowable causes." She says: "It was moral freedom at its purest. I saw it, I experienced it, I benefited from it, and I repeat it because there is nothing to add. Listen to me, don't take it apart, absorb it as I am telling it and remember it," she insists (108–109).

She continues directing her speech at the audience and predicts that "you" will object and claim there no true altruism, and she says, if that is the case, "freedom itself is a mere illusion as well" (109). Klüger addresses these comments now to "you." "You" is the American audience. They will read this story, she thinks, and disbelieve. This was not a kind act but a coincidence—luck, they will think. Nazis were evil. Klüger forces the audience to face the inaccuracy of such simplified, binary categories of good and evil in that direct address: This was goodness. Listen to me! Absorb it! You, who value "freedom" so much, believe that free will can exist in a place where so much evil reigned. So, believe this incident. Maybe it was because of "the perverse environment of Auschwitz" that "absolute goodness was a possibility," says Klüger but: "I am witness" (109). Klüger demands action and response as she deconstructs these binaries. Listen! Absorb! Rearrange your furniture—I bear witness to it. American audiences should reconsider the fragility of their own national identity as they consider their misconceptions about German identity in this history.

She wants audiences to know that this was a gendered experience, and bearing witness to it is a social activity. In another example, she relates her experience in the camp called Christianstadt (a subdivision of Gross Rosen).

She states that the female guards "addressed us in a normal, if somewhat strident, tone and used the polite form of address for grown-ups. It is hard to convey to English speakers," she adds, "the difference in respect or disrespect that is inherent in a switch from the formal to the intimate form of address. In the camps the prisoners were *du*, thou, and now this sudden return to a normality, a reminder of civilization" (115). Klüger makes the point that to delineate "guards" by gender allows a differentiation of male and female behavior to be seen as *constructed* as male and female. The female guards she encountered were pointedly *unlike* the guards described elsewhere without any specific reference to gender.

Further, Klüger tells the reader that, although they may know that there were female guards who guarded women prisoners, the term "SS women" is inaccurate. She says bluntly: "It's a misnomer, since there were no women in the SS. The SS was strictly a men's club. Everybody knows this, and yet the term remains in use, as if to make sure women get half the blame for an organization that was never theirs" (115). Women are invisible until they become visible for blame—why? Klüger implies that socially, women and men are *not* equal. When blame is meted equally in this case, it does not match the social reality. The term "Nazi," for instance (as she shows elsewhere in the book), is one that must be applied individually (as she applies "Nazi" differently to a helpful lawyer and an SS guard), changing its parameters when applied to women (and men). Their fragility causes them to be constantly under construction; this is why deconstructing the binary is so important. Klüger tells audiences to think about that repetition in a different light. In other words, these are consequences and implications of experience, representation, and history that are gendered—unique and complex.

Klüger says pointedly: Women did evil "but the Nazi evil was male, not female," and claims that whenever she says things like this she meets with "bitter objections" (115). People want to tell her that Nazi women were just as evil; they just didn't get a chance to commit as many crimes. People want to remind her of women cheering for Hitler ecstatically and about Ilse Koch with her lampshades of human skin. She says in reply, "It seems that we always pull the same names out of the hat when it comes to women, while the names of the men who committed atrocities are legion" (115). In using the term "we" she implies that issues of gender apply to everyone (including her). She wishes not to exonerate the women involved in the atrocities, but wonders, "How are we ever going to understand what happens when a civilization comes apart at the seams, as it did in Germany, if we fail to see the most glaring distinctions, such as the gender gap?" (115–116). For Klüger, any attempt to try to understand how and why these atrocities occurred will be unsuccessful if we do not include gender. And she talks directly to audiences as a whole using the "we"—we are part of the social construction of gender. We cannot turn a blind eye to its existence if we hope to change things. She seeks both audience participation and their willingness to re-orient themselves to history and to the stories of survivors.

By the late 1990s Ruth Klüger shares Hillman's sense that audiences will already know what Auschwitz is, even if they do not know the details. Klüger, however, takes this assumption of audience knowledge to another level by referring to what audiences "think they know" and speaking to them directly. She says, for example, that placing all the camps into one category: *death camps* is "easier to comprehend" for audiences but "in the process, we mythologize or trivialize them" (71), because no camp or experience was the same. Audiences may know a few names like "Auschwitz" she adds, but that does not require the "differentiation I am imposing on the reader right now" as she describes in detail her experiences in many types of camps and national locations.

Much like Hillman, Klüger tells her reader about each camp she was in and how they were different. "I insist on th[is], at the risk of alienating my readers (most of them likely to be female, since males, on the whole, tend to prefer books written by fellow males" (71). Klüger is constantly in conversation with her readers, directing them to think about how memorialization and public memory practices are problematic and how memorializing practices "constitute" things like gender, which she suggests is invisible or ignored. Klüger adds her deferred memories to the public realms in order to disturb public memory practices that have thus far only confirmed sexist gender structures or de-gendered that memory completely. The performative citational has allowed her to tell her story with a focus on that *difference*, space that deconstructs the binary between good and evil, men and women, and turning toward and away.

Anne Levy: *Kairos*, Political Reorientation, and Performative Subjectivity

Like the other two women in this chapter, the last author I explore in this chapter, Anne Levy (Ruth Levy's daughter), seeks connection with audiences because she is compelled by the *kairotic* moments in her present that exert force onto Holocaust public memory and her own survivor memories as yet unshared with the public. Like Klüger, Anne Levy is both a child survivor and a second-generation survivor, as the child of parents who both survived the Holocaust. While Klüger's context was a return to their historical legacy for young Germans and Americans, for Anne Levy, the historical context was one similar to her mother's—resurgence of Nazi ideology in the American South and the occlusion of public memory around the Holocaust. When Lincoln Rockwell was active in the 1960s, Ruth Levy was clearly affected, as

I explained early in this chapter. Her daughter Anne was also compelled to speak at this time, albeit only once.

Anne Levy had settled in New Orleans, Louisiana, with her survivor parents and her sister, Lila, shortly after emigrating from the Displacement (DP) Camps in Germany after 1948. New Orleans in the 1950s, like many southern cities, was rife with racial tensions and entrenched in Jim Crow segregation (as I noted above in Ruth's section). New Jewish immigrants, though they had suffered similar persecutions, were not ready to equate them with the racial inequality they saw on a daily basis, because, as new immigrants, they did not want to rock the boat too soon. Writing about the time period, biographer Powell says that, "like southern Jews generally, New Orleans's survivors also readily acquiesced in the dominant racial order, steering clear even of moderate civil rights action, leaving all of that to the next generation" (2000, 412). Fighting for their own survival in a new location seemed tantamount.

Ruth Levy bucked this trend of silence by dictating her story during the 1960s. When Ruth Levy tried to get her daughters, Anne and Lila, to also write about their experiences in the 1930s and 40s, however, they were uninterested: "They never wanted to recall their terrible childhood" (433), says Powell. During this period, as we recall from above, Rockwell was planning "hate rides" to counter the Civil Rights Freedom Rides in the South, and after his arrest in New Orleans, he made a statement to the press that the Holocaust had never happened. Anne Levy was strongly affected by this public statement and called her mother crying and saying "Momma, I have to do it" (433). By "it," she meant making her heretofore private memories public. On May 30, 1961, she wrote a letter to the *New Orleans States-Item* newspaper, a frightfully public venue for "the characteristically reticent Anne" (433), but this uncharacteristic action broke the binary of private and public. The letter says, in part:

> I could hardly believe my ears when I heard George Lincoln Rockwell say that the United States should have joined Hitler in World War II. If this statement wasn't enough, when a reporter asked if Hitler was right in murdering six million Jews, Mr. Rockwell had the audacity to say that it was a fabrication, that he (Mr. Rockwell) didn't believe that Hitler was responsible for mass murder.
>
> Sure, I am one of the lucky ones who wasn't in a concentration camp, but I do know what it means to live in the Warsaw ghetto. Although I was only a child, I saw more suffering and dead people than some grownups see in a lifetime.
>
> Since I am the mother of two children now, I would have hoped that my suffering could spare the children of the new generation the agony of hatred, but as long as we have people like th[is] Nazi, I am afraid that all the suffering of World War II was in vain. (433–434)

Anne Levy, like her mother, subverted the construction of gender roles that privilege the war memories of men to make her private memories public in this letter. Rockwell's public denial of the Holocaust made Anne feel she should speak out "now" to warn others; but it was only for a moment, for the suffering was too great. Anne Levy said afterward: "I don't remember writing that letter," and her war memories in general, Powell writes, went back "into hibernation" for another 25 years (434). Yet she initially wrote in order to speak into a space where people might hear and be warned.

Performative writing seeks action by becoming "writing as doing." Ruth Levy writes with performative evocation, imploring audiences to mark what happens in the present by re-marking the past. Audiences should re-see the past so they could dismantle resurgent racism in the American South in the present. Klüger uses the performative citational to repeat misconceptions of gender and the Holocaust with a difference (and an eye toward deconstructing the binaries of gender) and shifts orientations by disorienting readers with rearranged mental furniture. Audiences must reorient themselves to these new paradigms. As the collaborative auto/biography of the Levys' *Troubled Memory* moves to the second-generation story with Anne, it displays subjective performative writing because it does not refer to conventional mirror-reflections of Anne's auto/biography as a "coherent self across time," but rather as a "contiguous [. . .] relation between the writer and his/her subject(s), subject-selves, and/or reader(s)" (Pollock 1998, 86). This is most clearly seen as a literal disconnect between Anne's letter-writing action in 1961 and the subsequent total memory loss of that action. It is almost as if there were more than one person involved. Yet, it is not simply the self in plural that is performative, but the movement "forward and between selves to form multiple perspectives and relations" that marks the performative subject (86). In the examples below, I will show how over two decades, Anne's writing and public speaking about the Holocaust form these multiple perspectives and relations. Indeed, this multi-perspective relationship brings the writer and readers into critical intimacy, as the relationship must shift according to context (86).

In Anne's shifting contexts, her next engagement with the public would be two decades after she first wrote the letter to the newspaper. In her newer context in the 1980s, David Duke, the openly white supremacist politician, got elected in Louisiana. It brought national attention to the region and for Anne, became a *kairotic* moment that opened the necessity of a second public dialogue. The rise of Duke despite his affiliations with the KKK[37] did not seem to surprise or disturb anyone locally except the Jewish community. Klan affiliation was a shared but unexamined history for many families in Louisiana.[38] In this instance, it seemed only the

New Orleans Jewish community remembered Duke's neo-Nazi past with accuracy. Knowing of his neo-Nazi connections, the Simon Wiesenthal Center in Los Angeles offered the state capitol a traveling exhibit about the Holocaust called *The Courage to Remember* at a time they knew Duke would be canvassing in the area.

Anne Levy attended that opening ceremony in 1989 intending to simply bear witness to the Holocaust in her adopted home state. When she unexpectedly saw Duke, however, looking at the exhibit—looking at pictures he had claimed were not even real—standing "ramrod erect" as if in "parade rest" as if "he were conducting a selection at a railroad siding" (Powell 2000, 4), she was overcome by emotion. She confronted him: "I thought you said it never happened." The movement between the reticent Anne and this Anne who confronts Duke in public is performative, the subject/selves shift according to context. Her words will create action. Anne says she touched him on the shoulder two or three times, and then he replied vehemently: "I didn't say it didn't happen, I said it was exaggerated" (4). Duke told reporters later that what he had said in the past about the Holocaust did not matter to the present, but to Anne it was an affront to her personal story and the notion of shared history—those "common denominator" events that help facilitate intergenerational dialogue. Anne Levy's knowledge of the past collided with her emotions in the present to create a subjective performative memory with the *kairotic* force to compel her own unintended action, much as Ruth Klüger's performative began with an examination of herself.

Anne Levy confronted David Duke, in public, with the knowledge of her private story. She modeled not being a bystander—not stepping aside and not staying silent in the face of falsehood and wrong action. Duke's brazen, public denials of the Holocaust elsewhere, and literal whitewashing of those lies as he spoke to Anne Levy face-to-face were too much to bear. His denials were an affront to democratic civility and Anne Levy's identity as a new American, both of which she prized in her adopted home. The performance of her discourse in the public sphere here creates a community of witnesses to bear witness to the memories of those who had perished and were being erased by Duke's public denials of the Holocaust as well as to attend to the living survivors for whom this erasure reignited trauma.

MULTIPLE VOICES CREATE ACTION IN AUDIENCES

The Holocaust auto/biographers I discuss in this chapter disturb "degendered"[39] public memory by subverting binary (so-called neutral) gender constructions through performative writing. They seek to warn but also seek to inspire real action in audiences. They subvert gendered identity across generations by presenting shifts in voices and in time while following the threads of history that tie generations—they shift audience orientations to the past by re-orienting them to new narratives in the present that re-contextualize history as an ongoing process that involves connection and relationship. These authors ask their audiences to respond, and to act to dismantle gender or racial bias. But sometimes that action is real and immediate political action in the present, as we will see in Anne Levy's case.

What makes *Troubled Memory* such an interesting text is that it enacts the subjective performative through the multiple perspectives of Anne, but also the voice of Powell, voices of family and community members, and the voices of her mother. Powell constructs the text to move from Ruth to Anne and back again, which allows their voices to interact and blur chronological time. Each of their stories has its own *kairotic* force in a respective present, but Powell actively connects their voices across generations in his exposition sections. Powell's role in the collaborative auto/biography is as recorder and interpreter and as commentator. He performs a similar role as a "third Voice" with Anne's story.

For instance, when discussing why Anne told her story, Anne is often not quoted directly. Powell tells us that the drive to tell became more imperative for Anne because of the "increasing audacity of Holocaust deniers" (2000, 15). Powell leads with this claim and then provides evidence to bolster that claim. By the 1990s, according to a Gallup poll, the Holocaust was entering a realm of amnesia for many Americans (2). In a 1993 poll, over 50% of high school students nationwide could not explain the term "Holocaust," and in Louisiana, that percentage jumped to 90% (2). Not only was the Holocaust disappearing from Southern memory it seemed, but people were also beginning to openly and aggressively deny the Holocaust. Deniers were "propagandizing" among high school teachers and started taking out full-page ads in college newspapers to refute the "myth" of the Holocaust. "Denier activism had caused survivor children—the 'second generation'—and other social action groups to organize counter-movements." And the Chairman of the International Network of Survivor Children told *TIME*, according to Powell, that: "As children of Jewish Holocaust Survivors, we have a special obligation to make sure this doesn't happen again" (15). Holocaust denial was becoming a cottage industry. Based in pseudo-academic research, "revisionists" were calling the gas chambers fiction (15).[40] This second and more pointed assault on her experiences and the apparent occlusion of memory happening in her own backyard caused Anne to finally speak in public about the Holocaust and tell her story.

Perhaps because she was both a survivor and a second-generation survivor, Anne felt strongly that her experience should not be "defamed," especially by professors like Arthur Butz at Northwestern, whose most famous claims were that the six million dead was overestimated and "the forty thousand linear feet of documents on German genocide captured by the United States alone [...] had been planted" (16). In this auto/biography, Powell provides additional perspectives through research to underscore that Anne's feelings were based on real actions and facts, much as Klüger had done with her research on her father. Connecting new facts with emotion rearranged "the furniture" of her memory.

Powell writes that what was "more upsetting than anything" for Anne emotionally was "Butz's potential impact on the young." She went home and wrote a second letter, this time to *The Times-Picayune* on 28 April 1983,[41] which Powell includes as evidence of her own words:

> This story must be told and re-told, for in my own lifetime I have heard it said that the Holocaust didn't happen, that it was merely a fabrication of the Jews. Well, when you have witnessed death and starvation and see people comparing concentration camp numbers tattooed on their arms, how could anyone with any sense of compassion believe this never happened? The tragic history needed to be continually recounted, because this should never happen again to any people be they Jews or anyone else on the face of this planet. (16)

Like her mother, the anger Anne experienced turned into *fear* that the world would stand by once again—indifferent to a politician who openly disparaged Jews and blacks alike. Anne was angered most by Duke's white supporters, who seemed to care little about "Duke's anti-Semitism" (8). They often came into her shop and "they would never say anything to your face," she says, "but for the first time it made me stop and think [...] I felt uncomfortable" (80). Anne felt her own reorientation in this case. The antisemitism she was experiencing caused her to see with more clarity the racism around her. In the recession of the 1980s South, Duke preached moderation and economic renewal, and "born of firsthand experience, Anne's foreboding was deep and unshakable" (9). A famous study of a small town in Germany noted, locals "were drawn to anti-Semitism because they were drawn to Nazism, not the other way around." And Anne says, "When bad times come, somebody has to get blamed" (9).

Anne reacted to these contemporary events not just by telling her story, but by *acting* from her own private history in the public realm as an activist. She spoke out against David Duke in her community. She confronted Duke in public settings like the Wiesenthal exhibit at the capitol. Only after these very public events did Anne become committed to the continual re-telling of her story to children in local schools. It was as if once she had opened the door to her deferred memory and acted upon it in the public realm, it allowed her to shift more fluidly between her subject selves in her community through continued intergenerational dialogue. Anne's actions perform in the public realm in response to the fear that "history is repeating itself," and ask others to work with her public memory together to fight. By placing Anne's activism within the story of her mother's actions 25 years previously, Powell builds a bridge between them for readers. He showcases their voices, and his "third" voice as commentator, but he also highlights the voices of friends and community members, third-generation family members, and researched history to speak as well. The shifting voices become a chorus of shifting perspectives interacting with readers to tell the story of one family.

Performance and Gender: Intergenerational Dialogue

As we get further away from the actual event of the Holocaust, the act of bearing witness, the *phere* of listening and yielding (that I have been describing throughout this book) increasingly becomes the responsibility of the generations after who encounter these texts. Like Anne Levy. a child survivor and a second-generation survivor, Klüger has taken a long time to tell her story and by the time she does in 1980s Germany many survivors had already died, and taken their untold eyewitness accounts with them. Germans audiences were only beginning to be capable of listening to their own history. Thus, she describes the communication of this event across time as a "wall between the generations" as having always been there, but in Germany "the wall is barbed wire. Old, rusty barbed wire" (2001, 65).

As a result of this wall, Klüger does not represent a consistent listening audience and even underscores the lack of such a listener by describing her encounters with younger people who are far from responsive. She writes about her harrowing experience in the cattle cars. As a child, she witnesses someone urinating on her mother and how adults lost control mentally and physically in the heat, thirst, and crushing lack of space and air. She compares this with an experience she has visiting friends in Germany after writing the first book. These third-generation Germans discuss claustrophobia in the Chunnel and in elevators (92). Klüger notes that her experience of claustrophobia in the cattle cars comes back to her but she doesn't "contribute it, because if I had, I would have effectively shut up the rest of the company" (93). She would like to tell her stories, but no one wants to hear this and be bothered or uncomfortable (93). And thus, she states: "my childhood falls into a black hole" (93). She cannot validate her childhood experiences because of her inability to communicate them to her audience. No one "wants to hear"; thus, no conversation can occur.

Klüger knows that generations experience gaps in historical and emotional understanding. So, how do we bridge these gaps in memory in the gaps between a story in the past and a reality in the present to embody memory? In some way, we must all meet momentarily in the present, "time frozen in space, and space made human," she says (214). Klüger sees this in the close relationship between her 90-year-old mother and her four-year-old granddaughter. Her text seeks to bridge that generational gap by letting audiences into the process of building memory—one that is dialogic and active—but one that takes work. This work is not solitary; it is communal. Memories and histories must be retold; but the retelling is often forgotten generation to generation.

For Anne, though her mother had dictated that 1960s story about the family's Holocaust experiences, Anne had not read it and Ruth Levy had barely discussed the past with her children. Anne's "father had completely clammed up after the war," so Anne "realized I didn't know the names of either set of my grandparents or anyone else who perished in that beastly war" (Powell 2000, 14). She began to understand firsthand how quickly memory fades even across one generation.

With this same understanding, many survivors around Anne in New Orleans were becoming more focused on the moral imperative of remembering and bearing witness and were involved with the campaign to build the United States Holocaust Memorial Museum (USHMM). There was a growing realization by survivors that they must speak because their "tragic family history had greater than purely genealogical meaning" (15). That moral imperative to speak was felt by Anne's friend Shep Zitler, who said: "I survived in order to tell my story. Period" (15). Anne first shared her own story two years after the D.C. gathering. She told friends first, but that was easy compared to "forcing it on David Duke." Even though she felt compelled to finally speak, telling her story was difficult (17).

Her daughter, Robin, a third-generation survivor, told Powell in 1992 that her mother's confrontations with the neo-Nazi were personally traumatic. Robin says: "It's not like she is so articulate and composed. She's barely able to get very direct remarks out. She's a totally emotional package" (17). Robin described how Anne's language fluency in English "ebbed away when she was in a Duke-related situation" (17); the language of her home country suddenly deserted her, as perhaps she felt that her countrymen's memory of Duke's neo-Nazi past or the Holocaust deserted them (or simply did not cause them any discomfort). In this time period, though she was a private person, Anne was obsessed with Duke's public presence and tried to press him about the Holocaust in public whenever possible. He always brushed her off. Robin says of her mom's drive: "It sort of seems like my mom had no choice." Powell juxtaposes mother's and daughter's voices as Anne agrees: "I didn't mean to get involved, but something inside made me do it" (18).

First-generation Ruth Levy's behavior in the 1960s connects to second-generation daughter Anne's behavior in the 1980s, whose actions sparked connection to her third-generation daughter, Robin. These generations' connections allowed the communal performance of archive of memory for the next generation around them, firmly rooted in their local community. Their public interactions and private stories became a catalyst for others in the wider public realm, leading to real, political action. After Anne had repeatedly confronted David Duke in public, Beth Rickey, a Republican state central committee woman in Louisiana, who became part of the Coalition against Racism and Nazism, felt that many, in contrast, were stepping back from confronting Duke publically, especially on the Louisiana House floor. She was determined to expose his neo-Nazi book business, which was still active.

Rickey says with so many political setbacks related to discrediting Duke, "I was a little afraid of Duke as well. But then I thought if Anne Levy has got the guts to walk up to that man and ask him why he said the Holocaust never happened, I could certainly summon the courage to expose his Nazi book-selling operation" (19). Her press conference about his book-selling came a day after Anne Levy confronted Duke at the capitol, and Rickey feels like the impact of the press coverage impacted Duke's public persona in a way it would not have if she had waited—if she had done it in another time or place. This is the true meaning of *kairotic* force. Force, the pressure exerted on a historical moment, comes from the impact of a rhetorical act. In this case, the actions and voice of Anne Levy became that forceful rhetorical act; however, further action had to be communal. Anne Levy's "relationship to the countermovement that ultimately defeated Duke was always reciprocal" (19), Powell notes. She and others acted together in response to one another. It was never just one voice or action.

CONCLUSION

Action begins with one person and one act—but it can only expand through connection with community. Norman Robinson, an African American anchor who left CBS in Washington, D.C., to work for an NBC affiliate in his hometown of New Orleans, also confronted Duke publically many times during the same period as Anne Levy. The importance of working together as a community is a crucial choice: "At some point," he says, "you've got to stay at home and water your own grass" (Powell 2000, 493). Anne's story became public because she cared about her own past, but on a macro level it was because she cared about her community and her adopted nation. Klüger's telling also awaited a "community of witnesses" to listen in order to enact a productive dialogue about the memorial practices of communities and nations.

Performative writing as public memory work seeks to create action in its audiences; they must be disoriented in order to re-orient in connection with the other. Unlike collective memory, which is received by large groups, performative public memory is built by a variety of participants in a local context; without this communal work, we memorialize passively and certainly individually, if we memorialize at all. We likely become indifferent to the trauma around us—we turn away from the other, unlike the work of shifting orientations that builds us in relationship toward one another. One of the important mechanisms that stimulate participation in the construction of Holocaust public memory, as I have been describing it, is precisely the fact that artifacts of memorialization do not exist in a temporal void of "presentness," as is often the case with new media or even with iconic images or artifacts from the past. They are linked, sometimes intimately, often intergenerationally, to those artifacts or stories that have come before and may come after; the "linked-ness" is *relationship*. Our potential connections with others radiate both outward and inward. Like Ahmed's notion of orientation, there can be a turning toward others, but there also needs to be a turning inward, subjectivity and reflection that are nurtured so that we can connect deeply with others by doing honest self-reflection of the kind Klüger insists upon. When we engage in performative public memory work, we act *specifically in relation* to others and *in response* to history in our communities as the authors have shown here.

NOTES

1. Jewish women have a long history of political activism in the south since the Civil Rights era. See Debra Shultz's 2016 book *Going South: Jewish Women in the Civil Rights Movement*. The book is based on the oral histories of many of these women, and in some ways, this text can be considered a collaborative work in terms of voices.

2. I use this construction of the word "auto/biography" in the same vein as the *Journal of Auto/Biography Studies*. Depending on the format the writer uses, autobiography can sometimes blend with biography as a hybrid (as in Spiegelman's *Maus*; see also Costello 2006). Also, the term "auto/biography," constructed this way, defines the genre of life-writing broadly. See also Iadonisi on collaborative autobiography; he uses the term to refer only to the collaborators in the writing act in *Maus*, not in terms of "public memory (communal witnessing or audience response).

3. Memoirs and auto/biographies are considered "primary documents" that come from the eyewitness perspective, but chronologically they are also subject to greater

revision because they are "re-created memories" that are not written in the moment (as a diary would be) or given as testimony directly after the war. Many survivors like Primo Levi believed their purpose in writing memoir was to "counteract false belief and prove something to be true," but they also are aware that while they cannot present narratives that are completely factual (because memory is fallible), they do believe "they can be true to the essence of the suffering" (Waxman 2004, 496–497). Some memoirs have been discovered to be more fabricated than factual. *I, Rigoberta Menchú* (1984), a memoir by a Guatemalan revolutionary, and *Fragments: Memories of a Wartime Childhood* (1996) a Holocaust "memoir" by Binjamin Wilkomirski have both been discredited as "true" eyewitness accounts by scholars. Wilkomirski's memoir was almost entirely fabricated (Douglas and Vogler 2003, 34). The existence of these kinds of hoaxes add fuel to Holocaust deniers, but this does not mean that witness testimony loses its value, quite the contrary; witness testimony "demands special modes of attention and interpretation. What survivors are witnesses to is their own suffering, in the past as victims and in the now of telling as survivors" (34).

4. This also relates to Bahktin's dialogic speech act and Austin's speech as action.

5. Horowitz framed this concept in her presentation at the German Studies Association Conference in 2013. I was a co-panelist.

6. See Lucille Eichengreen's work, for instance, for one eyewitness narrative of such behavior in the ghetto. The work on gender and the Holocaust is filled with esteemed scholars, many of whom I note in the Introduction. The works span from the 1980s to the present. Joan Ringelheim did some of the early work and organized an influential conference on women in the Holocaust in the early 1980s. Other authors of note listed in this chapter's Bibliography include: Sara Horowitz and Atina Grossman. The 2013 book *Same Hell, Different Horrors: Gender and the Holocaust* is one example of a book published in the last five years. Nicole Ephgrave published an article on the topic in 2016. I will not be addressing these biological aspects of gender experience at length in this chapter. I focus on deconstructing perceived gender roles as strictly binary.

7. This kind of "deferred action" is at work in the deferred memories I discuss here, but because deferring their stories was conscious (these women chose not to tell for various but explicit reasons), the relation is implicit rather than explicit.

8. For Patraka the Holocaust performative has a built in "accountability" where play is limited. The two positions "(of reverentiality and play) comment upon each other: it is postmodernism that sees the deadness of that reverential gesture toward the Holocaust, but it is the Holocaust (and its goneness) that marks the point at which discursive play becomes a screen to keep the dead at a distance" (1999, 8).

9. Langer sees "never again" as an empty "moral" for audiences, even though it is used widely in educational programming around the nation and in many museums. He values Holocaust knowledge as an educational piece when he says: "there is educational merit in seeing how a culture writes into a rhetoric of pride" (2006, 120), which means building knowledge about discourse communities ad identities. "There is moreover, something bracing about the way in which writers, artists, memoirists, witnesses in their testimonies, and historians," he adds, "have rejected conventional eloquence and instead found a language and form to express more authentic verbal

and visual versions of the disaster" (120). I agree there is value to the "rhetoric of pride," but this resonates inside communities not necessarily outside them. What I argue for in this book is the necessity of engaging audiences on an active level across levels. Like Toporek, I feel knowledge about Jewish victims in the Holocaust is not just Jewish history or for Jewish audiences, it is human history that new generations, as authors, museums, and films of the Holocaust continue to recognize, need to connect and respond *in relation* to because knowledge in a digital world can be frighteningly passive, and sometimes very inaccurate.

10. See earlier notes on discussions of things like "validity" or "play" in the performative. Patraka importantly notes that the Holocaust performative must have a historical accountability to the facts and evidence. Thus, this play with "validity" does not apply, though the challenge to the binary does.

11. See Chapter One.

12. "Yizkor" according to the USHMM, were memorial books that "began as early as the displaced persons' camps, while others emerged later out of the painstaking efforts of the *landsmanshaften*, the immigrant mutual aid societies in Israel and North and South America. Their collective efforts created an estimated one thousand memorial books honoring the lost lives and destroyed communities of Europe" (ushmm.org, "Memorial"). Directly after the war, "Yizkor books also known as memorial books," were written to "chronicle the lives of Jewish communities destroyed during the Holocaust" (ushmm.org "Memorial"). Many survivors used these books to "reassemb[le] the pieces of their community's life and history" (ushmm.org).

13. See Atina Grossman's excellent work on gender and history in the Displaced Persons Camps and elsewhere.

14. Elie Wiesel's memoir, *Night* (1960), and Primo Levi's memoir, *Survival in Auschwitz* (1947), were some of the first memoirs to become well known in the United States. Even with the first translation it is clear how these written accounts, were framed to suit American audiences. Levi's original title in Italian translates as "If This Not Be a Man," a title that suggests the loss of a gendered, male identity and that underscores the dehumanization of the experience. *Survival in Auschwitz* (the American title) in comparison, suggests a victory over death and something achieved rather that lost. The strong sense of loss—of both identity and a moral compass—are no longer conveyed in the title. Similarly, Wiesel's memoir, though not re-titled, became most well known as a standing, single memoir, when, in fact, it is part of a trilogy. The memoir begins with his life before as a religious boy then details his deportation to Auschwitz. The book centers on Elie's relationship with his father in the camp and focuses on the way in which the camp degraded Elie's sense of respect for his father's strength and masculinity and eventually his own identity as a pious son. This memoir ends with both Elie's father's death but also with the liberation of the camps. Many memoirs end this way, with liberation, suggesting that the braking of bondage will mean freedom and revival. The second two books of Wiesel's trilogy suggest the opposite, however, and focus on how the survivor suffers with his own guilt and the apathy of those around him.

15. Excerpts from *Troubled Memory, Second Edition: Anne Levy, the Holocaust, and David Duke's Louisiana* by Lawrence N. Powell. Copyright © 2000 by the

University of North Carolina Press. Preface to the Second Edition © 2019 by the University of North Carolina Press. Used by permission of the publisher. www.uncpress.org.

16. See Felman and Laub (1992) and Chapters One and Two.

17. Ruth Kluger, excerpts from *Still Alive: A Holocaust Girl Remembered*. Copyright © 2001 by Ruth Kluger. Copyright © 1992 by Wallstein Verlag, Göttingen, Germany. Reprinted with the permission of The Permissions Company, LLC on behalf of The Feminist Press at the City University of New York, www.feministpress.org. All rights reserved.

18. *Dawn*, the second text, is a novel about enduring the follies of humankind. *Day*, the third text, is a novel about conscience and suffering. This book contrasts a fictional character's experience (implied) in the camps with his contemporary experiences in postwar Europe (this was published in 1960 as *The Night Trilogy*). *Night* bears witness in the ways described above, but the rest of the trilogy also bears witness to the after-effects of trauma and suffering, and these examples serve as a warning to those who think genocide ends with a liberation from physical captivity. Wiesel's trilogy, because the protagonist speaks about his suffering and depression, subverts the typical male gender role of stoic silence in the face of trauma. He has clearly been affected by his experiences. The protagonist both writes about mental illness like depression, and acts in a hyper-masculine way to counteract this perceived "weakness."

19. Although Western women writers worked through theses biases throughout the 19th and 20th centuries (think about auto/biographers like Virginia Woolf), these issues had to be reworked once again in the arena of Holocaust auto/biography, where gender and the Holocaust only became a legitimate subfield of Holocaust Studies 25 years ago. I have cited many of these groundbreaking texts in my Introduction. See Tess Cosslett's (2000) work on feminist autobiography, for general examples. See also Goldenberg and Shapiro's "Introduction" to *Different Horrors, Same Hell* (2013) for an excellent recent history of scholarship on gender and the Holocaust.

20. This is true also of memoirs about being gay in Nazi Germany and during the Holocaust. See Gad Beck's memoir *An Underground Life* (2000) and Richard Plant's *The Pink Triangle* (1988).

21. When Eichengreen submitted her first book, *From Ashes to Life*, for publication, the publishers wanted it to be more polished, but she says, "I wanted it to be harsh and abrupt."

22. See Erzahi (1980), Young (1988), Bernard-Donals (2009), Felman and Laub (1992).

23. *Night* did not see an English translation published until 1960, 15 years after the war. Wiesel has stated that his book was written 10 years after the war with a specific purpose in mind: "My principle goal, really, was to reach the survivors, my peers. Why? Because in the beginning they didn't talk. They didn't talk because nobody wanted to hear them. And I wanted to show them, 'Look, it's possible to talk, and even if it isn't, we must talk'" (Vinciguerra 2001, 165). Thus Wiesel's purpose is to tell the story to prove that audiences will listen and that these stories matter to history.

24. And Nemes in Chapter Two, and the authors in Chapter Five.

25. Hillman's title reflects her present context as well. In her interview with me, she said that she named it *I Will Plant You a Lilac Tree* because of a promise her betrothed made to her in the camps. The publisher in 2005 added the subtitle, "Memoir of a Schindler's List Survivor" so that readers might connect this survivor with a common memory that American audiences might have, thanks to the film, *Schindler's List* (see my discussion in Chapter Two).

26. Wineburg et al. corroborate this with interviews with second- and third-generation people with regard to the Vietnam War. There is a general sense of history but little detail as memory is passed intergenerationally.

27. See J. L. Austin's original work on speech acts. Felman and Laub have reiterated this concept eloquently in terms of Holocaust testimony.

28. Some memoirs were written in private but were not published for the public until much later. Charlotte Delbo, for instance, wrote her memoir in 1946 and did not publish it until 1972 (the English translation was published in 1995). Many other women survivors of the Holocaust were not ready to do as Ruth Levy had done and challenge gender stereotypes. Klüger feels that audiences would rather not hear her memories of the Holocaust, much as Wiesel felt decades ago, but Klüger adds another dimension: she feels that they don't want to hear her story partly because the social construction of gender tells them that war stories should come mostly from men. And yet she claims this ironically almost as she is telling her story now.

29. Though not many copies of the memoir were published, she was considered extraordinary for her time (the 1960s) according to both her daughter and the biographer, Lawrence Powell.

30. This anger together with the "imperative to bear witness" comes from "survivor guilt" (Powell 2000, 413).

31. These are the kinds of things that we also see today with low-income neighborhoods and bodies of color under surveillance by police. There are bodies under surveillance by the government at Guantanamo Bay in Cuba as well, for example. It is easy for Americans to remain bystanders because our neighborhoods are so segregated, and our terrorist policies are enacted overseas or in airports. It is simple to be ignorant and complicit but harder to admit that complicity and act to resist it. We think of ourselves as not racist but we uphold white supremacy now through inaction, much as many "white" Jews did in Levy's story in the Jim Crow South. Many whites and Jews importantly, in contrast, were active members of the civil rights movement. (See Shultz 2016.)

32. We are seeing this tendency to "flip" discourse and for extreme right groups to use terms associated with liberal actions or movements for their own "re-purposing." The aim is to take away some of the public, rhetorical power of those terms, or at least dilute their original meaning.

33. The Freedom Buses never made it to New Orleans on the planned day, but other events in New Orleans were making Jewish leaders call the hate ride a "calamity waiting to happen" (Powell 2000, 408).

34. In this chapter I will focus mostly on the English version. I have examined both versions with more depth in my article "Performative Auto/biography in Ruth Klüger's *Still Alive: A Holocaust Girlhood Remembered*" (2011). The translation

differences are interesting just in the titles. *Weiter Leben* could translate as "Going on Living," which has a despairing quality, while the English translation chosen "Still Alive" suggests something more hopeful.

35. As an American scholar of German language and culture, she traveled to Germany postwar, but she did not often visit her home country of Austria or Vienna, where she grew up.

36. See Wagner-Pacifici 1991.

37. Likewise, in fall of 2016, presidential candidate Donald Trump's affiliation with Duke and white supremacists did not seem to affect him negatively in the public, political realm or with many voters.

38. Occlusion applies also to second- and third-generation Southerners and their own historical links to the bigotry and violence of enslavement. The New Orleans white community (like other southern locales) remembered this past "in general" as heroic for whites, ignoring completely the details of its brutality against African Americans pre Civil War and into the present. For more on theories of whiteness, see Robin DiAngelo (2012).

39. Wodak addresses the gains made from seeing the constructed-ness of the sexes as Judith Butler does, but adds that this ignores the fact that "in our societies, biological sex is still used as a powerful categorization device" (1997, 12). This is similar to what many scholars of women and the Holocaust aimed to show: that biological differences resulted in abuse by the Nazis that targeted, for instance, pregnant women for immediate execution. I am indebted to this line of research and agree that biological differences still dictate inequality in some respects. In this project, however, I focus on how representations of memory reflect constructions of gender and, as a result, reflect the *process* of public memory discourse as "neutral" or "universal" when it is masculinist.

40. The issue of Holocaust denial remains an important issue. The recent release of the movie *Denial* indicates continued interest in the notion of truth and what reasonable doubt means to the general public. Deborah Lipstadt is a historian at Emory University, who went head to head with a British Holocaust denier. He filed a lawsuit for slander and subsequent evidence revealed his strong neo-Nazi ties, which caused him to lose the lawsuit.

41. The entire staff of this newspaper was fired on May 2, 2019, after it was bought by a rival. This paper has been in business since 1837, and the wholesale firing of Pulitzer Prize–winning journalists should be another warning to us that our free press is under fire (Kelly 2019).

Chapter Four

"Next Generation" Texts
Reclaiming the Body; Reclaiming Auschwitz

The ways in which the women in Chapter Three spoke into their present to share their deferred memories of traumatic experiences revealed their desire for political change and a shift in public memory; they felt the occlusion of memory in the community around them; therefore, they performed memory in the public realm to connect their stories to their community in the present. The forgetfulness of public memory results in part from people *orienting* themselves away from the suffering and experiences they see outside themselves to avoid connections that might be difficult or confrontations with the self that might be challenging. The implications of this privileged, self-protective detachment for public memory and the Holocaust are serious, yet the detachment and even denial of the suffering of other people in the past and the present seems to persist.[1]

In this chapter we will see the performative at work in contemporary film as well, but the visual texts in this chapter challenge the notion of public memory and the Holocaust in unique ways both corporeal and ephemeral. I will discuss primarily two films, the 2012 Israeli documentary *Numbered*, directed by Dana Doron and Uriel Sinai, and the 2009 Australian video *Dancing in Auschwitz* by Jane Korman, to show how second- and third-generation survivors reclaim gendered, degraded[2] bodies and locations in our memories and histories of the Holocaust to re-vision public memory. The traces of memory in this chapter are particularly material: they reside in bodies and on bodies and open memorialization practices to a non-binary that honors both death and life. The shifting of orientations in its cycle of disorientation/reorientation is acutely performative.

I first learned about the 2012 Israeli documentary film *Numbered* from a *New York Times* article that my mother sent me. As I have mentioned, my mother and I have read Holocaust memoirs and related nonfiction works for years together, and when she reads the newspaper, she sends me links and clippings, images—anything that relates to the Holocaust. We come from Polish immigrants who emigrated in the early 20th century with distant (often hidden) Jewish ancestors. We share the history and stories together across generations as those artifacts add themselves to our growing knowledge. Even though she is forgetting much of late, she remembers this connection we have. The feeling is what is most real about these memories. That *Times* review of the film described *Numbered* as providing a new perspective and another take on the stories of survivors: children and grandchildren of survivors were tattooing their grandparents' concentration camp numbers on their own bodies (Rudoren 2012). I have seen many survivor testimonies, documentaries, films, and read hundreds of memoirs, auto/biographies, and histories. They are never easy to watch or read. As I watched *Numbered*, however, I was unprepared for the emotions with which I was overcome. The camera lingered upon the tattooed numbers in several different frames for each story, as I might have expected, but I did not expect to find beauty in seeing the eyes of two lifelong friends, Hanna and Sarah, meet with love and the understanding of shared but unspoken memories as they embraced. I found myself sobbing, not with sadness but with joy, when I watched Ayal Gelles (28) and his grandfather, Abramo Nachshon (86), stroke each other's tattooed arms with loving acceptance and a bodily connection.

In this chapter I discuss gender and performativity as they relate to communal memory production and the insistence on the binary of memorialization that designate practices either as socially appropriate or inappropriate, to explore how second- and third-generation (what I have been calling "next generation"[3]) survivors create unique visual pieces to evoke affective responses from audiences that are atypical (not only based in mourning). I have theorized that visually based genres and gender are performative: they perform as interactive memory objects in dialogue with each other and audiences to respond to the present and to utilize the rhetorical force of *kairos*. Here I explore how some very recent visual memory artifacts use "standard" genres with unorthodox goals. The two films I examine, *Numbered* and *Dancing in Auschwitz*, change the memory landscape not only to reclaim location-based Holocaust imagery of degradation that has become "familiar," such as images associated with Auschwitz (much as the authors in Chapter Three), but they also use bodies to perform new memories across generations to dialogue in particularly affective ways with their audiences. These performances shift audience orientations so acutely that there is a danger that the disorientation may not lead to reorientation. Yet, second- and third-generation filmmakers reposition viewers radically enough that their methods might paradoxically bring us closer to the Holocaust though we are further away in time than we have ever been.

LOCATIONS: PERFORMATIVE AND ORIENTING

We have moved in this book from the original sites of destruction and digital space, to re-created sites and fictional stories, and to community and politics. This chapter shifts us back to the beginning—back to the original sites of destruction to rethink place. I have complicated the idea of location in terms of the gendered performative by asking: From which position, on which place, in which space? Nedra Reynolds has argued that based on the "theoretical frameworks of both cultural geographers and rhetoricians" it is important "to understand geographies as embodied, and how the process of social construction of space occurs at the level of the body, not just at the level of the city or street or nation." What we "normally take as 'sites' are not only constituted in a *situs* or fixed location"; sites are "made up of affective encounters, experiences, and moods that cohere around material spaces. This is why sites are not just seen, but (perhaps even more so) they are felt" (Edbauer 2005, 10–11).[4]

How we see (effect) depends on how we feel (affect). Ahmed has also theorized inside and outside as affective "orientations,"[5] in which we orient ourselves toward one another at the same time that we turn inward to reflect on how what we feel helps us to "know." Where we turn and how depend upon the *kairotic* force of memory. Memorial activity located on the body in the present exerts *kairotic* pressure and performativity through representations that challenge audiences to "see" and feel differently about the Holocaust as "the past." Performative writing (like *kairos*) "opens" to "incursion, permeation, multiplicity" as it also "requires its reading, writing, and written subjects to negotiate the claims of its respective forms" (Pollock 1998, 96). The filmmakers in this chapter embrace multiplicity and incursion to require audiences to negotiate their preconceptions about forms of public memory. The binary tension of either/or—either your public memory practices are appropriate or not—is challenged by performative writing that "recognizes its delays and displacements while proceeding as writing toward engaged, embodied, material ends" (96). Highlighting people connected by strong relationships in the present as they "re-locate" to degraded sites of the past enacts this performative tension. It directs audiences to reframe public memory to see the possibilities of love and life in places rife with death. Breaking these binaries by embracing both is a struggle but "performative writing is queer" because it refuses to choose, but it is also, Pollock says, "one way not only to make meaning but to make writing meaningful" (97); the movement is what brings about shifts in orientations and audiences' ability to make meaning.

RECLAIMING PLACE: PAST, PRESENT, AND FUTURE

As I explained in Chapter Three (and will explain in Chapter Five) collaborative auto/biographies (and museums) turn toward a strong focus on Jewish lives rather than focusing only on death. In some ways, this is a reaction to death camp sites and the graphic imagery of corpses and death that proliferate around Jewish bodies and so the Holocaust.[6] In auto/biography when we have a "before, during, and after" memory narrative, there remains an in-between space around these atrocities that overflows with bodies and un-reclaimed memories that have been degraded.[7] The notion of an in-between space suggests, as I have argued throughout this book, that public memory practices are not linear; meaning-making is recursive and dialogues across generations and temporal locations as performative and *kairotic*.[8]

Memory-making processes are performative because they claim these unstable, in-between spaces as new by repeating imagery that is known but recontextualizing those images and associations for audiences. These processes additionally are gendered because they interrogate public memory processes assumed as neutral and genderless, when they are not. In the second and third generations, Holocaust trauma is not gone; it continues to scar.[9] Patraka has theorized how visceral this "goneness" is. But there are non-binary ways to both honor and name trauma and death and celebrate the living. As we return in this chapter to the real sites of destruction (to which we saw first-generation survivors return in Chapter One), "next gen" survivors present the geographical fact of *place* by marking it on and through the body in positive and affective re-framing of that site or place.

Sara Ahmed reminds us "the repetition of images of trauma suggests a need to replay that which has yet to be assimilated into the individual collective psyche" (2015, 95).[10] In this chapter, we can observe again how the repetition of images, tropes, or artifacts allow audiences to locate themselves within the public memory realm to what is "familiar" (orientation) and then become disoriented in order to reorient. Next generation survivors reclaim their family's history and memories by changing the vantage points and the positionality of audiences, thereby influencing the ways in which the general public can remember the Holocaust past. These filmmakers reposition viewers by upsetting their expectations of what was historically considered Holocaust film imagery. I will look specifically at how these filmmakers re-vision Holocaust memories, examining reclaimed locations in *Dancing in Auschwitz* then reclaimed bodies and connections in *Numbered*. Finally, I will discuss how each film strives for revised "affect" from its viewers, a movement from the detached commemoration of those gone toward lived memory, relationship, and hope for the future.

RE-ORIENTING PERSPECTIVES: THE ORIGINAL FRAME OF REFERENCE PERFORMATIVELY RE-FRAMED

Dancing in Auschwitz and *Numbered* both represent nonfiction, documentary-style film perspectives like *Shoah*. These films, much like *Schindler's List* and *Son of Saul* (though these films are fictionalized narratives "based" on true stories) are filled with references and homages to Holocaust memory artifacts that have come before. These films and these filmmakers dialogue with the voices and images that have preceded them in ways that are specific to the genre, and as specific repetitions that exert either citational "counter-pressure" or *kairotic* force in the public memory realm. *Numbered* adheres more closely to the documentary genre, as we will see later, while *Dancing in Auschwitz* suggests documentary form stylistically while appearing more as a "real life" music video (which at the outset seems shockingly inappropriate, but I will address this shortly). All of these artifacts consider the Jewish survivor perspective, which as I noted in Chapter One was not always the case, especially in film. Who is filming and from what perspective is an important aspect of the binary, gendered imagery that has proliferated in public memory to sometimes occlude the experiences of the Jewish survivors. The filmmakers here use original documentary footage of the camps in order to establish a frame for how the sites of destruction have typically appeared as tropes permeated only with degraded Jewish bodies, then they performatively challenge these representations.

There is a power hierarchy at work in the original documentary footage because much of the film we have of the period—most particularly at the death camps—was not taken from the perspective of the survivor. Nazis took most of the film footage we have of the ghettoes and camps, and American, Russian, and British armies who liberated the death and concentration camps in Poland, Austria, and Germany in 1945 recorded most of the imagery of the Holocaust's aftermath (at the camps). The bodies of victims we see in this footage are mostly "degraded" through starvation and death. There is no counterpoint.

This Allied film footage was used to record visual "evidence" of the atrocities and was used in genres like newsreels for American and other audiences to view the atrocities from afar, and later as evidence for the War

Crimes trials in Nuremberg in 1948. This British footage is called *German Concentration Camps Factual Survey* with Sidney Bernstein supervising (1945, 2014). *Death Mills* was the American version directed by Billy Wilder (1945). *Nuremberg Trials* was the Soviet version directed by C. Sivlov two years later (1947). The purpose of this very particular genre was to provide visual evidence establishing "factual data" to explain an event that would come to be called a genocide.[11]

One of the most famous films using documentary film footage more stylistically was a French piece called *Nuit et broillard* (*Night and Fog* 1955), directed by Alain Resnais, which filmed abandoned camps like Mauthausen in 1955 and utilized stock, black and white footage. The film was difficult to make and difficult for audiences to watch because of its graphic nature. *The World at War* was a British television documentary that aired in 1974. It was not as graphic as *Night and Fog*, and its focus was not only on the Holocaust, but also on general World War Two history.[12] In order to establish "facts," these films eschew direct experiences to speak and view from a distance. We must, therefore, question how we are socially constructed to see the sites of destruction as a binary of good (Allies) and evil (Nazis) as so-called neutral observers when, in fact, these perspectives are gendered and sometimes nationalist. In many cases, the bodies of victims and survivors (Jewish for this study) appear mostly as degraded in death or distress, imprisoned, or in the case of women, hardly included at all.[13]

Lanzmann's *Shoah* (1985) was the first extensive use of the Jewish survivor perspective in the documentary-style film genre.[14] *Shoah* is especially notable for not using any other archival footage from the period, like many documentaries relied upon. *Shoah* used the sites of destruction in the present only to re-orient audiences and "defamiliarize" the old tropes.[15] Reclaiming bodies by placing them alive and sometimes speaking, in the sites of death broke with the tradition of the uninterrupted gaze on death, trauma, and victimization.

Dancing in Auschwitz and *Numbered* are starker, simpler, and shorter films that organize around testimony and Holocaust sites and do not use any archival footage. Lanzmann recorded traumatic, retold narratives of the past in order to insert them into the present to "mark" unfamiliar and unmarked spaces of death as performative "in-betweens." In contrast, filmmakers Dana Doron and Uriel Sinai (co-directors but a doctor and photographer by trade) and Jane Korman (the Australian daughter of a survivor) organize their work around the now "familiar" memory objects[16] of the Holocaust: the concentration camp tattoo and the extermination/concentration camp Auschwitz, in order to situate audiences initially within "traditional" memorialization modes. These traditional modes rely on sites, photo stills, books (and now films and museums) to which audiences might react with shock, disgust, horror, sadness, pity, disbelief, or anger. By using what is "familiar" to audiences, and then radically resituating those sites and objects, these filmmakers force audiences to rethink what they "know" or "feel." Let's first look at how *Dancing* relocates bodies to reclaim degraded spaces like Auschwitz for an affectively laden effect, one that disturbs audiences' expectations, and which has resulted in some controversy surrounding the "appropriateness" of the film.

DEBASING OR RECLAIMING BODIES? *DANCING IN AUSCHWITZ*

A film just over four minutes long, *Dancing in Auschwitz* is an art film created by a second-generation survivor, Jane Korman, that includes her father Adolek, a survivor, and her children dancing at several sites of destruction to the Gloria Gaynor song "I Will Survive." The film was originally exhibited at the Monash University gallery in Caulfield (near) Melbourne, Australia, in 2009. The director of the Jewish Museum in Melbourne said he would never display it because it "downplay[s] 'the significance of Auschwitz'" (Broder 2015). When it was posted a short time later to YouTube it went viral.[17] Since then it has been posted and taken down from YouTube repeatedly and had over one million hits. Broder notes the outrage that followed its debut, with charges of "tastelessness." Some see images like Adolek flashing a peace sign in front of the crematoria ovens (see figure 4.1) as inflammatory and disgustingly irreverent, so irreverent that many say the film debases the history. Others, however, such as Broder in the German magazine *Der Spiegel*, say that the film *Dancing in Auschwitz* broke some of the taboos of

Figure 4.1: Screenshot of Adolek posing in front of crematory ovens (Broder).

Holocaust commemoration in Germany, starting with the two words in the title that seem not to go together. Abraham Foxman, with the New York Anti-Defamation League (ADL) has said that celebrating survival is fine but that survival is "limited to those who survived."[18]

These critiques are relevant but fail to consider the long view of survival, which means the generations who follow.[19] Many Holocaust survivors see not only their survival, but also their children and grandchildren as a victory against Hitler. Adolek says this himself at the end of the film. Holocaust narratives should be serious and heavy, goes the traditional view; they should not trivialize or simplify the real event. Korman films her father Adolek, a Holocaust survivor, dancing with her and his grandchildren at a succession of camps in which he was imprisoned, like a music video. A superficial reading suggests this as a trivializing action. By returning to the sites of trauma and filming scenes that have historical precedent (like the barbed-wire photo or the crematoria photo), then juxtaposing the gendered movements of the body in motion and in loving *relation*, however, Korman re-marks these sites as places where people not only died but also survived, evoking the non-binary "both" at the same time. Korman reclaims the Auschwitz site in public memory by disrupting "genderless" memory practices that pose as universal in both perspective and affect. The sites of trauma are marked with mourning, but they are also reclaimed through the moving imagery of new bodies full of life and love and connection (and reproduction with the children); the binaries of is/is not or should/should not are blurred with the existence of both. The bodies in Holocaust documentary films have been seen mostly as victims, but that past is reimaged by the next generations. For Korman, it is not enough to be a body alive at Auschwitz. The body should be triumphant, in motion, to defy what has come before, as she sees the image of Adolek's peace sign in front of the crematoria as accomplishing.

Dancing evokes the documentaries of old; it uses the same sites, perspectives, and framings, but it also steps over the boundaries of "traditional" memorializing, which dictate only somber and contemplative responses. The orientation of audiences to Auschwitz as a familiar and destructive site is upended through the disorientation of what seems out of place in such a location: dancing. The out-of-place-ness[20] of that positive body then "re-orients" viewers (especially as they protest the inappropriateness of dancing in Auschwitz) to the out-of-place-ness of the original site. That such a site ever existed—a place in which millions of people were murdered as locals and governments and nations were silent bystanders—this is what is truly "inappropriate" and out-of-place. Yet so many said and did nothing.

DANCING IN AUSCHWITZ BREAKS THE BINARY

One method to perform memory and encourage a new "situatedness" or perspective from audiences is to position them somewhere in the middle, where they cannot simply receive the information passively; they have to work to decipher what they think and how they feel, and this work—this action—is performative. The title of the film *Dancing in Auschwitz* repositions audiences immediately by juxtaposing two seemingly incompatible ideas: dancing and Auschwitz. The two seem to be binary opposites, yet they are placed together suggesting a non-binary co-existence that might be ambiguous and even confusing. The film uses the Auschwitz-Birkenau memorial death camp site in the title (even though the people in the film visit more than one site), because it is a situated and familiar location that audiences associate with Holocaust trauma. In Ahmed's sense, it orients viewers to what they "know": many movies have been set in Auschwitz and there are iconographic objects that audiences also associate with this concentration/death camp like the *Arbeit Macht Frei* gate.

The term "Auschwitz" conjures the dark and heavy associations with imprisonment, loss, and death. The term "dancing," in contrast, is light; the body is in motion, and theoretically carefree. Audiences do not have any knowledge of dancing in relation to Auschwitz, and are therefore, disoriented. Both references in the title are embodied, however, at opposite points; death and trauma are embodied in the millions of victims who perished at sites like these, while the act of dancing is corporeal, joyful, and unrestrained. Immediately Korman places audiences in a quandary. What should they think about such incompatible things being placed together? Korman performatively shifts audiences' orientations by re-positioning their perspectives.

Dancing in Auschwitz "defamiliarizes" this locational site by repositioning its relationship to the viewer. When we see the *Arbeit Macht Frei* gate, it is usually from the perspective of a prisoner entering the gates. The barrier gate is rising, and the metal gates are opening. It is cold with snow on the ground. There are no prisoners in the archival photo typically, but we know that they were there. In contrast, one of the opening frames of *Dancing in Auschwitz*, set in the exact same location physically, comes from a completely different orientation prompted by the unfamiliar bodies and their poses.

Here, the gates are completely open (much as they are at the concentration camp site now to allow for large groups of tourists to enter the site). This image is in color, and there is no snow. But though the image is in color, the colors are very muted. The people in the photo are all related to Korman and include her survivor father, Adolek (second from left). The five people are lined up with about four feet between them with their heads bowed. Each

Figure 4.2: Screenshot of one of the opening shots from Dancing in Auschwitz *(Korman).*

wears a T-shirt that has a title: "survivor" or "third gen." Much as Korman has done with the title of the film, the idea of "labeling" bodies echoes the real historical fact of the Nazis marking Jews with the Yellow Star, the blue armband, or even the tattoo as we will discuss in a moment.[21] These "labels" are for the benefit of the viewer and confront our tendency to categorize bodies on screen as objects or en masse, rather than as unique people with subjectivity.

The family members are posed standing straight with their arms at their sides. The women have scarves over their heads. These poses are re-created at Auschwitz, as in this still, but also at Terezin and other sites to mark all the places where Adolek was imprisoned during the war. The opening chords of the pop song "I Will Survive" by Gloria Gaynor begin with the lyrics, "First I was afraid, I was petrified." Adolek, the survivor, and his family (the generations who have followed) then dance to this 1970s pop song. The pop song has echoes of African American struggle and diaspora. Some might say this re-appropriation is inappropriate as well, but the layers of possible meaning continue to make audiences work to make connections between the generations they see on screen and the generations to whom they are related in their own lives.[22] The film names and honors one survivor and then broadens that lens from the one to the many dispersed relatives and others who have been oppressed. The presence of surviving generations makes a strong statement about the living even in the shadow of those who have died.

As Gaynor's music fades in, and she sings: "I grew strong, and I learned how to get along," the five people begin to dance. The women remove their headscarves. The men look up. The dance moves have been choreographed, since all five people are attempting the same moves, but the moves clearly have not been rehearsed, as missteps abound, especially by Adolek. At several points, Adolek makes a mistake and walks away, causing the dance to immediately break up and a family member to embrace him. He and the others wave their hands in the air. The lack of rehearsal echoes the unrehearsed nature of testimony but also evokes the other side of that spectrum: the "staged" scenes in *Shoah* that are clearly not present here.

Once the openings shots have been established, the film continues to show the whole dance performed at each of the various locations. The various locations become part of the same dance, making clear that the parts make up the whole; instead of fragmentation of embodied motion, there is wholeness in these film clips as a related series. The dance is performed the same way (it is repeated but each "performance" is unique and ephemeral) at different camps with different tourists present. The dances are linked together by the song and choreography but each iteration and each location suggests how individual experiences in the "same location" were so very disparate. The performative citational echoes here with the repetition of something with a "difference." Though this film serves as a tribute to her father, by making each location a part of the same "narrative"—the song—Korman makes a memorial gesture toward not only her father and his experiences but to all those who experienced or died in these places, as a whole story, as a broad history embodied by reframing the more personal, material traces of memory.

At the end of the film, the Gaynor song fades out to a black screen and a moment of silence, and then words scroll onto the screen from Adolek: "63 some years later I never thought I would come back to Auschwitz with my grandchildren[.] I'd say 'what are you talking about? But here we are in a really historical moment" (Korman). This is the last line and the last frame of the film. The focus is on intergenerational relations and the ways in which audiences might begin to re-orient themselves to this history. We are survivors; we are still here.

RECLAIMING BODIES AND CONNECTIONS IN *NUMBERED*

In contrast *Numbered*, a longer film by Israeli directors Dana Doron and Uriel Sinai, does not use the Auschwitz site but focuses on camp tattoo numbers (that were largely administered at Auschwitz) to reposition the audience's relationship to a material trace connected to a "familiar" site. In *Numbered* bodies are not situated on or at the site; rather, the site is imprinted onto the bodies. This material trace of trauma makes literal Ahmed's claim that, "through emotions, the past persists on the surface of bodies" (2015, 202), especially as that past appears tattooed on the arms of first-generation survivors and reappears on the arms of their children and grandchildren, who have willingly tattooed themselves with their grandparents' concentration camp numbers. Doron and Sinai use survivor testimony to tell first-generation stories about concentration camp tattoos and include second- and third-generation survivors stories of those who have voluntarily tattooed themselves as a memorial act of respect for their grandparents' memories. The film echoes documentary footage of the past by presenting some of its material in black and white but *re-marks* it performatively by interspersing black and white stills with color footage of people in motion.

Auschwitz was the only camp that tattooed its prisoners (Li 2013), and that tattoo has stood for many things. Survivor and scholar Ruth Klüger has called it a silencing mechanism that shuts people down (2001). Others, like Ruth Bondy in the film, say people saw the number as "Darwinistic"; only the cruel survived, so she had it removed.[23] *Numbered* provides several perspectives of the relationship each person has to their number and how that number functions daily in their lives as a trace of memory. What is most important, however, is the way in which this film focuses on the tattooed number in positive relationship with others. Instead of being depicted as an object of judgment or pity, a thing that separates that person from the rest of "us" who are physically "unmarked" with trauma, the film shows the tattooed number as a connector. There are lovers, grandparents and grandchildren, parents and children, and survivor friendships. Relationships in the film are represented as physical, and this is one of the strongest ways it connects to audiences. All the bodies in this film touch each other. There are gentle caresses, the brushing of shoulders together, an embrace, and a kiss. These are gentle, intimate, accepting gestures, like the dancing, that are unexpected. Using gestures audiences might not typically associate with Auschwitz, as the act of "dancing" in Auschwitz embodied an "out-of-place-ness and viewers can see that as beautiful or horrific and even remain ambiguous, the film provokes them to feel."[24]

Numbered uses first-generation survivors as a central focus, as *Dancing in Auschwitz* does, but much more extensively. *The Jerusalem Post* calls *Numbered*'s vantage points "novel and compelling" (Corn 2012). Interwoven with the testimony from different survivors about the various ways each see their numbers is the testimony of children and grandchildren, who express a deep desire to memorialize their relatives in an embodied manner. This next generation viewpoint complicates that camp number as an "object." By choosing to tattoo themselves with their parents or grandparents' concentration camp number, the "next gens" have begun a new dialogue about what it means to re-appropriate or re-orient toward an object in order to challenge public memory practices. Co-director Doron says that for second generations and third, it is not only about "inheriting trauma" because "the number becomes a symbol of . . . 'I am here, I am life.' [It's a] life-affirming symbol instead of a death-affirming one. You don't necessarily have to talk about the transference of trauma" (Li 2013). Much as Adolek and Korman affirm life by presenting a family dance across camp sites, the tattooed number in *Numbered* affirms that they survived, had children, and those children had children. As generations—they are here.

In *Numbered*, although the body takes center stage, the film opens only with black screen and voices. A man recites his concentration camp tattoo number in German. A woman describes how her number is a "curiosity." Doron and Sinai seem to ask viewers to listen—before looking (much as *Shoah* and *Son of Saul* do); the *phere* of listening in order to bear witness is *kairotic*. The weight of that listening is a force that exerts pressure on the present; it does not simply depict chronological time.

Co-director Doron is a doctor by trade. She decided to do this film after she encountered a patient with a camp tattoo on her hospital rounds whose presenting and repeating symptoms seemed related more to her desire to talk to someone who might listen to her story than they did to an actual illness.[25] Doron decided that there were probably "others with a similar sense of isolation" (Corn 2012). She discovered many survivors with a tattoo who were ready to tell their story of living with it, and because of her lack of film experience, she brought Sinai in on the project. They envisioned it first as a photo essay but found that the interviews were beginning to tell a powerful story that they could not ignore. It would not be enough to see the tattoos; viewers needed to hear about and feel the relationships people had with these material traces.

From the disembodied voices of the black opening frames, the film moves to color frames of Leon Klinger holding his arm out and reciting his camp number in German. The next frame is of just a woman's arm, tattooed and adorned with jewelry, in black and white. *Numbered* continues in this vein, moving between photo stills and live interview footage. This opening sequence includes only the survivors, a choice that places the first-generation survivor at the forefront of the story, and leads the audience to expect this performance of memory to play out as a documentary about their stories alone.

That linear narrative, however, does not continue from person to person or even chronologically; instead it is an amalgam of voices, experiences, images, and time periods. The *kairotic* movement comes from this interaction of shifting time periods, punctuated with force by the appearance and re-appearance of a camp tattoo. The voices and the images alternate from sisters and lovers to grandfathers and grandsons. The languages shift from Hebrew to German to English and others. There is a combination of color and black and white, fully framed bodies, parts of bodies, and close-ups of faces. In the beginning, while these images cycle, there are voice-overs from survivors talking about their tattoos as "brands," "scars," even "a medal." This multiplicity is performative—incursion, permeation. Much like *Dancing* upset audience expectations by turning what they might "see" or associate with a Holocaust site upside down, this film also upsets expectations about what it means to have a camp tattoo and to tell a survivor's story in documentary style.

Dancing in Auschwitz re-visioned sites of trauma and death by embodying a rhetoric of both mourning and celebration. *Numbered* is performative in a similar way, albeit with more reflection and much less exuberance. *Numbered* focuses on the marked body but looks less at the site of trauma and more on how that site of trauma is inscribed, physically, on the surface of the body and how that inscription—that writing—creates performative connection to audiences. The screen often zooms in on the tattoo in motion, on an arm resting on a table, or on a leg walking. These bodies enact the performance of the "everyday," a wide range of behaviors that Michel de Certeau calls "'the practice of everyday life,' in which the role of spectator expands into that of participant" (Roach 1995, 46). As each of these survivors goes through their day, we go along with them. We might also drive, sit at our kitchen table, or feed our pets. The sites of meaning around the tattooed number multiply. Audiences are encouraged, as they were with *Dancing in Auschwitz*, to make new associations, as the tattoos are re-contextualized. The focus on the tattoo simultaneously marks the original trauma in the past for the first generation and re-frames it in the present for three generations together.

Bodies in *Numbered* are intimately connected because the sites of trauma—the camp and the tattoo—have actually brought them closer together. There are close-ups of the arms and the numbers, but these arms are also in motion and mostly shown touching someone else. Two friends embrace. A couple kisses. A grandson and grandfather sit side-by-side touching and examining each other's tattoos. The bodies in these images are not for passive consumption. The audience is brought into these embraces, gestures, and expressions of relationship. The survivors and their families talk to each other and talk back to us, challenging us to rethink that number and that body. It is not just a mark of shame or evil, it can be a mark of pride, love, connection, and life. Daniel, a survivor, (B2823) says he loves the summer, "when everyone can see my number." "Yeah," he adds, "it's a sign of prestige today. I have a number, I am a celebrity."

If the viewer is asked to look just at the tattoo, Doron and Sinai zoom the camera in on it to make the audience aware that they are looking at only one part of the whole body. Otherwise, the bodies and the countenances face the camera solidly and return the gaze of the camera[26] with a steady confidence. In an image of Vera Rosenzweig, she is shown looking at her tattoo, and then another photo fades in where she is looking directly at the camera. This insistence on looking back at the audience looking at you shifts the

Figure 4.3: Screenshot of Vera Rosenzweig: "It's cool" in Numbered *(Doron and Sinai).*

orientations. Audiences might be disoriented by Vera's pride in her tattoo. In the interview (in color), she describes going to a bank in the United States where the young clerk notices that she and her companion have consecutive numbers on their arms. "That's cool," the girl says. "That's right," we said, "it's cool. It's from another epoch in our life. It's cool." These interactions between generations (delineated by the movement between black and white and color) re-orient audiences to the present, and the discourses around the number—the ambiguous space between the past and the present—continue to be the centerpiece.

The ways that generations connect deepen 12 minutes into the film with the story of Leon Klinger's daughter (his image opened the film), Helen Rabinowitz. She decided to tattoo his camp number on her leg. The scene opens with scenes of a home, cut with images of her looking at a computer screen. She is listening to her father's oral testimony. This genre is layered behind her own testimony about the history that she is giving in the present, similar to the layering of testimony we saw with the autobiographies in Chapter Three. She explains: "The number was part of him […] like his freckles, his gray hair." The camera moves about her home as we listen to her father talk. It shows the framed photos on her piano. One is a replica of the gate image I discuss above. Her father at that moment is also describing the gate at Auschwitz and what the words mean. We see echoes of archival imagery, and how the repetition of those images in different settings performs with a citational "*difference*."[27] Audiences are being asked to see the same thing—the gate at Auschwitz—in a different way.

Similarly, the Auschwitz tattoo is familiar to audiences who know a little about the concentration camps. If they see the tattoo, they know what it means: audiences have seen the tattoo as a mark of pain, trauma, segregation, and death. They have probably also seen the tattoo on someone's arm who has survived, maybe in their community or in a museum. But the pride with which the tattoos in this film are displayed (and with purpose) gives agency back to the survivor (unlike in *Shoah* in Chapter One). These survivors choose to interpret the tattoo as *they* wish, not as others determine it. The generations who follow them in this film, make choices in this vein as well. These representations are distinctly performative, "*materializ[ing] possibility* in and through […] writing that recognizes its delays and displacements while proceeding as writing toward engaged, embodied, material ends" (Pollock 1998, 96). No one else dictates the meaning of the tattoo for them, which allows memory to be performed with the people around them (and viewers). The reclaiming of the tattoo reclaims the trauma and the place (Auschwitz) from which it originated. The "engaged and embodied ends" open the possibility of audience response to create action—the performance of memory that allows audiences to "re-see" what has become unseen and misunderstood, and sometimes even forgotten.

Helen's father used his camp number as the safe code on the luggage lock number, so she says, "the number was in our life," and when he was dying in the hospital, she realized that she wanted his number "tattooed on me too." The camera zooms then to her foot in motion under the table, the number tattooed on her ankle. "I just wanted the number etched on me," she says and the day after Shiva ended, she went to the tattoo parlor. She continues the story as she enters her car, turns it on, and begins to drive. This kind of activity, and we see it in all the other stories as well, leads audiences along her daily life. We participate in those actions with her. "Three days later, I had to open the family safe. I stared at the safe, then down at my leg and it hit me. I'd gotten the number wrong." She is angry that this familiar part of her father and her life, this ubiquitous number eluded her. With trauma, there is a displacement of the "familiar" that creates dissonance and gaps in the processes of memory, and this occurs for second-, third-, and fourth-generation survivors as well. When it was etched on her body, what she thought she "knew" got transposed in her mind with another number.

Helen says that her father would not have approved of the tattoo, and to have etched the wrong one, well, "he'd be pissed off," she laughs. She is driving to the tattoo parlor to have the first number inked out, and her father's placed below it.

When we next see her, it is toward the end of the film and she is reading a letter about Maurice Finsi. His was the number she had inked out. "He did not survive Auschwitz," she says slowly. "He died in 1942. He was 30. I erased him. I feel so sad all of a sudden." Her father's number has linked her to him,

Figure 4.4: Screenshot of Helen Rabinowitz with her two tattoos in Numbered *(Doron and Sinai).*

and inadvertently the other number has linked her to Maurice, whose photo is now pictured. Memory is performed across generations/across bodies to connect father to daughter through the etching of a tattoo, but it also unwittingly attaches her to other survivors like Maurice, and the audience watching becomes witness to that process as well. As Helen is disoriented by her own experience, so too is the audience.

We are encouraged by the filmmakers, however, to reorient to Helen and her attempt to address her inadvertent erasure of Maurice and shift our orientations toward the other, as she has done. The permanence of her connection through this material trace of memory—a permanent tattoo and the inking out of a permanent tattoo—creates an embodied performance, and that remembrance is made visible through the tattoo process. Memory is etched, physically, on the body to re-tell the story of being marked by the Nazis. The new tattoos make a mark that tells another, related story, adding performative multiplicity to the original. The stories and the bodies are intergenerationally linked—the tattoo tells many stories, not just one, and that memory process extends beyond the family to Helen and her father, to Maurice, to his family, and to the audience watching who become a shared community of witnesses through the affect they feel as a result of watching these scenes.

SHIFTING ORIENTATIONS: AFFECT IN AUDIENCES

As I have argued, for writers or artists creating new Holocaust artifacts, or revisiting old ones, one way to connect with audiences on a deeper level—and to revisit this history anew—is to defamiliarize the objects, images, or places through which audiences "usually" encounter the Holocaust. Remember Ahmed's observation that as subjects come into contact with objects, they interpret them as beneficial or threatening, and then respond with a turning toward or away. This is one of the disorientation processes. Public memory meaning-making results from these processes, in which the public assigns value and emotion to that object, which becomes "sticky, or saturated with affect" (2015, 11). Public memory of the Holocaust is based, in large part, on these "usual" or repeated encounters, which are almost always "sticky" with affect and emotion. Anne Frank's diary, as I have suggested, is a repetitive memory artifact because it is assigned in American elementary schools and has been reproduced on the stage. Her photo appears in exhibits on the Holocaust and in multiple Holocaust museums across the country.[28] It remains "sticky" because it is written from the perspective of an innocent victim—a child, which increases audiences' emotional response as a subject/narrative that is "non-threatening." Similarly objects like the train cars (in which victims were transported to camps) and the *Arbeit Macht Frei* gate at Auschwitz have been repeated enough in films, museums, and articles to become "icons" of the Holocaust that bring audiences quickly back to the event as "horrific" and "sad," mostly without any other context.[29]

Let us think about affect and the turning toward or turning away as the audience's shifting of orientation to objects or events, especially in terms of these new and unusual films about the Holocaust. Ahmed's orientation relates to stickiness: what we fear we turn away from while what we desire we turn toward. "Emotions involve readings of the openness of bodies to being affected," she says. Affect is not emotion but is linked to emotion in this way. "Fear reads that openness as the possibility of danger or pain; hope reads that openness as the possibility of desire or joy. These readings reshape bodies" (2015, 185). With fear the body shrinks and with hope the body expands. The emotion of hope broadens perspective and takes people out of themselves; it allows them to look toward futures but in ways that sometimes move them past the present. Hope in the present is the turning toward others with openness, joy, and connection. Yet, the question remains for many: "Does grounding hope in the present sound impossible to do with regard to the Holocaust and its memorialization?" The filmmakers I examine here think not.

If public memory is supposed to remain static as a "universal"—not performative, not multiple, not evolving, however, then responses are expected to stay the same (i.e., "appropriate") as well.[30] Take, for example, the response of Michael Wolffsohn, a German Jewish historian at the Bundeswehr Munich, who called *Dancing in Auschwitz* "tasteless" (AP 2010). Others describe grandchildren tattooing their arms with the camp numbers of their grandparents in *Numbered* as "shocking" (Rudoren 2012). To "queer" or shift public memory discussions challenges this binary of what should or should not be the "right" way to memorialize. Disturbing public memory processes and responses means that multiple and affective aspects must be considered, and they require a willingness to be opened to those possibilities, just as the performative does. We can turn toward (others and toward our inner selves) or away, or we can try to do both. In these films the creators ask audiences to consider death at the same time as they consider life.

In many scenes from *Dancing in Auschwitz*, places associated with death are "re-marked" with life. In front of one memorial to a destroyed crematory, Adolek and his granddaughter dance a waltz together. They touch and embrace and move. The film overlays their dance in a time-lapse fashion, so that we can see they dance an entire set of dances (a piece from each dance at each location is placed into a whole collage), and the people around them (other tourists) move in and out of the frame. By the end, those tourists have found a seat and watch the dance and then applaud. The relationship of connection and the positivity of applause in such a somber location seem grossly incompatible. Are they irreconcilable? Is this too surprising to apprehend?

Immediate reactions from media and some survivors suggest it was, who say the film trivializes horror. But Korman says her dad thinks they should be dancing and "affirming our existence." Their presence as a large family on that site reinforces this existence. Remember Adolek's words at the end that I noted above: "63 some years later I never thought I would come back to Auschwitz with my grandchildren" (Korman). Korman expected some people would be offended by her film, though it was not her intent. She says: "I explained to them [Holocaust survivors] that there's no intention of being disrespectful. It's about a new response, a fresh interpretation of history, the memory and the lesson so that these lessons keep on being remembered and not forgotten [sic], not become a numbing memory, but a very powerful memory" (Flower 2010). The dancing is exuberant and seems out of place among the dead, yet the audiences at those concentration camp sites in the film cheer for them, and the audience watching might want to dismiss and cheer at the same time. Ambiguity works in Korman's film as performative incursion; a way to move beyond the numbness that I have discussed many times in audiences confronted with some form of violence or trauma on almost a daily basis.

It is precisely this "out-of-place-ness" that makes this film so memorable. The dancers have labeled themselves with the T-shirts, and they embody that intergenerational relationship through dance and bodily connection. This repositioning of audiences encourages them to question what they think they know about the Holocaust concentration camp sites, or survivors and ask: "What's the 'proper' way to commemorate it? Can a survivor pay homage in a way that might be unthinkable for others?" (AP 2010).[31] Should it be remembered *only one way*? This single perspective view of commemoration is echoed in the irony that *Dancing in Auschwitz* might "owe [its] fame to neo-Nazi groups who posted the clip on their websites and turned it viral," Korman told the Associated Press in an interview (AP 2010). This audience of white supremacists finds odd agreement with audiences who find dancing at a death camp sites one of many ways to mourn, but obviously the two disparate audiences find the video appealing for very different reasons. The neo-Nazis seem to also feel there is a "right" way to mourn and memorialize and jeer at upending that. Audiences might feel shocked by the alignment of neo-Nazis with critics of the film, but each of these audiences aligns with two sides of a binary. Though this information made me deeply question why I find the video so compelling as a memory artifact, it also reminded me that breaking the binary remains difficult. The importance of connection that can result from celebrating death and life at the same time—the persistence of affect through hope—is an outcome that can re-orient us toward each other.

We are conditioned to construct public memory around the Holocaust in certain, binary ways, as these two groups I describe above clearly do. I engaged with a scholar at a conference in 2015 who said that she was prepared to be against the film as crass and inappropriate, but my analysis had shifted her perspective. This is the performative shift in orientations that this book argues for. Every time I watch the film I respond viscerally and emotionally. I cry each and every time. Through the whole video. As soon as it was done, I watched it again. And cried again. The turning away inclination some might feel tells audiences not to approve, while the turning toward inclination finds the loving gestures and embraces of Adolek and his family incredibly moving. The two can exist together, if we let them. Challenging ourselves to feel the complex spectrum of emotions might help us understand the "why" of how we feel about what we know or think about traumatic memory. That critical faculty can bring complex responses to a complex event. Do I want to be aligned with white supremacists? I do not; but knowing why I feel as I do when I watch this film helps me appreciate its power as an artifact of *hope* for new generations.[32]

Numbered has experienced similar reactions, some of disgust and many of consternation. *Numbered* has critics wondering why young people would willingly mark themselves with the concentration camp number tattoo so associated with the victimization of their forebears. The public "outrage" or "wonderment" at these perspectives on memorializing are part of what these filmmakers are striving for (I will discuss "wonder" more at length in Chapter Five). In the case of public memory, we remember the past through the memories of others, and as time goes on, this past becomes increasingly distant and remote from our present experience. Often, our encounters with these pasts are mediated through contact with repeated images, objects, or reference points until this past holds very little real or complex meaning. Audiences feel they can apprehend them as representations, even though they stand for something "beyond representation"[33] and they feel sad. Audiences know what is expected (how they are supposed to feel), but they are rarely asked to work to make meaning or to connect to that knowledge and to feel it personally, let alone to *do* something.

The films I discuss here, in the tradition of Lanzmann but in a much deeper and less binary manner, resituate audiences in their relation to concentration camp sites and survivors' bodies, demanding that audiences work to figure out what they see and how they feel. What are we turning toward, what are we turning away from, and why? Memory activity that performatively disrupts this process is public memory work that remains an ongoing process, interrogated by a variety of participants. Jessica Enoch suggests that "identities, communities, and interpretations, especially about gender" are constructed through public memory (2013, 63). By gendering bodies and places, the filmmakers prompt additional questions about the production of memory: by whom, for whom, and whose bodies count?

A good example of this comes in one of the last scenes in *Numbered*, between survivor, Abramo Nachshon (86), and his grandson, Ayal Gelles (28). Ayal has his grandfather's number tattooed on his arm, on the same arm and in the same place as Abramo. Perhaps in the same vein as critics who called *Schindler's List* overly sentimental,[34] Chang describes *Numbered* as "straightforward but inescapably emotional" (2012, par. 1). If we imagine "inescapable" emotion, it might be aligned with how audiences have described their emotional reactions in the USHMM: overwhelming sadness. Perhaps though, that overwhelming feeling could also lead to an affect that includes wonder, hope, and an increased sense of attachment to others.[35] What is inescapable in *Numbered* is a strong connection with others. We see relationships, love, respect, and openness: a willingness to listen to even the most difficult stories.

The scene between Ayal and Abramo (#15510) is arresting. It begins with the two of them sitting closely together. Ayal is looking at his grandfather's arm and number. The next frame shows them hugging. It is a long hug, and Abramo closes his eyes then looks directly at the camera like Vera. We cannot see Ayal's face, only his back and the tattoo on his arm wrapped around his grandfather. "You should go to university," says Abramo in Hebrew, then the film cuts to his story that begins, "Back at the camp…" where he describes being in charge of the corpses and being required to place two bodies in one casket. When they did not fit, he had to break the legs of the corpses to make all the parts fit. These details are gruesome, and although

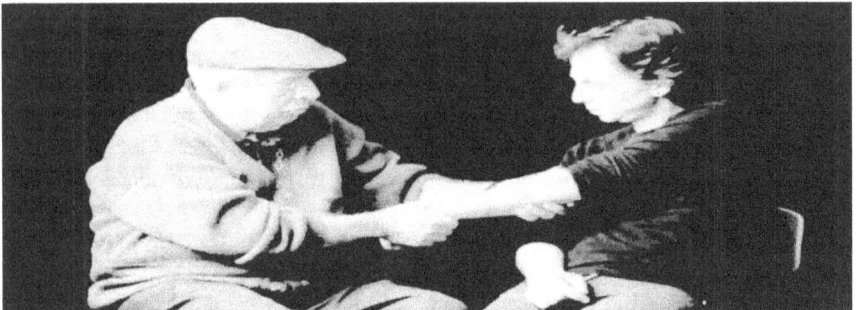

Figure 4.5: Screenshot of Grandfather Abramo and grandson Ayal in Numbered *(Doron and Sinai).*

Ayal covers his mouth and drops his head, he does not turn his body away from his grandfather.

In the next motion he reaches out to his grandfather. "Can you show it to me," Ayal asks his grandfather as he gently grasps his arm. He places one hand under his grandfather's and then cradles his grandfather's hand in his own to examine the number. "Was it with a pin and iodine?" he asks. The camera stays steady on them as they place their arms together and compare, arms touching, in silence.

Abramo asks his grandson: "Did you do it to remember me by? So that people who see it will never forget the Holocaust?" Ayal says, "It's so that *I* won't forget." Abramo takes his grandson's arm in his own and looks at it in silence. "You and all of us," says Abramo. He looks at the camera. "This is my victory. Him. My grandchildren, my great grandchildren," echoing Adolek. The sticky aspect of these films is not only the affect of mourning or sadness, emotions with which we are familiar even though audiences often find them uncomfortable, but also the joy of connection and the love and commitment to memory across generations of family. There is a place for both mourning those who have died and for celebrating those who live and how much they love each other. There is hope not only for the future, but also for action in the present. As Ahmed suggested, hope is not about the denial of reality by projecting something into the future; it is about staying open to the ways in which we can be better by *acting now*.

Part of the way my mother and I can manage to keep reading all of this Holocaust material over the years is that we do it together. Our ability to deeply mourn the loss of life comes from our equal ability to celebrate the lives of survivors and our lives as generations of strong women. We feel gratitude for our relationship in the present. We read and view these memories and histories as gendered people in relation to others: as mother and daughter, as grandmother with grandchildren. My sister sometimes reads my work on these topics. I am fearful that my writing will disappoint her for I admire her intellect. There is a vulnerability that comes from opening ourselves to others but also a strength (we saw this in all the preceding chapters). The relationships we see in *Numbered* show vulnerability, the turning toward others and the willingness to really listen, but also strength because it builds strong connections that are in a sense "unbreakable."

The primary affect in these films comes from intimacy, connection, and love, emotions with which we are not as familiar when coming to the Holocaust, but these are primary, affective aspects that deserve to be added to the public memory of the Holocaust. Affect is built in relation—we must come together communally to create that intimacy, because intimacy requires others, as it also requires an openness and willingness to listen: shifting our orientations by turning outwardly toward and inwardly within. The intimate relationship leads to the turn of self-reflection and critical thinking. The emotional connection, the investment of intimacy, makes audiences more willing to stay, to sit with the feelings and process them more deeply. This is what I have suggested elsewhere in this book, but I think the artifacts in this chapter are the most challenging for audiences but possibly also the most powerful in their ability to revitalize the past by opening conversations and the opportunity for reflection and action in the present.

BECOMING NON-BINARY: MOURNING DEATH AND CELEBRATING LIFE

I have argued throughout this book that performative public memory relies on the interaction of the object, producer, and receiver of memory. These practices vacillate between remembering and forgetting;[36] however, the relationships of and connections between these participants are more complexly layered. Edbauer reminds us that the rhetorical triangle, with just author, text, and audience, is insufficient because "distribution" crosses physical, spatial, and temporal boundaries (2005, 12–13). Felman and Laub (1992) posited the concept of the active listener in *Testimony*. Bahktin's (1991) dialogic model is the forerunner to this idea—suggesting communication across time and between a variety of interlocutors. When we think about memory in terms of gendered bodies and performance we see that de-gendered memory "norms" and memorialization practices, though they claim to express universals, also decide explicitly or implicitly "who counts," and these practices become reified through repetition.

By filming dancing at Holocaust sites of trauma, Korman challenges audiences to reckon with the binary of should/should not and consider that it can be both of those things—there is the possibility that repetition can be repetition with a difference (Ahmed 2015, 184; Pollock 1998, 92). The body of the Holocaust victim is no longer unnamed or lifeless in these films, but can be reclaimed in these new contexts as generations of survivors stand on the sites of death and touch the tattoo imprints of their families traumatic legacies. The familial connections are the emotional focus in both of these films. They both resonate with historical fact—Auschwitz was a death camp and the camp tattoo was forcibly imprinted onto prisoners by the Nazis, but they also resonate with emotion.

Audiences feel a myriad of emotions that are conflicting, ambiguous, and variable. The non-binary space in which audiences must position themselves will be uncomfortable, unfamiliar. But they will also be re-oriented to feel *hope* as they witness the connections between people. The films places bodies together in intimate, non-sexual relation—both the bodies in the film and the bodies watching the film as that contrasts with the knowledge of what Auschwitz will always be—a place of death. Holding both of those together causes discomfort for audiences because it is non-binary, but there is also a shifting reorientation in that public memory activity: it is ongoing, communal, and active and thus, becomes meaningful.

Breaking these binaries and refusing to choose between either/or but embracing both is a struggle. Much like Ahmed's orientations, however, "performative writing is queer" because it refuses to choose. It is, as Pollock says, "one way not only to make meaning but to make writing meaningful" (1998, 97). Korman and her family make these meaningful memories together and we share it with them, much as the audiences at the Auschwitz site do with them. *Numbered* shows us how survivors and their families talk about trauma and transmit it across generations. The tattoo is reclaimed by some and shunned by others, but the conversations about this material trace of memory are happening, bringing many generations together. These dialogues enact a rhetoric of mourning and a rhetoric of connection, reclaiming the previously degraded bodies and sites to which audiences have become "unnaturally" accustomed.

CONCLUSION

It might be hard for audiences to imagine that new artifacts, especially of the nature of those like *Dancing in Auschwitz* or *Numbered*, have a place in the Holocaust public memory "archive," a place where things are remembered because they have value for the future. What is "valued" in public memory—though often posited to be neutral or universal—is not neutral or universal because it leaves so much out; it is hindered by the limiting strictures of binary, gendered construction. When we imagine public memory as performative, we can locate the hierarchal structures that place value only on certain narratives and images and begin to challenge them and add to them. Public memory will still be constructed, but if audiences pay more attention to the performativity of the process, of "being acted upon in ways we do not always fully understand," and then acting in response "in politically conscious ways" (Butler 2009, xii), these processes can become recursive. We can see public memory in relationship to others as we connect our present to their past.

Foxman with the ADL in New York set a limit on who can celebrate survival, and yet the generations of families who follow those survivors (if the memory and history are to persist) must access those stories in ways that become meaningful to them and to their relatives, but also importantly with audiences who are not related at all. The occlusion of memory comes from willful forgetfulness, and public memory has a tendency toward avoiding the difficulties of representing the complexity of trauma. As they dialogue with family members and challenge the binaries of Holocaust public memory with an appeal to affect, these next generation filmmakers create public memory practices that are communal, ongoing projects that invite our participation. As we rethink the ways we can come productively to the Holocaust to remember and to respond, the question that might be asked is this: Is the celebration of life always in opposition to the commemoration of lost life? When it comes to the emotions evoked by memorial artifacts about the Holocaust, must those evocations always be somber and mournful in order to be "appropriate"?

The films in this chapter serve to record diverse stories and to connect those stories to new audiences by foregrounding the relationships between people and the non-binary co-existence of death and life. The viewing of a film, though sometimes solitary, is often a communal activity shared by a group.[37] On YouTube, communities are sometimes created around a posted item.[38] Though these types of communities can be ephemeral,[39] the social experience becomes part of the dynamic of public memory. Any performance does not cease to exist because it changes or goes away. It persists through repetition and memory. History and experiences persist in the same manner. We see the people in these films not only as survivors, but also as vibrant people with large, extended families. There are times when the absent family—the old family from the old country, the relatives who were murdered—comes to the forefront. They are remembered; but the focus does not remain there. The focus turns to the extended family, the second and third generations who resist the hatred of that era and the hatred they see today. It is not hate but love that persists across these generations, and with that persistence comes hope for those of us willing to listen and become a community of witnesses acting for good in the present. We will see this very clearly at work on a larger, spatial scale in the final chapter on local Holocaust museums, where real bodies move through constructed spaces as a performative, communal experience.

NOTES

1. When people learn what I write about, for example, their first question is usually: "Are you Jewish?" as if only Jewish people would care about the Holocaust (I am Jewish but many generations removed), not realizing that by not paying attention to the plight of the "other" because it is not you or "your people" is still an injustice, albeit a more passive one. Their next question is often, "How can you study that stuff? I stay away from all that; it is so depressing," not realizing that having a choice not to pay attention to issues of violence, gender, race, ethnicity means you are privileged, and though they would never classify themselves as bystanders to injustice, doing nothing affirms the wrongs others perpetrate. This is what this book is about: getting people to connect to the experiences and traumas of others. Especially as we get further away from events like the Holocaust, it is important to have evidence that the stories are still being told and heard, so that we are not forgetting to remember.

2. When I use the term "degraded," I mean that Holocaust bodies and sites are too often viewed in public memory as victimized and damaged. The images associated with these places and bodies are of death and destruction. I also use the term "degraded," however, as a word that suggests double meaning. The Holocaust memories themselves are degrading, or eroding in public memory as they are reduced to a few repeated images or stories like this.

3. The Holocaust Museum Houston uses this term for third-generation survivors, and I have used it to think about the generations after: second, third, and fourth.

4. Edbauer's theory is applied to a marketing message and the city of Austin. The work I do here has some echoes of the ecological rhetoric and networks of communication but with an ethical and historical imperative attached to it. My theories make visible how the powerful actions of survivors and their relatives interact with audiences, locations, bodies, and social constructions to perform memory and build connections. Over-theorizing any of these discursive practices as just "rhetorical" undermines their real impact on real people.

5. See *Queer Phenomenology* (2006).

6. Lanzmann did not focus on the degraded bodies but situated bodies in the present in the past in aesthetically constructed ways. *Schindler's List* showed degradation but in ways that were too simplified and objectified while *Son of Saul* challenged viewers to apprehend the destruction viscerally.

7. Art Spiegelman, another "next gen" survivor, visualizes this clearly in his comic book *Maus II* with drawings of these dead bodies filling up the space beneath his writing desk.

8. Young advocates finding "meaning" in the Holocaust, implying a universal meaning, and warns that scholars of the Holocaust should be concerned with the

"possible *consequences* of interpretation" for survivors and their families, suggesting understanding the past, not making new meaning from it (1988, 4). Re-making meaning based on evolving social contexts does not take away from historical and memorial activity but it queers it productively. Young complicates his own work in later studies of memorials and sites.

9. Thanks to Dr. Laura Carroll for this iteration.

10. Risa Applegarth has also suggested this in terms of genre.

11. I discussed this in terms of eyewitness testimony and its evolving functions in Chapter One.

12. This is obviously not a comprehensive list. I discuss only a few influential pieces that came out of Europe and opened up dialogue about the Holocaust that to this point was not common in public memory.

13. Barbie Zelizer's 2001 book *Visual Culture and the Holocaust* focused on images of female bodies and was a watershed moment in scholarship on gender and the Holocaust because the essays in the book did not take historical photographs as "objective evidence," but rather as subjective, gendered, and very partial depictions of complex settings and experiences. Where the photos were taken was always made clear, and who took them was often not noted.

14. Though it is categorized in the genre of documentary film, Lanzmann "insists that it is a work of art, an 'originary event' constructed with 'traces of traces'" (Liebman 2007, 4). See Chapter One.

15. Marianne Hirsch notes that feminist work on cultural memory has "defamiliarized and thus re-envisioned traditional modes of knowing the past," such that we can re-imagine history, symbols, and memory as constructions that need to be disturbed by new, feminist paradigms (2002, 11). Though Lanzmann could hardly be called a feminist, his methods did "defamiliarize" audiences' knowledge of the Holocaust by using never before seen testimony he recorded himself, as well as by documenting sites of the Holocaust that were less familiar to the public like the death camp Treblinka and the town and gas trucks of Chelmno.

16. See also how the auto/biography authors in Chapter Three and museums in Chapter Five use what is "familiar" to disturb limiting narratives and open public memory to broader perspectives.

17. According to Flower (2010) it got over 200,000 hits. According to Broder (2015), it had half a million hits in just a few days.

18. This suggests that the memorial activity of honoring death or celebrating survival is limited to eyewitnesses, a viewpoint that is at odds with the value expressed by the artists discussed in this book, of making the past become living history and memory for future generations. If you limit access to public memory only to those who experienced it, what broad relevance will it have for the generations who follow?

19. See Marianne Hirsch's extensive and influential work on the concept of "postmemory" that I have mentioned elsewhere and in the Introduction. This concept addresses trauma as generational and transferrable across generations.

20. I thank Dr. Carroll for this term.

21. In Chapter Two, we also saw in *Son of Saul* how *Sonderkommandos* were "marked" with a red "X."

22. In Korman's case, as postwar emigrants to Australia, the destruction of aboriginal people and lands echo in this instance. For American audiences it is (or could be) the genocide of the Native Americans, the enslavement of African Americans, the internment of Japanese Americans, the slave labor of Chinese immigrants for the railroad, etc. (the list is unfortunately quite long and even then incomplete; United States history is filled with these events). I say "could be" because many Americans, especially white Americans, screen out these domestic atrocities as they view atrocities from elsewhere.

23. Recall that these judgments were not uncommon from people who had no understanding of the "choiceless choices" prisoners faced in the camps (see Chapter Three), and wrongly judged them.

24. And similar to how I describe Saul's interaction with the boy's body in *Son of Saul* in Chapter Two.

25. This recalls Laub and Felman's testimony as a speech act to one who listens and the women in Chapters One and Two who had waited to be truly "heard."

26. The male "objectifying" gaze in film was first posited by Laura Mulvey in 1975. Doron and Sinai do not fall prey to the objectifying or marginalizing gaze of the camera lens at any point in this film.

27. See the Introduction for the first appearance of this term related to the performative citational. It is repetition with "a *difference*," so that writing "does something" to create action (see Pollock 1998).

28. See Chapter Five for more details of her repetitive but productively iterative and performative image.

29. I discuss this in Chapter Three about belated narratives; the authors assume that audiences know certain things so long after the war like what the place "Auschwitz" is. Marianne Hirsch has used the term "surviving images" with regard to photos (2001); I see them as *artifacts of memory* because they have come to encompass such a wide range of artifacts that exceed the limits of just image. The effect of them is the same, however: they resonate with audiences.

30. I have taken college students many times to the Dachau camp outside Munich, and there are appropriate behaviors associated with these sites. My thesis in this chapter does not propose that reflective and respectful behavior should *not* be expected at these sites. As an artistic piece by a second-generation survivor, Korman's work is designed to provoke us out of apathy, much like Klüger's direct address. Korman can claim direct experience as a second-generation survivor through her father, Adolek.

31. "If someone else were to do it, I would find it highly inappropriate," says Piotr Kadlcik, head of Poland's Jewish community. "But in the case of someone who is Jewish and who is a Holocaust survivor […] these people lived through things that we, fortunately, cannot imagine" (AP 2010).

32. I must also say that an audience filled with fear (white supremacists) might applaud the film's seeming lack of respect for the dead. They lack respect for these murdered people themselves, and they project that lack of respect onto what they "think" they see but clearly do not feel. They miss the point of the film entirely. Adolek basically says "F-you" to Hitler. That is worth some joy.

33. See Bernard-Donals and Glejzer's edited collection of essays (2001) for more on this concept.
34. See Chapter Two for more on *Schindler's List*.
35. See Chapter Five for more on the USHMM.
36. See Blair, Dickinson, and Ott (2010), Bernard-Donals (2009), and Vivian (2012) as three examples.
37. As I pointed out in Chapters One and Two.
38. Remember the implied community online with Netflix in Chapter Two.
39. See Rice (2014) and "18 Pop-Ups."

Chapter Five

Performing Gender in Local Holocaust Museums

Memorial Spaces and Community Places

I have suggested throughout this book that because of the global reach of the Holocaust, its multiple sites of trauma, and the proliferation of objects and narratives about the Holocaust,[1] that the nature of Holocaust public memory has moved increasingly from private and individual to public and communal.[2] The performative piece of this public memory making is important to discover how memory creates action and response. As I noted earlier, the increasing digitization at the USHMM and the oral testimony archives like the USC Visual History Archive that make them more accessible to the general public have disrupted the locational stasis of public memory. So too, we have seen how the range of memorial practices have expanded knowledge and perspectives through representations that challenge the notion of public memory practices as gender neutral or "universal," shifting audiences' orientations to public memory away from the binary, especially of the gendered feminine or masculine and the self or the other. In this chapter we will see how affective anchors and calls for social responsibility perform memory by directing bodies through spaces and recontextualize the past as a *kairotic*, consequential force in the present that requires audience response.

Twenty-five years ago I visited my first Holocaust museum, Yad Vashem in Jerusalem, the first museum of its kind and now the largest in the world. One of the reasons I was in Israel was because I was working on a kibbutz. My mother and I had discussed how important it would be, given my proclivity for study of the Holocaust, to spend time in both Germany and Israel. I stayed on the same kibbutz as an old friend of hers, and I think this might have been the only reason she approved my solo travel at such a young age. My first impression of Yad Vashem was its enormous size. It took me two days to walk the grounds and see the exhibits, and I still felt rushed. At the end of the first day, I remember sitting on the steps of the museum with my head in my hands feeling physically and emotionally drained. I was crushed by the weight of the content I had just witnessed and by the spectrum of emotions I experienced in response to that information. Museum experiences can be overwhelming both physically and emotionally, and part of the reason for this is that it feels like there is too much to take in and it's hard to know what to feel. The binary, socially constructed hierarchies of emotions as good or bad or masculine or feminine, which many public spaces tend toward, diminish the complexity of experience and the spectrum of emotions. Much as I discussed in Chapter Four with the binary of appropriate and inappropriate memorial artifacts and processes, how I feel in a very public memory space is perceived by others as appropriate, or not, based on those constructions, and in a communal space that assessment by others can feel intimidatingly real. What we are "moved by," thus becomes influenced by the people around us. What I knew as a result of being at Yad Vashem multiplied like a network of related pieces, sharp and detailed; based on my observations of others, it was clear that I should feel as overwhelmed as I did, and that I was not alone.

I had a store of knowledge about the Holocaust, but the images I had seen and voices I had heard with so many other people made that information newly visceral and multifaceted. In *Preempting the Holocaust*, Lawrence Langer argues that, "Only by multiplying voices can we begin to present the moral complexity of the Holocaust experience to individuals accustomed to basing their conduct on stable value systems" (2000, 190). Holocaust museums provide those multiple narratives as a way to suggest the non-binary aspects of both moral complexity and conflicting emotions. Audiences react physically and emotionally in museum spaces, and this interaction can be a powerful way to bear witness to educate.[3] After being at Yad Vashem, what I thought I knew no longer sufficed. I felt moved, depressed, enlightened, and overwhelmed, but holding on to all of these feelings at once brought me into deep connection with the experiences of the people to which I had just borne witness, as it also prompted me to self-reflect. The wonder I felt in that space aided those connections.

As I have been discussing in previous chapters, Ahmed suggests productive ways to shift orientations that involve the stickiness of affect. What is sticky is that which "moves us." It is hard to connect to atrocity on the scale of the Holocaust, but without connection public memory will tend toward forgetfulness and turn away from the difficult emotions that result from it: fear, uncertainty, guilt. Museums are spaces built specifically to engage with the public in person. How can the stickiness of affect work in spaces so large and overwhelming? Patraka adds this key point about how museums consider the overall *effect* of their content on visitors: "Ideally this contradiction opens a space of possibility for the spectator to consider how representative democracy operates in the present with regard to genocides elsewhere, rather than entirely soliciting a sense of disillusion, betrayal, and despair about the past" (1999, 144). But for affective attachments Ahmed suggests that "wonder" might be a path to open spaces of possibility (2015, 180). Furthering the concept of "contradiction opening space," affect and performance encourage audiences to hold on to the paradox of the non-binary "both/and."

Ahmed's concept of queering orientations reiterates the need to connect to others so that we turn toward instead of away, movements I have been calling "shifting orientations." These shifts depend on performative and *kairotic* "in between" spaces that leave invitations to audience affect and communal connection. As Segal suggests, as we focus more and more on independence and individuality, "it allows no space for [...] dependence; it is also quintessentially shallow and self-centered" (2012, 179). Segal refers to aging and dependence, but I would recast this as the passage of time and interdependence in terms of traumatic memory. We need to be connected to each other much more than we acknowledge, and public memory can be a strong and shared connector. We have talked about the ways in which the performative and the *kairotic* open apertures for audiences to enter into a dialogue, but the question remains: Will they? Books and films can create an intimacy ripe for personal and sometimes communal response as I outlined in the previous chapters. Although performative memory work encourages active response, it is never a given, especially when audiences must do difficult inner and outer work to respond. These artifacts only open spaces for that *possibility*.

The bulk of scholarly discussion focuses on national Holocaust museums such as Yad Vashem and the United States Holocaust Memorial Museum (USHMM) and the impact of their Holocaust history and memory.[4] In the United States, however, there is also a proliferation of regional Holocaust museums, which have similar missions but have engendered much less scholarly discussion.[5] Like national museums, regional Holocaust museums are repositories for oral histories, artifacts, and archives, but they also can be spaces that reflect and build a special relationship between history and memory within particular communities through wonder and the performative consequential. In museums communal experiences are tangible. I will examine the particular richness of possibility for affect and connection that resides in these spaces.

MUSEUMS: THE AFFECT OF WONDER

For museum spaces, it is useful to think of affect as "wonder" and the performative as "consequential" to see how space and content interact to bring audiences closer to the past. When we think of wonder, we may think of starstruck awe for something larger than we are or something awe-inspiring. But wonder might also result from not knowing or understanding, the expanse and the weight of what is not, or cannot, be known. This is what many have said about knowledge and the Holocaust. This was my experience at Yad Vashem. The Holocaust is trauma so large it cannot be understood, represented, or known yet memorial practices persist.[6] "To wonder" brings something palpable to the body as in the feeling of amazement; wonder often comes from seeing something incredible for the first time. Ahmed posits that wonder can be conceptualized not only as the "new," and the "radical present" (2015, 180), but also as a relation to the past that lives "anew" in the present; wonder can also represent a deeper spectrum of feelings that include sadness and hope.

As we have seen thus far, expanding available experiences and performing memory viscerally allows audiences to connect more readily. In the museum space, this visceral experience is physical and literal but also emotional. Though I will briefly explore the USHMM as a benchmark for national, public memory about the Holocaust, in this chapter I will primarily focus on the ways in which public memory becomes performative through local museum culture. We will see the divergences and convergences of Holocaust memory at the various local Holocaust museums and how the communal nature of memory work in museums both reifies and resists a universal narrative based on geographical location and spatial, gendered subjectivity.[7] This analysis looks at the ways local museums perform memory as gender in place and space, through material artifacts as anchors of affect and audience orientation that turns toward social responsibility. I include data from four sites: Dallas, Houston, St. Petersburg, and Los Angeles,[8] but first I will establish museums as "texts" that are rhetorical, and then the ways in which local museums are performative and gendered.

MUSEUMS AS RHETORICAL, PERFORMATIVE, AND GENDERED

Although many scholars have analyzed Holocaust memorials and museums across Europe and the United States, James E. Young was one of the first to suggest (echoing Wagner-Pacifici and Barry Schwartz), that the "initial impulse to memorialize events like the Holocaust may actually spring from an opposite and equal desire to forget them" even in large, very public spaces (1993, 5).[9] Recent rhetorical scholarship on public memory, separate from this rich history of Holocaust scholarship but certainly reliant on it, reminds readers of this human impulse to both remember and forget, especially in terms of public spaces and the Holocaust.[10] It is important to remain reflective about what might be seen or unseen in these spaces—and why these things are remembered or forgotten.

A rhetorical framework illuminates both the seen and unseen because it allows evaluation and interpretation with competing perspectives and contexts (Blair, Dickinson, and Ott 2010, 2).[11] A rhetorical reading of space also positions memorialization as a social genre because space promotes human interaction in its specific local context. Reading sites like rhetorical texts continues to be crucial to public memory because making "an event of the past—what the memorial marks—relevant to the needs and desires of the memorial's own present" continues to be "one of the most profound rhetorical challenges faced" by designers of these spaces (Blair and Michel 2000, 33). Memorial artifacts such as films, texts, and archives are easily seen as objects that can be analyzed. Spaces are trickier because they resist objectification. Magali Sarfatti Larson provides an excellent base method with which to analyze architecture in her piece on the USHMM, in which she reads architecture as an object that makes meaning (1997, 65–67). Sarfatti Larson uses sociology and semiotics to define architecture as an object that communicates a message. I go further, however, to suggest that the form of the building and the content of the exhibits work together not just as an object, but also as a text that can be analyzed rhetorically to discover the patterns of communication that emerge.

Elements of performative theory work well to provide a connection to issues of representability[12] distinct to the Holocaust (a crucial aspect Sarfatti Larson does not discuss), by revealing how a museum as text can perform to create action in its visitors. Examining the performative aspects of public memory allows me to examine writing that "is meant to make a difference" (Pollock 1998, 95). The histories and memories of the Holocaust are constantly re-contextualized in the present in the museum setting through repetition, yet they are also de-stabilized with the constant motion and interaction of bodies in these spaces. These non-binary interactions help history become "lived memory" built communally through a dialogic that becomes more dynamic and less limited in gender expression. For this final chapter, I will specifically apply Pollock's performative consequential.

The performative consequential is especially rhetorical in the "sense of rhetoric as a '*productive* force,' and, most definitely and performatively, as *force*" (1998, 95), which marries the performative and *kairos* as rhetorical action and a temporal force, which I have elucidated in the previous chapters. In museums particularly, because they exist in a constant place with shifting spaces, the performative consequential "recasts rhetoric as a constitutive aesthetic" that appeals not to "given audiences" but instead "names a new public" that is capable of deconstructing established norms (95). The shifting of audience orientations is powerful in museum spaces because it is almost impossible to physically turn away from what is represented. The question is whether or not the museum content and purposes can disorient the viewer with productive force.

Museums create audience response differently than written texts do because, although they both address "mass" audiences, texts have an intimacy between author and reader that museums do not. The interaction of a physical exhibition space with its spectators, however, is naturally performative because the notion of "action" is physically enacted or "dramatized" by spectators with their movement through the space, their reception of the artifacts and representations of history and memory, as well as their interaction with other spectators within that space. Public memory narratives or images in these spaces can be, however, "simplified [or] overgendered in ways that play to stereotypical notions of gender or rendered genderless" (Zelizer 2001, 8). These genderless representations that play to the binary can be more prevalent since these spaces are designed for broad audiences[13] and they attempt to provide chronological "coherence"[14] in the Holocaust narrative for those large audiences.

So-called "genderless" representations "suggest disturbing findings concerning the inability of atrocity to reflect the nuances, complications, and contradictions that exist in gendered experience," Zelizer argues (8). I suggest that it is not the inability of atrocity itself that is reflected but rather the unwillingness of the creators of public memory spaces to challenge the entrenched, binary systems of gender and power. Remember that Hirsch posited feminist memory work as "counter-history" that could "account for the power structures animating forgetting, oblivion, and erasure, and thus to engage in acts of repair and redress" (2012, 16). Much public memory has moved away from this feminist ideal, but performative memory work and the shifting of orientations can help audiences deconstruct binary representations that uphold hierarchies and embrace the non-binary elements they experience in these spaces as "redress."

If these spaces[15] enact productive rhetorical force that challenges binaries, these performative texts can act as a "mode of cultural, historical action," engaging audiences in "reflexive" activity. By making themselves highly "*visible*," museums can break the binary of representation by making audiences interactively confront both the other and themselves: the museum space is made both vulnerable to displacement by the instability of performance as it simultaneously strengthens its own "capacity for political, ethical agency" (Pollock 1998, 95–96). It speaks directly to the "affective investment of one who [...] has been there and has a stake in the outcome of the exchange" (96). Indeed, local museum spaces have a special relationship with the surrounding community that can be a highly productive force. I will begin my analysis with the USHMM in Washington, DC, as a baseline example because it is the largest and most well-known Holocaust museum in America with more than 500,000 student visits annually and creates a national narrative that contrasts with the local narratives in local Holocaust museums.

THE USHMM: A NATIONAL PLACE AND SPACE

The idea of a communal or shared purpose in relation to the *place* of the surrounding community is paramount to a museum space, but in a national museum the context must also be rooted in national identity, which is itself complex and shifting. In the example of the USHMM, the building of a museum to commemorate the Holocaust in the United States was one of the directives stipulated by the members of President Carter's Commission on the Holocaust created in 1978 as a federal action. This Commission was created in the period of resurgent interest in the Holocaust in the United States. The president later wrote about the Commission's report that:

> Of all the issues addressed by the Commission, none was as perplexing or as urgent as the need to ensure that such a totally inhuman assault as the Holocaust—or any partial version thereof—never recurs. The Commission was burdened by the knowledge that 35 years of post-Holocaust history testify to how little has been learned. Only a conscious, concerted attempt to learn from past errors can prevent recurrence to any racial, religious, ethnic, or national group. A memorial unresponsive to the future would also violate the memory of the past. (USHMM "Excerpts")

Thus, from the very beginning, the USHMM has had a directed, pedagogical purpose that looked toward the future. The intent to teach visitors about the past so that they might learn from "past errors" seeks actions from its audiences (as citizens of a nation) that should be the result of visiting the museum.

The unique context for a Holocaust museum in the United States is that its geographical *place* is so far away from the original "sites of destruction" (to use Lanzmann's term from Chapter One). As I pointed out in the Introduction, as more narratives about the Holocaust became public, public memory around the Holocaust in America shifted from the story of victims to the story of survivors. The USHMM continues this with a strong, "context of survival, of a 'living memorial' *by* the living (as framers, funders, and visitors) that those in the devastated landscape of Europe can never possess."

Additionally, the location of the USHMM on the Mall in Washington D.C. serves as "a reminder of the dark side of humankind's civilized works," according to the USHMM committee's chairperson, Harvey Meyerhoff (Patraka 2001, 142).

The building design *space* is another element contributing to a museum's meaning-making potential for audiences. The USHMM's architect, Ingo Freed, says that a building that houses memory should be "sufficiently ambiguous and open ended *so that others can inhabit the space, can imbue the forms with their own memory*" (Young 1993, 339). The idea that interaction with audiences "imbues" a space with their collective memories and experiences is novel, because memorials (especially of the war type) typically involve passive viewing.[16] This is the unique aspect of both the national Holocaust museum and the local museums: they interact with the audience and community with the intention of preventing intolerance and promoting education *through collaboration* and a *physical engagement* (i.e., inhabiting the space).

The USHMM's location as both place and space thus, continues a nationalist dimension of the Holocaust that was complicated and not always positive: American soldiers helped liberate the camps, but America also had severe restrictions on Jewish immigration and did not make bombing the death camps a priority (Young 1993, 338). But in its broad, mostly binary representations it reverts to ambivalence: the critique-able American response is present but subsumed by the need for a larger, more coherent national narrative around the Holocaust and gender. In contrast, local museums with their smaller size and local audiences, tend to narrate less of an identity and encourage more of a de-identified communal response to the tragedy that ends with a return to directly addressing each individual's imperative to social responsibility, building an experience more akin to Ahmed's shared community of witnesses.

LOCAL MUSEUMS: THE PERFORMATIVE CONSEQUENTIAL IN COMMUNITY CONTEXTS

There are 16 Holocaust Museums in major metropolitan areas around the country and a multitude of smaller sites (educational centers, etc.) in other locations.[17] We might be tempted to see these local sites as smaller "versions" of the national museum, with a ripple effect like a pond. The stone drops into the center (the USHMM opens in D.C.) and the effects ripple outward to other "locations" around the country.[18] The opposite, in fact, is true. Each of the sites I visited has a distinctive origination date, some of them predating the USHMM.[19] I would like us to imagine, rather than a linear progression of time or buildings, museums as linked dynamically like a constellation of pressure points on memory. Each site exerts a *kairotic* force on its community through the performative consequential. The repeated performance of a generalized history with images, audio testimony, and artifacts speaks to the real, "affective investment" of its audience in that history, but because of its local focus additionally, it speaks directly to its community—those who theoretically have a "stake in the outcome of that exchange" (Pollock 1998, 96). With each museum opening (and in the case of two of the museums in this study, the moving and re-opening), a *kairotic* force of memory is exerted on the community. A rhetorical moment creates a new opening for dialogue. Because these museums interact so intimately with their locations and communities, they challenge scripted gender narratives and the notion of national identity as it relates to Holocaust memory. These local museums perform memory to create wonder through affective anchors that are both global (Anne Frank) and local (community survivor artifacts and stories) and by ending with calls for localized, social responsibility.

To each of the local museums I visited, there belongs a rich and unique community history of its creation. What they have in common is a core community of Holocaust survivors, who served as the original impetus for a memorial site and/or education center. It is important to set out the community history and context briefly for each museum, so that readers are reminded that it is a mistaken assumption to think of local museums as being extensions of the national site, or places where people might go if they cannot get to Washington D.C. The relationships that local museums have with their community are intimate, broad, and intergenerational, with a dedication to preserving memories of the history particularly as it pertains to their community members. We will explore the site history to discuss the affect of wonder, affective anchors, and social responsibility.

Dallas

According to my interviews with Dr. Sara Abosch, Senior Director of Education, and Dr. Charlotte Decoster, Assistant Director of Education in May 2015,[20] Dallas Holocaust Museum (DHM) is one of the oldest regional museums in the United States (personal interview). The museum began as a memorial space for the survivors to remember the dead, but they moved toward wanting to educate the community around them.[21] Their Jewish Community Center (JCC) Building opened in 1984. The Dallas Survivor Association of 1977 founded and opened the original Memorial Center in 1984, which remained open until 2005 though was shut down in 2004 and moved

Figure 5.1: Dallas Holocaust Museum, outside view (Costello).

to a transitional space in 2005. In 2014 DHM purchased a site, because they wanted it to be permanent. The DHM employees I spoke with made clear that the museum operated independently of the national site.

Houston

Like DHM, Holocaust Museum Houston (HMH) was built because of local survivors.[22] When I spoke with Carol Manley,[23] Director of Collections and Exhibitions at HMH, in May 2015, she stressed that local survivors and their testimony were at the center of everything they do at the museum (personal interview). The museum has an extensive history of the site that was published in house.[24] In 1981, Siegi Isakson, a survivor and Houston resident, went to a survivor conference (like Anne Levy did) in Israel and

Figure 5.2: Holocaust Museum Houston, outside view (Costello).

had an "epiphany": his peers (other survivors) would soon pass away. He began to organize a Speakers' Bureau of Holocaust Survivors to go out into community settings and into classrooms in the Houston area.[25] Because the Houston Jewish community saw themselves as broad and inclusive, they sought a location in the centralized museum district. But there were other, specific and local reasons for seeking a place in this district. The HEC Board rejected the idea of a site at the Jewish Federation (at the center of the Jewish community) because from the beginning they wanted the museum to be accessible and central to a multicultural Houston community (HMH 2005, 16). It was not just about a central or urban location, though: "the site asserts that there are associations between a horrific event that occurred in the distant past, on another continent, and the life of contemporary Houston. It warns that prejudice, intolerance, and hatred can occur anywhere at any time, that apathy and indifference can lead to disaster" (17). They broke ground on the museum in October 1993,[26] but it took several intense years to design the space.[27]

St. Petersburg

The website for the Florida Holocaust Museum (FHM) calls it "One of the largest in the country," and a museum that embodies the concept of a "living memorial" since 1992. They moved their location to St. Petersburg in 1998 and had 65,000 visitors in that first year. In 1994 Florida became the first state to mandate Holocaust education in schools. FHM is not affiliated with the USHMM in any way, though they have a strong partnership with Yad Vashem in Israel. They serve the southeast as a region and have the largest

Figure 5.3: Florida Holocaust Museum, outside view (Costello).

library collection; it is not available online, but that access is in progress (personal interview).

Los Angeles

Los Angeles Museum of the Holocaust (LAMOTH) is the oldest Holocaust Museum in the United States, according to their website (Los Angeles).[28] Their website states, similarly to FHM, that the museum is based on the experiences of survivors, who are the "living embodiment of history" (LAMOTH). It started in 1961 at Hollywood High when survivors were taking ESL courses, and they discovered each had a primary source item from the Holocaust. These artifacts needed a permanent home to be displayed and they wanted a place "to memorialize their dead and help to educate the world so that no one would ever forget" (Los Angeles). Some of these survivors are still active on the Board today. On 14 October 2010, LAMOTH opened the doors to its new building in Pan Pacific Park.

The contexts of *place* add important nuances to the sense of *space* in each of these local museums. As genres that tell multiple histories, these museums must aim for a level of objectivity, and indeed this is the expressed goal of many museums (like LAMOTH). In order to engage audiences in the *space*, however, there is a need to infuse that space with subjectivity, gender, and affect, so that memory can perform communally with its audiences. This is why so many of them also express the strong commitment to telling local stories and base their exhibits and outreach on the local community.

Figure 5.4: Los Angeles Museum of the Holocaust, outside view (Costello).

LOCAL MUSEUM DESIGN: ANCHORING THE PAST THROUGH SUBJECTIVE AFFECTS

I have outlined above the importance of the interaction of space and bodies as performative and rhetorical. If we allow ourselves to reside in non-binary thinking and experience we might see the world with more "wonder"—we might be open to see "as if" for the first time (Ahmed 2015, 179). Seeing "anew" however, does not mean that the history changes radically or that it can be challenged in the consistency of its details, as some deniers would like to claim. As recently as July 26, 2017, Siegal noted in the *New York Times* that: "Museums that preserve and present the truth are also fighting revisionists and Holocaust deniers who are increasingly vocal on the internet, and who are confusing the public, at a time when firsthand accounts of the Holocaust are fading" (par.10). Though wonder might seem to require an "erasure of history" or what has come before, Ahmed claims that wonder "allows us to see the world *as made*, and as such, wonder *opens up* rather than suspends historicity" [my emphasis] (2015, 179).

In comparison to the other genres I have described in this book, museum spaces (because they are less intimate and are designed for wide audiences) while naturally performative can have a distancing effect. One element of the distancing is the tone of the narrative that guides the visitor. Unlike a film or a text that is very subjective and might include self-reflective interruptions that cause audiences to pause, respond, and reflect in connection with the speaker as I described in Chapters One, Two, and Three, visitors are directed through a space (often chronologically) and through a historical narrative that is both textual and visual.

Local Holocaust museums, I argue, are stickier with affect because they enhance affective experience by creating "wonder" in audiences who may come with little general history of the Holocaust (if any), and are confronted with new stories and details. Many of these local stories appear only in the museum space having never been published or displayed anywhere else, firmly rooted in the place in which visitors stand (St. Petersburg, Dallas, etc.). We can be surprised by emotion, and what we see or experience can become extraordinary as a result. This is the "stickiness" of *affect* that comes from emotional *connections* with people and places in your precise corner of the world.

The design of local museum spaces uses artifacts in specific ways to direct and anchor sections of the exhibits for the audience. I call these artifacts *affective anchors*, rhetorical objects that move audiences emotionally and physically in directed ways. What is ordinary can sometimes not really be "seen," claims Ahmed, but it can nevertheless be familiar or comforting.

Even in a space as potentially alienating as a Holocaust museum (alienating because it will elicit feelings of discomfort, guilt, sadness, etc.) there must be a sense of the familiar to "anchor" a space for visitors, something to which they can immediately connect. In the USHMM, this is accomplished on the fourth floor of the museum (where the exhibit opens) with a floor to ceiling photograph of the liberation of the camps (i.e., national identity like American[29]). Local Holocaust museums use another kind of anchor: Anne Frank. Her image and her story are familiar (and therefore comforting) to visitors who may find the Holocaust museum space (and confronting trauma) uncomfortable.[30] Like national identity narratives that assure us we are not *very* implicated, Anne Frank's story has always reminded Americans that we can have "hope" even when humanity seems to have lost its sanity. The "familiarity and openness to identification" that an image of a child can bring, especially a girl who might be seen as even more "innocent," allow audiences to "project themselves directly into the image" and "bring its murdered subject out into [our] present world with extreme ease" (Hirsch 2012, 156). Local museums seek to represent a broad history of the Holocaust, but they want audiences to be able to connect immediately with the content. Each location frames this affective anchor of Anne Frank's image differently.

ANNE FRANK AS AFFECTIVE ANCHOR

Anne Frank is one example of how the repetition of the performative citational works. Her image or her story appears in every Holocaust museum I have visited in the United States (thus far). Anne Frank's image and story might serve as an example of what Blair identifies as the "rhetorical features we *should* be identifying [—] those that link and differentiate discourses according to the rhetorical work they do" (2001, 283). When objects, images, and content, as well as socially constructed identities, repeat, they send a message of importance. The repetition of Anne Frank's image becomes a productive force that is supposed to make something happen; audiences are supposed to easily connect to her. Hirsch argues that this mutual reflection, we look at Anne and she looks back, mediates our entry into "postmemory"[31] precisely because it is such a "readily available public image." But is this familiarity too easy to "mark the gravity" of the event, she asks? (2012, 161). In local museums, I argue that Anne Frank becomes an affective anchor that roots American audiences in what they "already know" (and that part is "easy") but then challenges them to feel "wonder" as they approach what they do not yet know. Wonder opens a *kairotic* aperture for audiences to participate and learn more. What's more, Anne Frank as this primary, repetitive anchor highlights gender as visible (not "genderless") and therefore also an important focus in public memory and the Holocaust.

Anne Frank's image and story serve as a reference point for many Americans. One reason is that *Anne Frank: Diary of a Young Girl,* is taught in schools around the country, sometimes mandated by law;[32] thus, hundreds of thousands of school children have encountered her story. For many even as they grow into adults, hers might be the only Holocaust story they know. Her face is something that is "familiar" and even friendly to audiences (she is often shown smiling) and her perspective as an innocent child makes her story particularly compelling. August 1, 2014, was the 70th anniversary of her final diary entry, and many national newspapers reflected on this date (Eleftheriou-Smith 2014). For all these reasons, perhaps, every museum includes her, but we must ask if this is its only rhetorical function (Blair 2001, 282).[33] How might the repetition of Anne Frank or her story disturb the genderless memorial narrative of the Holocaust although it appears to be telling the same, single story over and over again? Pollock's citational performative writing is helpful here to further the idea of repetition. Because identity cannot escape its construction, performative elements can exert "counterpressure" where the repetition is a "repetition with a *difference*" (1998, 92).[34] I will look at how the image of Anne Frank may exert counterpressure to scripted memorialization practices in these three spaces through a re-contextualization of both the construction of the "passive" victim and the construction of gender to help audiences feel that opening up of *wonder* in seeing information in a new context, "as if" for the first time.[35]

Dallas Holocaust Museum

In DHM the Anne Frank image is presented to audiences from their first steps into the museum exhibit. Her image appears at the end of several iconic photographs of the Holocaust from the Nazi rallies, book burnings, and deportation centers. Her placement here is "expected," because it is placed among other well-known images. This serves as an effective way to introduce the Holocaust to audiences with varying levels of knowledge. I watched several tours with middle grades and high school students, and this section was used to talk about the Holocaust in general and to glean what they knew and what they might still need to know during the tour. DHM presents a "standard" narrative in this section: it contains pictures/events we might be familiar with while also presenting an overly gendered picture of the Holocaust: lots of masculine, military imagery and images of large groups of victims from afar. No women are prominent, only the girl Anne Frank.

Figure 5.5: DHM and Anne Frank image in entry (Costello).

Although this DHM representation seems standard, there are many elements to this context that exert a performative counterpressure. As one of the final photos before the visitor enters the larger exhibit, her image represents the movement from the scripted to the unscripted narrative that is about to come. If one only encounters this iconic text, it certainly does not tell the "whole story," and yet even the diary itself was not originally the "whole diary." Her diary was edited for publication by her father, who took out passages critical of her mother and others. It was published with these passages only years later. Additionally, Frank's story has become a stage play, and an opera, re-appearing in new contexts almost constantly, as she does in these museums.[36] These repetitions (even if the audience is not aware of them) exert counterpressure to single representations. Indeed, the DHM example may embody what the Director of the Anne Frank Museum in Amsterdam wishes for Anne Frank's story and memory: "We want to make sure that Anne Frank isn't just an icon, but a portal into history" (Siegal 2017). In the DHM her image opens up one of the most singular exhibits on the Holocaust I have seen.

Holocaust Museum Houston

The image of Anne Frank in HMH does not appear at the beginning of the exhibit, as at DHM. Instead, Anne Frank's image appears in chronological time; the time period of the escalation of Nazi discrimination in occupied territories to the west, and the escalation from discrimination to murder in the east coincides with the Frank family going into hiding. The panel on Anne Frank is labeled: "False Identity and Hiding." Her photo appears among several other panels that discuss resistance, fleeing, and rescue. This representation of Frank works as an affective anchor in a different way than it did in DHM.

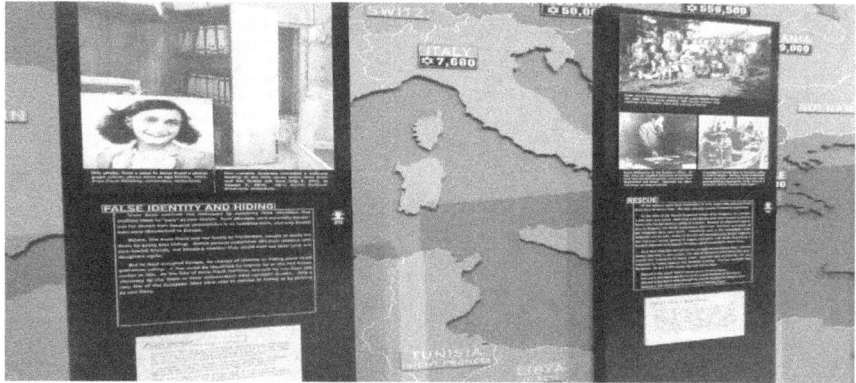

Figure 5.6: HMH and Anne Frank image (Costello).

Audiences have begun to experience images of violence and death in the exhibit, so Anne Frank's image, since it often resonates with hope for visitors familiar with her, acts as a counterpoint to despair. Additionally, because of its placement among resistance, fleeing, and rescue, HMH frames Anne Frank as part of the larger narrative of active resistor instead of passive victim. Fleeing, juxtaposed with resistance and rescue, reframes it as heroic (as perhaps witnessing is in this historical moment as well). In this photo she is shown smiling in the foreground and her hiding place in the Annex is the background image (next to her panel is one on "Rescue"). The depiction of Anne Frank in this section does not orient the viewer to a "familiar" victim or image as it did in Dallas's opening section. Her image placed among these others "re-contextualizes" her and the act of hiding as agency and power. She is not presented as a victim; this performative citation, the repetition of Anne Frank's image, reasserts a gender and cultural identity for the audience that is newly gendered. She is not just the innocent little girl. Visitors have just passed through sections with graphic photos of victims. Anne Frank, a "victim" for most audiences (she has a fatal end that is often "forgotten"), is now re-scripted as a fighter, a heroine, and a person in resistance who happens to be female. Visitors are also reminded, as Frank's image is surrounded by images of the dead, that she did not survive.

Los Angeles Museum of the Holocaust

The LAMOTH represents Anne Frank in a setting similar to the one at HMH. The second to last exhibit room is called "World Response, Resistance, Rescue." Anne Frank's story placed here highlights her actions again as resistant

Figure 5.7: LAMOTH and Anne Frank images (Costello).

and heroic. Unlike HMH but like FHM, her story is linked with the rescuer action of Miep Gies, the woman who helped hide the Frank family and saved Anne's diary. The added category of "World Response" also situates audiences as members of that "world" that knows about Anne Frank now, but did not respond then (American response). The affect at work implicates those who might identify (proudly) as American.[37] How might Americans have been implicated in the deaths of Holocaust victims as we engaged in this war and ignored their plight?

The photo of Anne Frank is one of the largest, which allows the audience to become anchored to a familiar story before they read the numerous other stories presented in this room, not all of them familiar. There is the story, for instance, of Varian Fry, a journalist who witnessed the mistreatment of Jews in Germany in 1935. He argued vocally against United States immigration policies at the time, and the United States did not support him. He was part of a group that rescued 2,000 in Vichy, France. The exhibit has another citational counterpressure in this story, because it references Schindler specifically, another famous rescuer. It says that Fry rescued all these people, but had "no benefits like Schindler." In 1994, Yad Vashem recognized him as the first American in the Garden of the Righteous (where Schindler is also recognized). Anne Frank is an iconic symbol of the Holocaust; thus she stands for what is "true" and known about the Holocaust, but in all these examples Anne Frank is also an affective anchor that is performatively citational. The repetition of her image with a *difference* allows audiences to make new historical and gendered associations that can create affective wonder and connection to the broader, less known local narrative.

Florida Holocaust Museum

In the FMH, there is a marked absence of Anne Frank imagery, though her story is still told. While Dallas framed their exhibits at the beginning with a Frank reference to anchor audiences with something familiar, and Houston and Los Angeles re-contextualized her as heroic by placing her among fighters, FHM ends their exhibit with this familiar story, but the re-contextualization is similar to HMH's and LAMOTH's approach. FMH has a special interactive section at the end of the museum called "heroes" in which audiences can use a screen to call up the biographies of several heroes (rescuers like Wallenberg). The images here are mostly headshots with extended texts that encourage the audience to focus on the actions that person took to resist. Although Anne Frank does not actually appear here, Miep Gies the woman who helped hide Anne Frank and saved her diary, does. Frank's story is thus told *through* the courageous actions of this woman. The performative counterpressure of this representation is the focus on relationships and how we are connected with others. Focusing on how people helped through small actions (even though this event was so large) challenges the audience to think about the ways in which they might act as they come to the end of the exhibit, and think about how someone then might have resisted the temptation to be a passive bystander. This shifts their orientation to turn toward the other represented as it is also performative: it asks audiences to think directly about what they could *do*.

Anne Frank, thus, appears here as an indirect affective anchor. She returns visitors who have experienced many new stories to one they might already

Figure 5.8: FHM without Anne Frank image but with Anne Frank story (Costello).

know. The end of the museum, in a way, brings visitors back to the beginning of their knowledge. But now, as they prepare to leave the space, they are confronted with a woman who tried to save Frank; she was unsuccessful ultimately but was not deterred from that heroic action. She also had the fortitude to save the written evidence that Frank left in the Annex. The anchor affect in FHM comes from the placement: the link of heroism to sustained action on behalf of others comes at the end, suggesting that visitors might also choose to do the right thing—fight discrimination even if it seems futile. This might create a sense of wonder for audiences who may not have considered the impact of those who were *not* bystanders and yet still were thwarted in their efforts to save lives. Does this failure make their actions meaningless or alert us to the agency of choice? Taking responsibility implies action, and the ways in which local museums focus visitors at the end of their exhibits on social responsibility in the community enacts the performative consequential.

LOCAL MUSEUMS: PERFORMING MEMORY AS SOCIAL RESPONSIBILITY

Above I described how Anne Frank is used to anchor audiences to what they know so that they might more easily enter into learning new knowledge or "seeing for the first time" as affective wonder, so they might shift orientations. In local museums, there is also a performative consequential at work such that audiences are turned toward their responsibility as a result of being in the museum and learning about the Holocaust. I will use one artifact from the DHM as an example of both at work.

In the DHM the last exhibit uses a freight boxcar artifact as its anchor to discuss the deportations and camp experiences. This section is filled again with Dallas survivors' experiences. But there is another important element at work in this section. Displayed next to the train car, extended material explains how Germans contracted with European trains for the cheapest way to transport humans, which were fixed at a "per piece" price, full price for adult and half price for children. Jewish prisoners were made to pay their own fare. The collaboration of the Nazi government and corporations to profit from slave labor and murder is highlighted here. Boxcars were the cheapest transport method and the most inhumane. The boxcar as artifact has become an iconic symbol of the Holocaust, but the details about how many people and institutions willingly participated for profit and eagerly made the Final Solution possible are not very well known.[38] This kind of information might be new to visitors so they might feel wonder: Can anyone be neutral in a war? Are there moral dimensions to profit? These questions of wonder are critical especially for American audiences, who are rarely, if ever, encouraged to reflect on the vagaries of greed and capitalism. They may begin to reflect on the role of corporations in exploitation and atrocity, perhaps for the first time. This kind of reflection can lead to a greater sense of responsibility in the present.

When visitors finish their experience at the USHMM, they are asked to reflect on global genocide and the things that people are doing now to mitigate these crises. Similarly in the local museums, there is a turn toward direct action in the world, but the focused use of contemporary local history in these museums creates a particularly "sticky" affect; audiences cannot continue to view the Holocaust as something distant that does not affect their lives. They must turn inward to reflect, which is another aspect of shifting orientations. Audiences in museums may not experience disorientation as they do in the examples in Chapters One through Four but they are asked to move through orientations that include turning toward and then inward—not away. These final sections in local museums are also performatively consequential because they bring audiences in as participants with a "stake in the outcome" of what happens in their community. Audiences are not allowed to finish their experience passively with broad reflections on the horror of the Holocaust and the "past-ness" of it. The contemporary local contexts put that into relief.

In DHM the last section is called Dallas/Ft. Worth April 19, 1943, and it turns the audience's perspective back onto themselves. It shows articles from local newspapers from the same day that have stories about the war. There are big headlines about ships and bombs and convoys, and tiny entries on back pages about Jews starving to death in Europe while the Germans are the best fed. Local newspaper front-page photos show "nurses being neat in Australia" and a young boy plowing a victory garden, mundane or "happy" story foci that ignore the European catastrophe in progress completely. The final entry in this exhibit is the headline: "Negro pinches white woman: gets 200 days" and this, with a wall-sized photo of a sign for a "Colored waiting room" effectively juxtaposes our racism and segregation here and the murders in Europe to bring audiences' critical eye on discrimination and violence into the local setting. Visitors are not only challenged by the non-chronological re-telling of this history, but also implicated in it.[39] This narrative suggests audiences need to reconcile their own local history with this history abroad, and the final call to act on daily basis in their community demands communal action (as we will see in the last section of this chapter).

Throughout all the exhibits in HMH there is a Houston connection. Many of the photos (including the one of Anne Frank) note a person who is well known and juxtaposes it with someone unknown, often someone who has a connection to Houston. The audience is asked constantly, therefore, to be negotiating space with place. In HMH, there is a focus on artifacts and quotes from local survivors that stand next to general information on these same camps: Siegi, one of the museum's founders, says, "the best way I can describe Auschwitz is the fact that I saw death every second of the day." Remmy Bowman talks about religious holidays in Auschwitz. Morris Cweigenberg (pushed off a train to Madjanek) is shown with photos of kids in Auschwitz and Mauthausen. Louise Joskowitz talks about starvation and her spoon and bowl from Auschwitz are displayed. Rose Fogiel worked with the underground to bomb the Auschwitz crematorium. She upends the notion of rebellion being strictly male, as she is also the survivor talking about the danger of being pregnant above. She was one of 700 women to survive a death march. The specific details from these survivors who live in Houston make their past experience live in the present for audiences. The subjective nature of their experience cannot be "neutralized" in the mass of numbers or deaths. They become gendered bodies that represent life—not at the expense of memorializing the dead—but as a strong narrative of connection to the present.[40]

This museum, as DHM does, ends with the testimonies of local survivors. This video plays for about 90 minutes. The common message from the survivors is: "let the museum speak for us," which projects its impact into the future. From here, the HMH exhibit officially ends outside, unlike FHM and DHM, but like LAMOTH. As they finish the exhibit with those who acted, audiences are encouraged to leave the museum with the idea that resistance begins with one and radiates outward. Here they have a Danish rescue boat donated by the Danish government in 2008. There is a Memorial Room with a Wall of Tears. When the sun filters through the glass, it looks like tears falling on the ground. There is a Wall of Remembrance and Wall of Hope that face each other; one is dark and one light. These are performatively consequential spaces because they are designed to encourage visitors to quietly reflect upon and negotiate their thoughts and feelings. There is a wall for those who perished (relatives of Houston survivors), and survivors who have died since the Holocaust are memorialized with an eternal flame, which links visitors both to the past and the future they can imagine. HMH's exhibit ends purposely by having visitors go outside and resituate themselves in the center of a Houston suburb (over the walls you can see the neighborhood around you). The message is that you *can* use your experience to imagine and engage in action that betters your community—and you should.

The end of the exhibit at FHM is similar to the one at DHM focusing on the local community and the racism prevalent there. There are several newspaper clippings about racist acts in Florida in the same time period. Florida Jim Crow laws are highlighted. Unlike in Dallas, however, FHM also turns this local focus strongly toward the present. There is a timeline that tracks the changes to racist policies postwar. It lists laws and lawmakers that challenged segregation and other racist practices. It suggests that progress has been made but that much more must be done. As audience orientations are shifted—they look inward (perhaps) to consider racism at home—they are then faced with a digital counter of global genocides happening right now. Unlike the other sites, FHM's exhibit does not just suggest action; it confronts audiences to ask directly: What will *you* do?

An extended section on their "Upstander Program" follows, in which community members can come together to create positive change by orienting themselves outward toward others, which exemplifies the performative consequential as creating agency both socially and politically, areas where apathy has often set in. While HMH finishes with some quiet reflection (which can be omitted by visitors if they choose not to go outside), FHM is forthright in its expectation that visitors will want to do something. They provide a clear avenue to action. FHM also has Tampa area survivor testimony at the end of the exhibit. Survivor testimonies are a constant presence at all the museums. At FHM, the video includes not only survivors, but also third generation survivors, talking about "why we need to remember." This design creates a performance of memory because it is not only about what can or cannot be known; it is about connecting with the experiences of others in order to be "moved" and to be attached, over generations, to the past.

In the atrium of LAMOTH the hallway heads downhill and gets darker as it leads to the first room. In the hall cases along the wall, there are *Los Angeles Times* articles from 1933 on about Nazi actions. The use of local papers is similar to the other museums I have mentioned in that it brings audiences' awareness to their local setting, but LAMOTH places these newspaper articles at the beginning of their exhibit (and place them throughout). Though they do not wait until the end to confront audiences with the issues in their local contexts, they also focus more on the war story rather than the stories of racism at home. The next few rooms detail the rise of the Nazis, ghettoes, and deportation.

Room Four on the death and concentration camps is another one of the unique aspects of the LAMOTH exhibits. This is the darkest and most isolated room, and by its design, it "limits the viewer to a single spectator," (LAMOTH) re-orienting them to seeing one camp at a time. Viewers move inside this room from screen to screen. In contrast to this larger room about the camps with more general information is an adjacent room that holds a detailed diorama of the Sobibor death camp that focuses exclusively on the local experience of survivor Thomas Platt.

This camp is not well known by audiences, which creates an element of wonder, and the diorama table also includes a video monitor above it, in which Platt narrates his experiences in this camp including *Selektions*, shaving, zyklon B. He talks especially about the *Sonderkommandos*, who had the hardest job (it was physical, end of the line, and they often saw family members as we recall from Chapters One and Two). Platt marks other important details about the uprising in the camp, highlighting resistance as a major theme. He explains how they planned the uprising: they led guards through their greed, got guns, cut off electricity, and set mines. Of the 250 prisoners who escaped, only 50 survived. Platt was only 15 years old as he followed the path of the mines. This brings viewers back again to a "connection" similar to the one they had with Anne Frank. Platt is a boy, and as a child "victim" who is less individualized, it is easier for audiences to project themselves onto him and connect with his story.

The broader presentation of camp experience next to the focused presentation of camp experience disorients viewers by shifting them between distance and intimacy. The Nazis bulldozed Sobibor, but LAMOTH notably includes research from 2016. Scientists have a new machine that has found gas chambers and jewelry buried at this site. This example of local experience detailed in a model built by Platt himself brings the local experience of the past directly into the present for visitors. Also, like DMH, this exhibit reveals how local museums' exhibits can be very responsive to new research in their design and content.

Orientation can mean simply a "turning toward" instead of a turning away. But it also means that one can re-orient both to turn toward others and turn inward to self-reflect. These dual behaviors create affective connections that can radiate outward to build community actions. Because these local museums have all evolved from small memorial spaces for Jewish memory to larger spaces that both memorialize loss and celebrate the living (through education) with broader audiences, they encourage those audiences to respond and make choices that lead to responsible action. Lately though, the "right" response or the "moral" response seems to depend more and more on each individual's position—how they are oriented toward or away from others—rather than toward the position of the community good. The "community good" can be framed, however, in very exclusive ways.

In Nazi Germany, being a good citizen (where people designated as Jewish actually lost their citizenship and Roma never had citizenship) meant being loyal to the Nazi Party and turning in neighbors and friends to the *Gestapo*. The moral aspects of "responsible citizenship" in this era were deeply contextual but also rigidly ideological with violent results for some of the population. This should resonate with audiences in the present with American immigration policies that echo this time period: anonymous citizen reports to ICE, deportations, and violent family separations that end in death. Right action can begin with one person, as these local museums constantly repeat, but finding that "right" becomes harder and harder, especially for younger generations who might feel a sense of detachment from their community even in the present, let alone from the past that seems so distant and unrelated to their lives.

Local museums focus on the responsibilities of citizens in their community for this reason. These local museums provide a great deal of education to schools, even in states without educational mandates. These museums include a wealth of educational programming that is broad in reach.[41] In local museums people and events are re-contextualized to encourage audiences to consider the past in the present or to consider the details of gendered subjectivity in contrast to the tendency to universal or genderless narratives. This may disorient viewers in order to reorient them to the experience of the other, to create deeper attachments to multiple, gendered perspectives. As I discussed in the beginning of this chapter, Ahmed sees a way for us to connect more intimately with one another; through "wonder" we can form "attachments" (2015, 180). This is one way that audiences can also connect to public memory narratives, but it is important that the knowledge they acquire in a museum move from knowing, seeing, or saying, *to doing*.

LOCAL MUSEUM OUTREACH: PERFORMATIVELY CONSEQUENTIAL

The educational focus and interaction with audiences in these locations resides firmly with communal experiences in physical spaces as well as actions that resonate outside the museum in the local community as performatively consequential. Archival material is variously available at these museums but not yet on the scale of the large archives I mention in Chapters One and Two.[42] At the close of exhibits, visitors are encouraged to see themselves as stakeholders in creating a world that is less prejudiced and violent. Visitors are presented with clear evidence of the programs that are available to local schools (evident first of all by the many tours of local schoolchildren that are ever-present at these sites) and community members (like tolerance training for police forces).[43]

FHM said that teachers can "over-teach" (using material that is above grade level, for example, an Auschwitz survivor talking to a 5th grade class), therefore the trunk program solves that problem by designating teaching material according to grade level with special local features. For example, there is a large laminated photo of a survivor. This is part of a project called "Fragments," in which survivors pulled out a line or two of their own testimony to hand-write under their photo. The educational piece is moving for many students, especially those who can come for field trips. FHM also has a robust "Upstander Program," which is designed for all visitors, not just young students. It guides visitors to think about what it means to stand up for right action instead of being a bystander. This is an important message to place at the end of the museum for reflection on action in the community.

DHM offers teacher trainings and trunk programs that are produced in-house. They came a little late to the trunk program according to my interview, because their site often featured larger trainings from USHMM and Yad Vashem that tended to overshadow local efforts. As they build their resources and staff, however, these trainings are expanding. The site gives tours to local students by the thousands every year. The DHM provides many docent-led tours with student-groups, and I witnessed several on the days I visited. Like FHM and the trunks, the tours are specifically targeted by age. Younger kids, for example, do not listen to the extensive audio program because it contains too many graphic details. A tour for 6th graders ends with a survivor talk with Max Glauben. The idea of contextualizing history and memory in these museums is so crucial at the early stages of learning. For kids creating wonder and the desire to learn more sometimes means protecting them from feeling too afraid. This particular survivor talk started with the story of Max Glauben and the power of the positive in humans. His testimony mixed with the classroom teacher's commentary to explain why we teach the Holocaust and what we can learn. He ends with the fortunate circumstances of liberation and life in the United States, but he notes that there is still evil in the world that we must fight against.

The HMH has many of these student educational programs as well. HMH also is doing a great deal of work around generational memory linked to local survivors. They are in the process of recording stories from second-generation survivors. Their "Next Gen Project"[44] recruits third-generation survivors to become active in the museum as docents or by telling their stories on film or in schools. HMH actively supports the creation and preservation of intergenerational memory. HMH also has curriculum trunks, but Ms. Manley told me that technology challenges have hampered the delivery of these. With teachers relying so heavily on computers, they want material uploaded to tablets and this is costly (interview). HMH has an Upstander Program like FHM, but theirs is focused on immediate action in one month: "30 days – 30 acts." They have 40–50,000 K–12 students coming through the museum and this program each year.

LAMOTH is likewise focused on the future and education as a way of broadening knowledge and bringing people together in connection. The final exhibit in the museum focuses, much as the beginning did, on sound. The last room is small but has an enormous wall filled with a metal tree of life sculpture. At the end of each branch is a video monitor on which plays a survivor's testimony. Through a partnership with the USC Shoah Foundation, the screens are linked to the USC Visual History Archive and show all 52,000 testimonies on a continuous loop. The links between these two projects and locations brings the two local settings together and provides even greater access to this archive for Los Angeles students and residents.

Like HMH, FHM, and DHM, LAMOTH also has generational activities for second- and third-generation family members, many of whom work at the museum sites. At LAMOTH, there is a group called 3G, which focuses on connection activities between audiences and survivor stories. They have a *Voices of History* project, in which students interview survivors and make short films, theater performances, and music compositions reflecting the survivors' experiences (Brown, personal interview). In 2014, LAMOTH began some new academic partnerships like the "Ambassadors of Memory" Project in which middle-school students help unpack artifacts on loan from Auschwitz-Birkenau. To be on site discussing these objects and the history with staff and survivors, while being in physical contact with the objects, is an unusually visceral and enriching experience for the students.[45]

All of these have a strong focus on Jewish lives as they commemorate suffering and death, but they are also committed to having audiences experience the history viscerally so that they will be inspired—even compelled—to go out and teach others. LAMOTH's website says: "we believe your visit to the museum will strengthen your personal commitment to making the world a better place," and this call to action is a primary part of the mission for all the museums. These sites are performatively consequential because they seek action from the stakeholders around them and use "rhetoric as a '*productive* force,' and, most definitely and performatively, as *force*" (Pollock 1998, 95) with *kairotic* effect and wondrous affect.

CONCLUSION

Local Holocaust Museums are special spaces about Jewish history that have a non-binary focus on both life and death, much as the artifacts in Chapter Four did. Museums often begin with artifacts and stories about the lives of Jewish families before the war,[46] and end with the local community and the growing generations of survivors and their families, and the responsibilities of viewers, citizens, and witnesses to these atrocities.[47] Though bodies move through these museum spaces, negotiating, learning, and feeling wonder, and the museums' missions seek community action and response, is there a guarantee that this museum experience creates action? Some of the written museum responses from visitors suggest it does. Although I did not include the St. Louis Holocaust Museum and Education Center in this chapter, this was one museum where I was able to read actual visitors' comments after moving through the exhibits.[48] Audiences have responded with a high level of emotion. In 2011, visitor comments included: "should be required for all students (IL)," "informative and liked the St. Louis ties" (MO), "moving" (various), "makes you think" (MO), and "emotionally compelling" (MO). In the teacher surveys, many teachers agreed that a visit to the Museum created a "greater desire to teach about those who are persecuted/oppressed" (earlier responses may differ, and I plan to return to these surveys). Such responses suggest that direct action might be the result of this museum experience, especially when the visitors are locals, precisely as the mission statement of the museum has intended.

The exhibits and the programming at local Holocaust museums ask visitors to act now in ways small and large in their local contexts to fight intolerance and to prevent prejudice and violence in their communities. But these local sites do not remain statically local in their perspectives. As they bring visitors to confront themselves and their actions in their communities, they ask them also to look outward and consider atrocity in the world at large enacting the performative consequential. This performs memory in ways that subvert the false notion that the "public sphere in which collective memories are articulated is a scarce resource" such that public memory is an identity struggle (as I have noted in this book) that is a "struggle of recognition in which there can only be winners and losers" (Rothberg 2009, 3). Rothberg suggests that memory can be multidirectional, "subject to ongoing negotiation," much as the rhetorical and feminist scholars I have noted here. The fight against intolerance, racism, and violence is ongoing, as is our communal public memory negotiation of those eras and events. The work we do here involves relationships and a conscious shifting of orientations to the past and to others.

The act of turning toward and turning inward as a means of reorienting visitors is the final step of this shifting of orientations. Affect relies on emotion, and Ahmed describes "emotions as *doing things*." For her, "emotions involve different movements towards and away from others, such that they shape the contours of social as well as bodily space" (2015, 209). Museums are social spaces that hold bodies within them. The emotional affect can be powerful in a positive way. Museums hold large outcomes for action that rely on hope for the future. "The moment of hope," says Ahmed, "is when the 'not yet' impresses upon us in the present, such that we must act, politically, to make it our future" (184). Museums perform consequentially to spark action in their visitors. To connect to others and to act for good are messages for everyone, not just Jewish visitors, turning all people toward honoring the dead by celebrating the living in order to make the world less bigoted and less violent. The focus on *teaching* about atrocity in the past has an explicit message about *acting* against atrocity in the present. Without the hope that things can change, there is apathy about ever affecting change. With hope, there is the sense that we "must" and we can act to change our future.

NOTES

1. Some might even say it has become an industry or has led to the "end of the Holocaust." (See Cole 2000; Rosenfeld 2013).

2. Samantha Power's thesis in *A Problem from Hell* (2003) shows that America has a history of denying genocides (and in legal terms, this includes the Holocaust) as a way to sidestep the need to act against contemporary genocides and is worth noting. This adds an interesting political layer to American Holocaust memorialization, but this is not the focus of this book.

3. This is usually part of the stated mission of these museums. See my next manuscript for a deeper analysis of museum missions, including the USHMM and local sites.

4. See Bartov 1996; Ofer and Weitzman 1998; Patraka 2001; and Young 1993; 2002; 2008.

5. Stier is one exception (2005).

6. See Friedlander in the Introduction about the "limits of representation," for example (1992).

7. Though it must certainly be noted that these locations are less resistant to the nationalist narrative of the United States, and while not the focus of this book, this is an important aspect that may limit their inclusivity of and reach toward international audiences.

8. I visited each of these sites and did extensive interviews and onsite research between 2015 and 2016. I am only utilizing a tiny portion of the research data I gathered here. A second book is in progress that focuses on these museums and the materiality of memory and rhetorical performance at these rich memorial sites. I thank all of the people I interviewed for their candor and willingness to spend time with me.

9. See also Pennebaker and Banasik 1997; Peterson 2002; Rensmann 2004; Wohl and Branscombe 2004.

10. See Michael Bernard-Donals's *Forgetful Memory: Representation and Remembrance in the Wake of the Holocaust* and discussions in Chapter Two.

11. In her work on the Civil Right Institute, Victoria Gallagher cites Tamar Katriel's work on heritage museums in Israel, which focuses on the "social functions

that are performed through visitors' experiences" (1999, 305–308). Similarly, this chapter focuses on the performance of museum space.

12. See the Introduction on issues of representation and the Holocaust.

13. This is similar to films as I noted in Chapter Two with *Schindler's List*.

14. I noted this in Chapter Three as well with the auto/biographical self. The performative self is in flux while "typical" auto/biographies attempt to portray a coherent self across time. To present coherence in atrocity erases much of the complexity and ambiguity, while binary simplistic representations are easier for audiences to digest and leave them less "implicated" as I will discuss later in this chapter.

15. A distinction between space and place is important according to Patraka, because museums tend to vacillate between space and place in the process of memorializing, where "place" has an inherent narrativity that entails mostly passive apprehension, and "space" allows for the re-negotiation of narrative through multiple interpretations and spectator perspectives, which is essentially a performative activity (1999, 139–141). Therefore, when I use the term "place," it will mean geographical and static. When I use "space," it will mean multiple, performative, and dynamic. Museum design vacillates between place (passive) and space (active), but I argue that they become open to audience response through the use of purposeful, performative choices that require the audience's critical collaboration.

16. Museums, in general, have become increasingly interactive, but Holocaust museums specifically have because of their expressed mission to educate about and prevent atrocity.

17. These sites are the subjects of my next book project, for which I have collected extensive data.

18. Gail Beckerman in *The Jewish Daily Forward* writes that, "those who defend the existence of the regional [Holocaust] museums do so on the grounds that they serve populations that cannot visit the nation's capital" (2009, 1). The national museum agrees that the "smaller local organizations" are "on the ground everyday in their communities" (2). Yet, I would suggest these museums do much more than work "on the ground" to serve populations that would rather go to D.C. The mission and purpose of these local museums makes them a particular form of testimony that *does* tie into the national narrative as a general Holocaust history, but they also *enhance* that narrative by multiplying the stories that are told to "present," as Langer suggested, "the moral complexity of the Holocaust experience" (2006, 190).

19. I would like to extend my thanks to all the museums' staffs, who welcomed me as a visiting scholar and everyone who allowed me to interview them about their work and their sites. I appreciated the valuable time and information that was shared with me. My second book will involve more work with these sites and further site visits.

20. I am grateful for their time in May of 2015. They are both historians. The DHM is in the process of moving to a new site, which is set to open late in 2019.

21. The evolution from memorial space to educational community leader (and the merging of these two goals) is echoed at each site. I do not have the space to do so here, but I examine this progression at these sites looking at the design, exhibits, revisions to their missions, and the community outreach programs that result, at greater length, in my book on museums (in progress).

22. The above photo was taken in 2015. HMH is currently undergoing extensive renovations at a new location.

23. I am thankful to Carol Manley for taking the time to talk to me in May 2015. Our interview was extensive, and her library and museum staff was incredibly accommodating, allowing me to share their workspace for one full day.

24. According to this Holocaust Museum Houston text, *10 Years: Remembrance, Education, Hope* (2005), the museum works toward the paradox of devoting itself to producing "good memories" about a history that has so few. The book includes museum "lessons" for visitors to take home with them, such as: "remember that some people risked everything to be perpetrators" and "remember that some people risked everything to be resistors" (5). The DHM, in contrast, as of 2015, did not have any compiled works (internal or external) that recorded its institutional memory, and therefore the original history is less detailed.

25. He brought the idea for a center and memorial museum to Houston's Jewish Federation but they tabled it. In 1990 Sandra Weiner, President of the Federation, embraced Izakson's idea, and "she established the Holocaust Education Center and Memorial Museum. She chose "Martin Fein, the son of survivors, as the Center's first director" (HMH 2005, 9). The acronym became HEC.

26. HMH is also moving to a new location in 2019. I look forward to researching these new sites and exhibits as well.

27. Just before it opened they changed the name to Holocaust Museum Houston, and opened in March 1996. Siegi said during the ceremony: "I thank G-d for letting me live to witness this day after thirteen years of hope. It means the Holocaust is going to be told through education and memorial" (HMH 2005, 11).

28. According to Dr. Vladimir Melamed, (former) Director of Archives at LAMOTH, the website is necessarily simplified; when the museum first opened, it was not meant to be a museum with artifacts but a way to represent genocide and memorialize the dead.

29. In the USHMM, even though visitors have been given the identity card of a victim of the Holocaust upon entering the museum, beginning at a historical point with which Americans might be most familiar: the liberation of the camps, causes visitors to immediately identify, not with the victim on their card, but with the liberators. Philip Gourevitch agrees that "opening the show from this vantage point will also comfort Americans by identifying them immediately as heroes. An odd spin, this: clutching their I.D. cards, museumgoers are asked to identify simultaneously with the victims and their saviors. Placing the American liberation of the camps in the foreground of the exhibition also nudges to the background the third role visitors are being asked to consider: that of the bystanders who participate in history by an acquiescent failure to act" (1993, 6).

30. Siegal's 2017 article may seem to undercut this with her exposition of interviews with visitors to the Anne Frank museum in Amsterdam who are unclear about who Anne Frank is, or even if she was Jewish. I posit, however, that the familiarity of Anne Frank is a reality for Americans, many of whom read her diary as part of the public middle school curriculum. They may have occluded this memory (lost the

details of it) as I mentioned in Chapter Three, but most will be able to at least identify her photograph or story.

31. See my discussion of postmemory in the Introduction. Traumatic memory is passed intergenerationally and is not something that only happens within survivor families.

32. Florida and Illinois, for instance, have state mandates to include the Holocaust in social studies education. But, these state mandates, at least in Florida, depend on donors and state funding, which are dwindling.

33. Blair discusses the repetitive practice of naming the dead at national memorials (2001, 282).

34. Pollock cites Homi Bhabha in *The Location of Culture* as part of this explanation of the citational.

35. This works also in other genres. When Anne Frank's story is produced in a play or a film, the context changes.

36. Hirsch notes this as a disturbing reality but also says that because children are less individualized, they "invite multiple projections" that can be universalized. She and I agree that this "universalization" can end up being simply disguised as "neutral" when it is in most other cases primarily male (2012, 162).

37. One section in the USHMM details to what extent the United States government ignored the plight of the Jews from the early years and well into the years of deportation and extermination. By placing the government's willful ignorance in this section, Patraka claims that the museum, "constructs a localized historical contradiction to its own ideological claims about how democracies respond to genocides, thereby complicating the narrative of our national identity" (2001, 144).

38. The national German train service, *Deutsche Bahn* (DB), has built and dedicated a memorial to the deported victims of the Holocaust at the Grunewald Station outside Berlin. They have made formal and public apologies, unlike some other German corporations who collaborated with the Nazis.

39. Patraka adds this key point: "Ideally this contradiction *opens a space of possibility* for the spectator to consider how representative democracy operates in the present with regard to genocides elsewhere, rather than entirely soliciting a sense of disillusion, betrayal, and despair about the past [emphasis added]" (2001, 144). This is why this section is effective at the end. The implication of complicity serves as a "take away" for visitors to act bravely in their own communities.

40. It must be noted, of course, that this movement toward connection and action is designed and intended; this is what I am theorizing. But there remains the real fact of distance with a few visitors. As I observed one of the final sections called "Terrifying Testimony," there are survivors speaking about being separated from their children, babies being placed in sacks and shot, and a woman who suffocated her crying child so that the group of people hiding with her would survive. I overheard one high school student say at this point to a friend: "It [this exhibit] was so long, I stopped paying attention." This astounding lack of empathy can only result from a conscious turning away to which he admitted. It would be hard to *really* listen to these testimonies and not feel some kind of affect. The lack of connection on the part of this student makes me sad, but is probably not unusual in each student group. Many more students (and

visitors) are affected by the experience, as my section on Education and Outreach will note.

41. I do not mean to imply that the USHMM does not have this focus on community in their programming. They have a wonderful police training program, for example, which extends to D.C. and Virginia. My point here is to suggest that not having the imperative to this programming in addition to making a message national or based in broad theories of democracy, actually specifies outcomes for audiences effectively in the local setting. Visitors can participate *and do* as soon as they walk out the door.

42. LAMOTH has the largest archival material available (online) to the public of all the museums I visited. They also have full access to the USC Visual History Archive. The videos play on an endless loop at the end of their exhibit. The other local museums I visited (according to my interviews) struggle with archiving and digitizing because of staffing and funding issues. The USC Visual History Archive has programs to help local sites digitize material, and I would like to be involved in mediating these relationships as I work on my next book that focuses only on museums.

43. I talked with a museum staff member at FHM who is a second-generation survivor and has worked at FHM for decades. FHM has an active trunk program and provides tolerance and diversity training for local police.

The USHMM has piloted police trainings locally in DC as well as I note in endnote 41.

44. I have used this terminology to refer to third-generation survivors in Chapter Four.

45. LAMOTH also prides itself on providing open access to research materials to the public. LAMOTH's collection on Modern European History, for example, is a singular online archive according to Dr. Melamed, and visitors can download and print for free. High-resolution items need permission, but the intent is that information should be easy to get at the site for both young students and scholars.

46. In the Jewish Museum Berlin, visitors first encounter images of Jewish lives before the Nazis with family photos, jewelry, and prayer books. Holocaust Museum Houston and the St. Louis Holocaust Museum begin their exhibits with Torah scrolls, family photos, and the stories of lives in progress.

47. In addition to trainings for police and community members, this focus on action is also a focus on message and behavior, and these new generations are asked to become bodies in motion—agents of change.

48. For my second book on museums, I plan to obtain visitor comments from all the locations.

Conclusion

It has been almost two years since heavily armed white supremacists, neo-Nazis, and alt-right supporters marched violently in Charlottesville, Virginia. The president of the United States did not denounce them. The white supremacist politician, David Duke, embraced this absence of condemnation as support, and he is right. Ruth and Anne Levy in Chapter Three knew an absence of condemnation is as good as support. Only three months ago, there was a mass shooting at the Tree of Life synagogue in Pittsburgh and precisely three months before International Holocaust Remembrance Day 2019. Hundreds of newspapers and leaders worldwide marked this event with speeches and articles. This year, the United States executive branch was not silent but marked the day with others as antisemitic acts are rising exponentially around the globe.[1]

In the Introduction I talked about the occlusion of memory and the competing desires of audiences to both remember and forget the Holocaust. Recent polls have found statistics even more shocking than those I cited from 1993. According to the ADL, antisemitic incidents increased by "57% in the US in 2017," the largest increase in one year, and 2017 was also the year that "cases were reported in every single state since 2010." In a disturbing statistic about the evolution of authoritarian power today, "fifty-two percent of Americans said incorrectly that Hitler came to power through force." For Americans engaging or not engaging with the Holocaust, "forty-one percent of Americans and 66% of millennials couldn't say what Auschwitz was." And the most disturbing of all perhaps is that "the survey also found that 22% of millennials said they had never heard of the Holocaust or weren't sure" (Cranley, 2019, pars. 12–14).

I have spent years studying the Holocaust, talking to people, and visiting sites and museums; it seems we should know what the Nazis and others did.

Yet so many it seems, do not. The world has also largely ignored subsequent genocides in Rwanda and the Sudan, as well as previous genocides like in Armenia and of Native Americans in North America for many reasons but often political ones. Rothberg notes that, "because of the Holocaust's salience to the relationship of collective memory, group identity, and violence, an exploration of it is ongoing public evocation" (2009, 6) for comparative national contexts, as he notes, or in its lack of evocation by many who veer into historical amnesia, the analysis of its contribution to public memory practices remains vital.

Even in 2019 again and again we seemingly "confront" bald hatred and unapologetic racism in the public sphere in America, yet it persists overtly and in the shadows. Is this our destiny as humans? Are we wired to hate enough to kill? Through the lens of violent and tragic events like mass genocide, it seems as if the answer would be "yes." Through the lens of the small community of Charlottesville, Virginia, where a violent rally left one counter-protester dead and several others injured, it seems too that the answer is "yes." Speaking out meant death for one protester and this was how the Nazis operated in 1930s as well. Fear and propaganda were their tools of control.

Nevertheless, I know that when humans connect and are open to each other's differences we have hope and we enact change. This is why finding a way to connect with Holocaust public memory and shifting our orientations have real import for the world. I am afraid of what will continue to happen if we continue to turn away from our connection with other people as unique human beings and reject relationship and community on a large scale in favor of hate, segregation, and violence. This book is about the ways in which we can find connection to the past and to the people around us now. This book is about orienting ourselves to others so that we can listen, empathize, and be open. I find the rhetoric of disrespect, hatred, walls, and degradation disorienting—terribly so. But maybe, if I adhere to what I advocate in this book, I need to experience that disorientation in this precise historical moment in order to reorient *myself* to the actions I value in the world: those that are ethical, kind, and fair and gender, religiously, and racially inclusive. Maybe I need to reapply vigor to my public self and double my efforts at speaking out. The *doing* itself is a performance that reifies or disturbs the modes of public knowledge. Remembering and honoring the memories of those gone is necessary and dynamically connected to the present. We must choose to return to the past, to see, to hear, and to feel—and apply that knowledge to our present contexts to honor those memories as we also act for good in the present.

When I talk about the performance of memory in this book, I mean that modes of writing and visual communication that transmit memory *do something*, a concept Della Pollock has so eloquently argued. The performances of memory I have described (and that exist numerously elsewhere) create action by disturbing reified public memory around gender and the Holocaust. They confront audiences with new depictions and framings, challenging them to do something with their broader access to knowledge and the blurring of binary representations. What does it mean to mourn, memorialize, and educate? What does it mean to have gender representations embracing a spectrum instead of a binary? The authors in this book define these variously, but what they have in common, however, is their desire for change. They want audiences to see *and feel* differently such that they might reorient themselves, hopefully toward connection with others. That action, though, requires a subject, a person who chooses and who does; the dialogic of history and memory as interactive requires those participants to engage in relationship and emotion together over time and with effort.

Is there a way to come together when we seem so divided? As we saw in many of the chapters in this book, Holocaust public memory has not remained statically present in form or degree; there are reifications, regressions, additions, and disruptions over time. People continue to be willing to revisit this history: the firsthand witnesses and their families, the next generations of audiences and artists, continue to confront knowledge about the Holocaust and what that means in new contexts, and this is hopeful. But readers may ask: why? We have revisited this history and continue to memorialize it and yet white supremacists are empowered to march in Charlottesville, Virginia, in 2017. Police continue to shoot unarmed black men and women despite the powerful voices in Black Lives Matter. The Tree of Life synagogue in Pittsburgh, Pennsylvania, suffered a mass shooting just three months ago. Does knowing more about violence and genocide change any of this in the present? If these views persist more than 70 years after the National Socialists took power in Germany, does communal memory work even matter?

For me, it not only matters; it matters *more* in light of such events. We know that when intolerant views become public and are multiplied, they become normalized. I have argued this very point about the repetition of forms or gender representations in Holocaust memorialization. A strict binary of language or emotion or representations (the either/or) does not depict our complicated world anymore; in fact, it may never have. Yet, it persists because it is simple, even if it is inaccurate. To assert that Hitler was evil and the sole reason for the Holocaust is simple but not exactly true. Many people around Hitler helped the Holocaust happen. Researchers have proved this, yet the "the evil ruler" myth persists because it is easier to dismiss it as a human anomaly. But this normalization process (public memory as binary) can be disturbed with review, analysis, and dialogue that challenges the simplistic binary of either/or.

The difficulty of non-binary representation (the both/and) is that it *is* complicated, ambiguous, and difficult. In terms of the Holocaust we have to review what we know, revisit the past in the present, and remain in constant dialogue with that knowledge. When we use terms like "bystander" and "collaborator," what did those terms mean then and what do they mean now? Contexts change, and we are at our best when we address the needs of those changing contexts. What we know is bolstered by facts, which can change based on new research; Ruth Klüger knew this intimately with her room full of memory furniture. Bumping into that rearranged furniture can be uncomfortable and even painful, and many of us do not want to know more. What happens when we choose to know less? If we shift our orientations to this past, the concept of orientation itself, as Ahmed points out, can be the "site of an encounter" (2006, 5), where we increase our affective connections to make meaning together with other witnesses.

I have discussed the notion of orientation with regard to our relationships with others. This book has argued again and again that if we orient ourselves away from others, we become immune to their suffering. Thus, we *choose* not to know, as if our lives—our individual perspective is what matters most (and we can think of this on a personal and also a national basis), in addition to deluding ourselves that we are not all connected in some way. But the human experience is not about just the self. It is about community. It is about how we work together and how we come to know each other. Orienting away from ourselves and toward others is sometimes quite hard and thus, avoided. Sometimes, it requires disorientation from what we think we know or understand or care about, in order to re-orient: to others and to facts, or inwardly to emotions and reflection. Queer orientation, as Ahmed has suggested about sexual orientation, is about turning toward not away. Shifting orientations in this text is about moving in the direction of places and people, thoughts and feelings, and non-binary gender representation about the Holocaust in order to become connected to new knowledge.

We must consider, however, how much can be held or remembered. To "archive" is to save for the future. It is to decide that certain artifacts or memories or events have value. In the traditional sense, the archive is about who has the power to make these decisions about what matters to the future of public memory. Rhetorically, I have illuminated how public memory is under construction and contested across borders of all kinds. Rothberg calls memory an "open-ended field of articulation and struggle," from which he posits memory as multidirectional (2009, 21). When memory is social and communal and gendered, public memory becomes more than a repository of things to be "saved" and is not bound by these hierarchies as strongly. By challenging genderless narratives in the public realm, performative public memory becomes an ephemeral space with lived, performed memory at its center. Audiences can encounter memory and engage with it as an embrace and a struggle.

Edbauer reminds us that the rhetorical triangle, with just author, text, and audience, is insufficient because "distribution" of this sort crosses physical, spatial, and temporal boundaries (2005, 12–13). We might consider this patchwork spatially as a "whole landscape" of witnessing where a growing network of connections might create listeners, who might become students, who might speak, who might take responsibility or action. Each is connected to the other. This book situates spatial location historically and temporally in terms of the *kairotic* force of memory work.[2] Memorial activity exerts *kairotic* pressure, performative counterpressure, through representations that challenge audiences to "see" and feel differently about the Holocaust over time. We have moved in this book from the original sites of destruction and digital space, to re-created sites and fictional stories, to community and politics, and finally to space versus place discussions in which we can re-see "degraded" bodies as gendered, living memorials to the past. Chapter Five completed the trajectory of discussion by moving us firmly toward education and social responsibility in Holocaust museums. In thinking about "how" public memory works within these different frames, we have complicated the idea of location in terms of the gendered performative. If we ask which position, on which place, in which space, we must also ask how many times and how does it change?

If a network theory of "affective ecologies" complicates the elements of the rhetorical situation, as Edbauer argues, then we are able to "more fully theorize rhetoric as a public(s) creation" (Edbauer 2005, 9). The rhetoric of knowing, however, entails facts and emotion *together* as non-binary knowledge; this is what I mean by a whole landscape of witnessing—a network of interaction between history and memory. Discerning between fact-based and emotion-based knowledge has seemed more and more difficult in the public sphere lately. My theory accounts for continuous movement and meaning making over time in a space that is public, as a network of sorts, but one that is in constant movement by being more accessible and open. As we isolate and divide ourselves from one another in digital or political spaces, it becomes increasingly important to do more than just theorize or recontextualize the rhetoric of that public space and memory. We must think about ecologies and networks more so, as Ahmed does, as purposeful orientations: conscious movements toward, away, and inward to align what we feel with what we know—not to solidify our extreme positions away from each other but to understand and embrace difference. The *actions* we take as a result are what matter in the end.

The performance of public memory seeks action and requires repetition but with attention to gendered difference. In the power hierarchy of the gendered binary, for example, "feminists who speak out against established 'truths' are often constructed as emotional," and therefore failing in reason and good judgment. But to claim rationality instead merely brings us back to the binary. "We need to contest this understanding of emotion as 'the unthought,'" says Ahmed, "just as we need to contest the assumption that 'rational' thought is unemotional, or that it does not involve being moved by others" (2015, 170). The "sociality of emotions" that Ahmed describes attaches itself to objects, objects that accumulate affect (218). The Holocaust public memory artifacts I discuss here also have this accumulated affective value. The non-binary truth of both emotional and rational engagement with these artifacts can bring us together. The performative elements of Holocaust memory, connecting past, present, and future, invite many participants and build many layers that seek to hold multiple perspectives. The pieces I have analyzed in this book show evolving rhetorical strategies to reach audiences because they perform differently in each iteration. That space of ambiguity and difference, the "in-between," the not knowing, opens a space *to know*; a non-binary, gendered framework that allows for both. The performance of memory is an invitation—to participate and intervene, to turn toward others instead of away. I refuse to be a bystander to hate, division, and violence.

This is one of the ways I connect with the world but also with my mother, whose own lived memories are becoming fainter and fainter with advancing age and dementia. I smile when I see another newspaper clipping about the Holocaust arrive in my post box with her beautiful handwriting on the envelope. She remembers this connection we have even if she does not remember talking to me on the phone just days ago. This realization that she is disappearing to herself is hard to turn toward. But if I remember, and my siblings remember, her life retains a lived meaning that grows in the present as it is re-lived, applied, and valued. We have to choose to work through and with memory and to seek knowledge of what was and what might be; it is not always easy. In terms of the traumatic history of genocide and hatred, that work is even harder. It remains up to us, however—individually and communally—to make that choice to connect and to be in relationship with people across the spectrum. This is the only way we can salvage our feminist attachments, by embracing the rational and the emotional to build hope and wonder instead of fear and isolation.

NOTES

1. I have already discussed Deborah Lipstadt and her book *Denying the Holocaust*. As Stephens notes, we might have hoped that hers was the last that needed to be written, and yet antisemitism persists and grows. Her new book is called *Antisemitism: Here and Now*. Antisemitism rises again with ferocity in many countries and in Germany as well, a country once admired for its ability to confront its Holocaust history. One example is Angelos's exploration in "The New German Antisemitism," May 21, 2019.

2. Rothberg calls this "epochal change," historical moments when Holocaust memories enter the public sphere (2009, 27).

References

Abosch, Dr. Sara, and Dr. Charlotte Decoster. 18 May 2015. *Dallas Holocaust Museum* (Personal Interview).

Adorno, Theodor W. 1984. *Aesthetic Theory*. New York: Routledge & K. Paul.

Ahmed, Sara. 2006. *Queer Phenomenology: Orientations, Objects, Others*. Duke University Press.

———. 2015. *The Cultural Politics of Emotion*. New York: Routledge.

Akcan, Esra. 2010. "Apology and Triumph: Memory Transference, Erasure, and a Rereading of the Berlin Jewish Museum." *New German Critique*. Vol. 110, no. 37.2: 153–179.

Alter, Ethan. 2015. "*Son of Saul*." *Film Journal International*. Vol. 118, no. 12 (December): 92–93.

Anti-Defamation League. 2019. *Anti-Defamation League online.* www.adl.org.

Angelos, James. "The New German Antisemitism." *The New York Times Magazine*. NYTimes.com. 21 May 2019. https://www.nytimes.com/2019/05/21/magazine/anti-semitism-germany.html.

Anzaldua, Gloria. 1999. *Borderlands/La Frontera: The New Mestiza*. San Francisco: Aunt Lute Books.

Applegarth. Risa. 2014. *Rhetoric in American Anthropology: Gender, Genre, and Science*. Pittsburgh: University of Pittsburgh Press.

Ash, Timothy Garton. 2007. "The Life of Death": *Shoah*—A Film by Claude Lanzmann." *Claude Lanzmann's Shoah: Key Essays*. Edited by Stuart Liebman. Oxford University Press. 135–148.

Associated Press. 2010. "Eerie Dance of Holocaust Survivor at Concentration Camps." 16 July 2010. NDTV.com.

Austin, John Langshaw (J.L.). 1975. *How to Do Things with Words*. Harvard University Press.

Bachrach, Susan. Project Director. 2004. *Deadly Medicine: Creating the Master Race*. Edited by Dieter Kuntz. Washington D.C.: United States Holocaust Museum.

Baer, Elizabeth Roberts, and Myrna Goldenberg, eds. 2003. *Experience and Expression: Women, the Nazis, and the Holocaust*. Detroit: Wayne State University Press.

Bakhtin, Mikhail. 1991. "Discourse in the Novel." *The Dialogic Imagination: Four Essays*. Translated by Caryl Emerson and Michael Holquist. University of Texas Press. 259–434.

———. *Speech Genres and Other Late Essays*. 1986. Edited by Caryl Emerson and Michael Holquist. Translated by Vern W. McGee. University of Texas Press.

Balog, Katalin. 2016. "Son of Saul, Kierkegaard, and the Holocaust." The Opinionator-Opinion Pages. *New York Times*. 28 February 2016. https://opinionator.blogs.nytimes.com/2016/02/28/son-of-saul-kierkegaard-and-the-holocaust/.

Bartov, Omer. 2000. *Holocaust: Origins, Implementation, Aftermath*. London; New York: Routledge.

———. 1996. *Murder in Our Midst: The Holocaust, Industrial Killing, and Representation*. Oxford University Press.

Baumel, Judith Tydor. 1998. *Double Jeopardy: Gender and the Holocaust*. London: Vallentine Mitchell.

BBC. 2015. "Auschwitz 70th Anniversary: Survivors Warn of New Crimes." Europe page. 27 January 2015. https://www.bbc.com/news/world-europe-30996555.

Beck, Gad, and Frank Heibert. 2000. *An Underground Life: Memoirs of a Gay Jew in Nazi Berlin*. Translated by Alison Brown. Wisconsin University Press.

Beckerman, Gail. 2009. "Local Holocaust Museums Grow Amid Worries about the Future." *The Jewish Daily Forward*. 23 December 2009.

Bernard-Donals, Michael, and Richard Glejzer. 2001. *Between Witness and Testimony: The Holocaust and the Limits of Representation*. New York: State University of New York Press.

Bernard-Donals, Michael. 2010. *Forgetful Memory: Representation and Remembrance in the Wake of the Holocaust*. New York: State University of New York Press.

Blair, Carole. 2001. "Reflections on Criticism and Bodies: Parables from Public Places." *Western Journal of Communication* 65: 271–294.

Blair, Carole, Greg Dickinson, and Brian L. Ott. 2010. "Introduction: Rhetoric/Memory/Place." *The Places of Public Memory: The Rhetoric of Museums and Memorials*. Edited by Greg Dickinson, Carole Blair, Brian L. Ott. Tuscaloosa: University of Alabama Press. 1–54.

Blair, Carole, and Neil Michel. 2000. "Reproducing Civil Rights Tactics: The Rhetorical Performance of the Civil Rights Memorial." *Rhetoric Society Quarterly*. Vol. 30, no. 2 (Spring): 31–55.

Bock, Gisela. 1983. "Racism and Sexism in Nazi Germany: Motherhood, Compulsory Sterilization, and the State." *Signs*. Vol. 8, no. 3 (Spring): 400–421. *Jstor*.

Brittain, Vera. 1957, 1985 (reprint). *Testament of Experience*. Virago.

Broder, Henryk M. 2015. "Dancing Auschwitz: Holocaust Survivor Becomes YouTube Star." *Der Spiegel*. http://www.spiegel.de/international/world/dancing-auschwitz-holocaust-survivor-becomes-youtube-star-a-711247.html.

Brown, Jill. Communications Director, LAMOTH. Personal Interview (e-mail). April 2019.

Butler, Judith. 1993. *Bodies that Matter: On the Discursive Limits of "Sex."* New York: Routledge.

———. 1995. "Burning Acts—Injurious Speech." *Performativity and Performance.* Edited by Andrew Parker and Eve Kosofsky Sedgwick. New York: Routledge. 197–227.

———. 1990. *Gender Trouble: Feminism and the Subversion of Identity.* New York: Routledge.

———. 2009. "Perfomativity, Precarity, and Sexual Politics." Lecture given at Universidad Complutense de Madrid. AIBR. Revista de Antropología Iberoamericana. Volumen 4, Número 3. Septiembre–Diciembre 2009. Pp. i–xiii, Madrid: Antropólogos Iberoamericanos en Red. 8 June 2009. http://www.aibr.org/antropologia/04v03/criticos/040301b.pdf.

Camper, Fred. 2007. "Shoah's Absence." *Claude Lanzmann's Shoah: Key Essays.* Edited by Stuart Liebman. Oxford: Oxford University Press. 103–112.

Carr, Steven Alan. 2016. "*Son of Saul* and the Crisis of the Holocaust." *Film Criticism.* Ann Arbor: Michigan Publishing, University of Michigan. Vol. 40, no. 3: 1–3.

Caruth, Cathy. 1995. Introduction. *Trauma: Explorations in Memory.* Edited by Cathy Caruth. Baltimore: Johns Hopkins University Press. 3–12.

Celan, Paul. 2002. *Poems of Paul Celan: A Bilingual German/English Edition*, Revised and Expanded Edition. Translated by Michael Hamburger. Persea.

Chabad Lubavitch Media Center. 1993, 2017. "The Stages of Jewish Mourning." https://www.chabad.org/library/article_cdo/aid/282506/jewish/The-Stages-of-Mourning-in-Judaism.htm.

Chang, Justin. 2012. "Review: *Numbered.*" *Variety.* U.S. Edition. 11 July 2012. https://variety.com/2012/film/reviews/numbered-1117947885/.

Chevrie, Marc, and Herve Le Roux. 2007. "Site and Speech: An Interview with Claude Lanzmann about *Shoah.*" *Claude Lanzmann's Shoah: Key Essays.* Edited by Stuart Liebman. Oxford: Oxford University Press. 37–50.

Cole, Tim. 2000. *Selling the Holocaust: from Auschwitz to Schindler: How History is Bought, Packaged, and Sold.* New York: Routledge.

Colotla, Victor A. and Samuel Jurado, Ph.D. 2014. "Silenced Voices." *American Psychological Association.* Vol. 45, no. 11. December 2014. http://www.apa.org/monitor/2014/12/silenced-voices.aspx.

Corn, Benjamin. 2012. "Holocaust Film Numbered Reminds Us How Much People Count." *The Jerusalem Post.* Opinion Editorial. 8 August 2012. https://www.jpost.com/Opinion/Op-Ed-Contributors/Holocaust-film-Numbered-reminds-us-how-much-people-count.

Cosslett, Tess. 2000. "Introduction." *Feminism and Autobiography: Texts, Theories, Methods.* Edited by Tess Cosslett, Celia Lury, and Penny Summerfield. New York: Routledge. 1–22.

Costello, Lisa. 2006. "History and Memory in a Dialogic of 'Performative Memorialization' in Art Spiegelman's *Maus: a Survivor's Tale.*" *Journal of the Midwest Modern Language Association (JMMLA).* Vol. 9, no. 2 (Fall): 22–42.

———. 2011. "Performative Auto/biography in Ruth Klüger's Still Alive: A Holocaust Girlhood Remembered." *Auto/Biography Studies* vol. 26, no. 2: 238–264.

———. 2013. "Performative Memory: Form and Content in The Jewish Museum Berlin." *Liminalities* 9.4 (December). http://liminalities.net/9-4/index.html.

Cranley, Ellen. 2019. "Trump and Other Leaders Mark International Holocaust Remembrance Day Amid Rising Anti-Semitism." *Business Insider*. 27 January 2019. https://www.businessinsider.com/trump-marks-holocaust-remembrance-day-2019-amid-rising-anti-semitism-2019-1.

Damasio, Antonio. 2014. "Understanding Testimony: Emotion, Storytelling, and the Human Universals: How personal stories can evoke deep empathy for human tragedy." *PastForward*. USC Shoah Foundation. (Spring): 18. http://sfi.usc.edu/pastforward.

Davidowicz, Lucy S. 1975. *From that Time and Place: A Memoir 1938–1947*. New York: W.W. Norton & Company.

———. 1986. *The War Against the Jews: 1933–1945*. New York: Bantam.

Dear, Michael, and Greg Wassmansdorf. 1993. "Postmodern Consequences." *Geographical Review*. Vol. 83, no. 3 (July): 321–325.

DeBruge, Peter. 2015. "An Unblinking Horror: Laszlo Nemes's *Son of Saul* bears witness to the Holocaust through the Eyes of a Morally Complicit Prisoner." *Variety*. Vol. 330, no. 10 (December): 64–65.

DeCerteau, Michel. 1984. *The Practice of Everyday Life*. Translated by Steve Rendall. Berkeley: University of California Press.

Delbo, Charlotte. 1995. *Auschwitz and After*. Translated by Rosette C. Lamont. Yale University Press.

Devitt, Amy J. 1993. "Generalizing about Genre: New Conceptions of an Old Concept." *College Composition and Communication*. Vol. 44, no. 4: 573–586.

Diamond, Elin. 1995. "The Shudder of Catharsis in Twentieth Century Performance." *Performativity and Performance*. Edited by Andrew Parker and Eve Kosofsky Sedgwick. New York: Routledge.

DiAngelo, Robin. 2012. *What Does It Mean to White? Developing White Racial Literacy*. London: Peter Lang International Publishing.

Didi-Huberman, Georges. 2007. "The Site, Despite Everything." *Claude Lanzmann's Shoah: Key Essays*. Edited by Stuart Liebman. Oxford University Press. 113–124.

Doron, Dana and Uriel Sinai. 2012. *Numbered*. Israel. Directed by Dana Doron and Uriel Sinai.

Douglass, Ana and Thomas A. Vogler, eds. 2003. *Witness and Memory: The Discourse of Trauma*. New York: Routledge.

Douthat, Ross. 2016. "Testimony from Hell." *National Review*. Vol. 68, no. 5 (28 March 2016): 47.

Doward, Jamie. 2017. "New Online Generation Takes Up Holocaust Denial." *The Guardian*. 21 January 2017. https://www.theguardian.com/world/2017/jan/22/online-conspiracy-theories-feed-holocaust-denial.

Edbauer, Jenny. 2005. "Unframing Models of Public Distribution: From Rhetorical Situation to Rhetorical Ecologies." *Rhetoric Society Quarterly*. Vol. 35, no. 4: 5–24.

Eichengreen, Lucille. 2011. *Haunted Memories: Portraits of Women in the Holocaust.* Publishing Works.

Eleftheriou-Smith, Loulla-Mae. 2014. "Anne Frank Arrested 70 years Ago Today: Read her Last Diary Extract." *Independent-UK.* 4 August 2014. https://www.independent.co.uk/news/people/anne-frank-arrested-70-years-ago-today-read-her-last-diary-extract-9646390.html.

Ellsworth, Elizabeth. 2002. "The U.S. Holocaust Museum as a Scene of Pedagogical Address." *Symploke: A Journal for the Intermingling of Literary, Cultural, and Theoretical Scholarship.* Vol. 10, nos. 1–2: 13–31.

Enoch, Jessica. 2013. "Releasing Hold: Feminist Historiography without the Tradition." *Theorizing Histories of Rhetoric.* Edited by Michelle Ballif. Southern Illinois University Press. 58–73.

Ephgrave, Nicole. 2016. "On Women's Bodies: Experiences of Dehumanization during the Holocaust." *Journal of Women's History.* Vol. 28, no. 2 (Summer): 12–32.

Epstein, Julia, and Lori Hope Lefkovitz, eds. 2001. *Shaping Losses: Cultural Memory and the Holocaust.* University of Illinois Press.

Erzahi, Sidra DeKoven. 1980. *By Words Alone: The Holocaust in Literature.* Chicago: The University of Chicago Press.

Fast, Omer. 2003. *Spielberg's List.* Digital Video. Directed by Omer Fast. The Met New York.

Felman, Shoshana, and Dori Laub. 1992. *Testimony: Crises of Witnessing in Literature, Psychoanalysis, and History.* New York: Routledge.

Fink, Ida. 1989. *A Scrap of Time and Other Stories.* New York: Schocken Publishers.

Finkelstein, Norman G. 2000. *The Holocaust Industry: Reflections on the Exploitation of Jewish Suffering.* New York: Verso.

Florida Holocaust Museum. https://www.flholocaustmuseum.org.

Flower, Wayne. 2010. "Melbourne Family's Dance Video Sparks Auschwitz Outrage." *Herald Sun Melbourne.* 13 July 2010.

Fortunoff Archives at Yale. "History." http://www.library.yale.edu/testimonies/about/index.html.

Franklin, Benjamin. 1996. *The Autobiography of Benjamin Franklin.* Dover Thrift Edition. Dover Publications (first edition 1791).

Franklin, Ruth. 2018. "Transported: How Should Children's Books Deal with the Holocaust?" *The New Yorker.* 23 July 2018. https://www.newyorker.com/magazine/2018/07/23/how-should-childrens-books-deal-with-the-holocaust.

Friedlander, Saul. 1992. "Trauma, Transference and 'Working Through' in Writing the History of the Shoah." *History & Memory: Studies in Representations of the Past.* Vol. 4, no. 1 (Spring–Summer): 9–59.

Fuchs, Esther. 1999. *Women in Jewish Life and Culture.* Lincoln: University of Nebraska Press.

Gallagher, Victoria J. 1999. "Memory and Reconciliation in the Birmingham Civil Rights Institute." *Rhetoric and Public Affairs.* Vol. 2, no. 2: 303–320.

Hitchcock, Alfred, and Sidney and Naron Bernstein. 1945. Film/DVD. *German Concentration Camps Factual Survey.* Directed by Alfred Hitchcock and Sidney and Baron Bernstein. Great Britain. (1945, 2014).

Gilbey, Ryan. 2016. "Your Close-up on Hell." *New Statesman* (29 April 2016): 53.

Gire, Dan. 2016. "Son of Saul Makes the Human Cost of Nazis the Focus." *The Daily Herald.* 28 January 2016. https://www.dailyherald.com/article/20160128/entlife/160128958/.

Goldberg, Jeffrey. 2015. "Is It Time for the Jews to Leave Europe?" *The Atlantic.* Accessed 15 April 2015. https://www.theatlantic.com/magazine/archive/2015/04/is-it-time-for-the-jews-to-leave-europe/386279/.

Goldberg, Tehilla R. 2010. "Dancing at Auschwitz." *Intermountain Jewish News.* 29 July 2010.

Goldenberg, Myrna, and Amy Shapiro, eds. 2013. *Different Horrors, Same Hell: Gender and the Holocaust.* Seattle: University of Washington Press.

Gourevitch, Philip. 1993. "Behold now Behemoth." *Harper's Magazine.* 1–12.

Greene, Joshua, and Shiva Kumar. 2011. *Witness: Voices from the Holocaust.* New York: Free Press Publishing. Simon and Schuster.

Grissemann, Stefan. 2015. "Atrocity Exhibitionism: Why Son of Saul is an Opportunistic and Highly Problematic Work of Meta-exploitation." *Film Comment.* 51.6 (November/December): 26–29. Accessed 15 June 2017. https://www.filmcomment.com/article/son-of-saul-lazlo-nemes-con/.

Gross, John. 1994. "Hollywood and the Holocaust." *The New York Review of Books.*

Grossman, Atina. 2007. *Jews, Germans, and Allies: Close Encounters in Occupied Germany.* Princeton University Press.

Halberstam, Jack. 2005. *In a Queer Time and Place: Transgender Bodies, Subcultural Lives.* New York: New York University Press.

———. 2011. *The Queer Art of Failure* (A John Hope Franklin Center Book). Durham: Duke University Press

Hansen, Miriam Bratu. 1997. "Schindler's List Is not Shoah: Second Commandment, Popular Modernism, and Public Memory." *Spielberg's Holocaust: Critical Perspectives on Schindler's List.* Edited by Yosefa Loshitzky. Indiana University Press. 77–103.

Hardman, Anna. 2000. *Women and the Holocaust.* Holocaust Educational Trust Research Papers 1.3.

Harpine, William D. 2004. "What Do You Mean, Rhetoric Is Epistemic?" *Philosophy and Rhetoric.* Vol. 37, no. 4: 335–352.

Hartman, Geoffrey H. 1996. *The Longest Shadow: In the Aftermath of the Holocaust.* Bloomington: Indiana University Press.

Haskins, Ekaterina. 2007. "Between Archive and Participation: Public Memory in the Digital Age." *Rhetoric Society Quarterly* 37: 401–422.

Hawhee, Debra. 2004. *Bodily Arts: Rhetoric and Athletics in Ancient Greece.* University of Texas Press. ProQuest.

Haun, Harry. 2015. "Inside the Inferno." *Film Journal International.* Vol. 118, no. 12 (December): 24–26. http://www.filmjournal.com/features/son-of-saul-laszlo-nemes-geza-rohrig-interview.

Heinemann, Marlene E. 1986. *Gender and Destiny: Women Writers and the Holocaust.* Greenwood Press.

Hilberg, Raul. 1971. *Documents of Destruction; Germany and Jewry, 1933–1945*. Quadrangle Books.

———. 1992. *Perpetrators, Victims, Bystanders: The Jewish Catastrophe 1933–1945*. Harper Collins,

———. 1985. *The Destruction of the European Jews*. Teaneck, NJ: Holmes and Meier.

Hillman, Laura. 2005. *I Will Plant You a Lilac Tree: a Memoir of a Schindler's List Survivor*. New York: Simon & Schuster Books for Young Readers.

——— 2004. Personal interview. 23 December.

Hirsch, Marianne. 1997. *Family Frames: Photographs, Narrative, and Postmemory*. Cambridge: Harvard University Press.

———. 2002. "Feminism and Cultural Memory: An Introduction." *Signs: Journal of Women in Culture and Society* vol. 28 no. 1: 1–19.

———. 2003. "Mourning and Postmemory." *The Holocaust: Theoretical Readings*. Edited by Neil Levi and Michael Rothberg. Newark: Rutgers University Press. 416–422.

———. 2001. "Surviving Images: Holocaust Photographs and the Work of Postmemory."*Visual Culture and the Holocaust*. Edited by Barbie Zelizer. Newark: Rutgers University Press. 215–246.

———. 2012. *The Generation of Postmemory: Writing and Visual Culture after the Holocaust*. New York: Columbia University Press.

Hirsch, Marianne and Leo Spitzer. 2007. "Gendered Translations: Claude Lanzmann's *Shoah*." *Claude Lanzmann's Shoah: Key Essays*. Edited by Stuart Liebman. Oxford University Press. 175–190.

———. 2006. "Testimonial Objects: Memory, Gender, and Transmission. *Poetics Today* 27.2 (Summer): 353–383.

Holocaust. 1978. Television miniseries. United States.

Holocaust Museum Houston. 2005. *10 Years: Remembrance, Education, Hope*. Houston, TX:. Holocaust Museum Houston.

Hooper-Greenhill, Eilean. 1995. "Introduction." *Museum, Media, and Message*. Edited bt Eilean Hooper-Greenhill. New York: Routledge. 1–12.

Horowitz, Sara. 1997. "But Is It Good for the Jews? Spielberg's Schindler and the Aesthetics of Atrocity." *Spielberg's Holocaust: Critical Perspectives on Schindler's List*. Edited by Yosefa Loshitzky. Indiana University Press. 119–139.

———. 2000. "Gender, Genocide, and Jewish Memory." *Prooftexts* Number 1&2 (Winter/Spring): 158–190.

———. 1997. *Voicing the Void: Muteness and Memory in Holocaust Fiction*. New York: State University of New York Press.

Hsu, Hua. 2017. "Stir It Up: the Battle over Bob Marley." *The New Yorker*. 24 July 2017.

Huyssen, Andreas. 1995. *Twilight Memories: Marking Time in a Culture of Amnesia*. New York: Routledge.

Iadonisi, Rick. 1994. "Bleeding History and Owning His [Father's] Story: *Maus* and Collaborative Autobiography." Re-Evaluating the Boundaries of Autobiography: A Special Issue of *The CEA Critic*. Vol. 57, no.1 (Fall): 41–56.

Imdb website. www.Imdb.com.

Internet Encyclopedia of Philosophy. "Gorgias." Accessed 1 July 2017. https://www.iep.utm.edu/gorgias/.

Jackson, Mick. 2016. *Denial,* DVD. Directed by Mick Jackson.

"Jewish Historical Institute, Warsaw." 1998–2017. *Jewish Virtual Library. A Project of American–Israeli Cooperative Enterprise (AICE).* 1998–2017. Accessed 25 May 2017. https://www.jewishvirtuallibrary.org/jewish-historical-institute-warsaw.

Jockusch, Laura. 2007. "*Khurbn Forshung*: Jewish Historical Commissions in Europe, 1943–1949." *JBDI/DIYB. Simon Dubnow Institute Yearbook* 6: 441–473.

Kelly, Keith J. "Entire New Orleans Times Picayune Staff Axed after Sale to Competitor. NYpost.com. 3 May 2019. https://nypost.com/2019/05/03/entire-new-orleans-times-picayune-staff-axed-after-sale-to-competitor/.

Kilday, Gregg. 2015. "Making of *Son of Saul*." *Hollywood Reporter*. Supplement Awards Playbook. (November): 42–48. Accessed 15 June 2017. https://www.hollywoodreporter.com/features/how-son-saul-defied-dangers-838149.

Kimmel, Michael, and Tristan Bridges. 2011. "Masculinity." *Oxford Bibliographies.com*. 27 July 2011.

Klüger, Ruth. 1992. *Weiter Leben: Eine Jugend.* München: Deutscher Taschenbuch Verlag.

———. 2001. *Still Alive: A Holocaust Girlhood Remembered.* New York: Feminist Press.

Knoblach, A. Abby. 2012. "Bodies of Knowledge: Definitions, Delineations, and Implications of Embodied Writing in the Academy." *Composition Studies*. Vol. 40, no. 2: 50–65.

Kobrynskyy, Oleksandr, and Gerd Bayer, eds. 2015. *Holocaust Cinema in the Twenty-First Century: Memory, Images, and the Ethics of Representation.* London: Wallflower Press.

Koch, Gertrud. 2007. "The Aesthetic Transformation of the Image of the Unimaginable: Notes on Claude Lanzmann's *Shoah*." *Claude Lanzmann's Shoah: Key Essays*. Edited by Stuart Liebman. Oxford University Press. 125–134.

Korman, Jane, dir. 2009. Digital video. *Dancing in Auschwitz*. 2009. YouTube.

Kosofsky Sedgwick, Eve. 2003. *Touching Feeling: Affect, Pedagogy, Performativity.* Durham: Duke University Press.

Krekó, Péter. 2014. "Testimony in Action: Anti-Semitism in Hungary: Education is Necessary to Combat Hungary's Troubling Rise in Anti-Semitism." *PastForward*. USC Shoah Foundation. (Spring): 30–31. http://sfi.usc.edu/pastforward.

Kremer, S. Lillian. 1999. *Women's Holocaust Writing: Memory and Imagination.* University of Nebraska Press.

Langer, Lawrence L. 1991. *Holocaust Testimonies: The Ruins of Memory.* Yale University Press.

———. 2000. *Preempting the Holocaust.* Yale University Press.

———. 2006. *Using and Abusing the Holocaust.* Bloomington: Indiana University Press.

Lanzmann, Claude. 2007. "From the Holocaust to 'Holocaust.'" *Claude Lanzmann's Shoah: Key Essays.* Edited by Stuart Liebman. Oxford University Press. 27–36.

———. 1985. *Shoah*. DVD. Directed by Claude Lanzmann. France.

———. 1985/2012. "Shoah Outtakes." *Steve Spielberg Film and Video Archive*. Purchased October 1996. Accessed 1 June 2012, July 2017. United States Holocaust Memorial Museum (USHMM), Washington, D.C.

———. 1996. "Shoah Outtakes—Paula Biren," 1985. *Steven Spielberg Film and Video Archive* (Film ID: 3105–3108). Purchased October 1996. United States Holocaust Memorial Museum (USHMM), Washington, D.C.

———. 1996. "Shoah Outtakes—Ruth Elias," 1985. *Steven Spielberg Film and Video Archive* (Film ID: 3112–3118). Purchased October 1996. United States Holocaust Memorial Museum (USHMM), Washington, D.C.

———. 1996. "Shoah Outtakes—Malka Goldberg," 1985. *Steven Spielberg Film and Video Archive* (Film ID: 3869–3870). Purchased October 1996. United States Holocaust Memorial Museum (USHMM), Washington, D.C.

———. 1996. "Shoah Outtakes—Ada Lichtman," 1985. *Steven Spielberg Film and Video Archive* (Film ID: 3270–3277). Purchased October 1996. United States Holocaust Memorial Museum (USHMM), Washington, D.C.

———. 1996. "Shoah Outtakes—Filip Mueller," 1985. *Steven Spielberg Film and Video Archive* (Film ID: 3206–3215). Purchased October 1996. United States Holocaust Memorial Museum (USHMM), Washington, D.C.

———. 1996. "Shoah Outtakes—Getrude Schneider," 1985. *Steven Spielberg Film and Video Archive* (Film ID: 3221–3225). Purchased October 1996. United States Holocaust Memorial Museum (USHMM), Washington, D.C.

Levi, Primo. 1961. *Survival in Auschwitz: The Nazi Assault on Humanity.* Translated by Stuart Woolf. Collier. Re-Published by Blurb. 2019.

Li, Sherrie. 2013. "A Film Showing Grandchildren of Auschwitz Survivors Who Tattoo their Number on Themselves," *LA Weekly*. 26 April 2013. https://www.laweekly.com/arts/a-film-showing-grandchildren-of-auschwitz-survivors-who-tattoo-the-numbers-on-themselves-4183733.

"Liberation of Nazi Camps." N.d. *Holocaust Encyclopedia*. USHMM. www.ushmm.org.

Liebman, Stuart. 2007. "Introduction." *Claude Lanzmann's Shoah: Key Essays*. Edited by Stuart Liebman. Oxford University Press. 3–26.

———. 2015. "*Son of Saul*." *Cineaste*. 41.1 (Winter): 46–48. Web. Accessed 15 June 2017. https://www.politeianet.gr/magazines/-xena-periodika-cineaste-volume-41-issue-1-winter-20152016-253138.

Libermann, Oren. 2019. "A Holocaust Diary is Reborn on Instagram." *CNN*. Cnn.com. 2 May 2019. https://www.cnn.com/2019/05/02/europe/evas-story-holocaust-instagram-intl/index.html.

Ligocka, Roma, and Iris von Finckenstein. 2003. *The Girl in the Red Coat: A Memoir*. Delta.

Lipstadt, Deborah. 1994. *Denying the Holocaust: The Growing Assault on Truth and Memory*. New York: Plume Reprint.

Los Angeles Museum of the Holocaust. http://lamoth.org.

Love, Meredith. 2018. "Call for Papers." *Conference on College Composition and Communication*, March 2018.

———. 2007. "Composing through the Performative Screen: Translating Performance Studies into Writing Pedagogy." *Composition Studies*. Vol. 35, no. 2 (Fall): 11–30.

Manley, Caroline. Director of Collections and Exhibitions. 2015. *Holocaust Museum Houston* (Personal Interview).

Marcuse, Harold. 2010. "Holocaust Memorials: The Emergence of a Genre." *American Historical Review*. Vol. 115, no. 1: 53–89.

Mastin, Luke. 2008. "Sophism." www.philosophybasics.com. 2008.

Matchan, Linda. 2014. "Schindler's List: Still the 'Definitive Holocaust Drama.'" *Boston Globe*. 26 April 2014. https://www.bostonglobe.com/arts/movies/2014/04/26/schin/JdBVJcVSSF5Iugh2PCM3cP/story.html.

McKenzie, Jon. 1998. "Genre Trouble: (The) Butler Did It." *The Ends of Performance*. Edited by Peggy Phelan and Jill Lane. New York: New York University Press. 217–235.

Melamed, Dr. Valdimir. 2016. Director of Archives, *LAMOTH*. Personal Interview. 17 February 2016.

Menchú, Rigoberta. 1984. *I Rigoberto Menchú: An Indian Woman in Guatemala*. Edited by Elisabeth Burgos-Debray. Translated by Ann Wright. Verso.

Metz, Walter C. 2008. "'Show Me the Shoah!': Generic Experience and Spectatorship in Popular Representations of the Holocaust." *Shofar: An Interdisciplinary Journal of Jewish Studies*. Vol. 27, no. 1: 16–35.

Miller, Carolyn. 1984. "Genre as Social Action." *Quarterly Journal of Speech* 70: 151–167.

Mintz, Alan. 2001. *Popular Culture and the Shaping of Holocaust Memory in America*. The Samuel and Althea Stroum Lectures in Jewish Studies. Seattle: University of Washington Press.

Modlinger, Martin. 2015. "The Ethics of Perspective and the Holocaust Archive: Spielberg's List, the *Boy in the Striped Pyjamas* and *Fateless*." *Holocaust Cinema in the Twenty-First Century: Memory, Images, and the Ethics of Representation*. Edited by Oleksandr Kobrynskyy and Gerd Bayer. Wallflower Press. 161–182.

Mulvey, Laura. 1975. "Visual Pleasure and the Narrative Cinema. *Screen*. Vol. 16, no. 3 (Autumn): 6–18.

Murphy, Mekado. 2016. "Laszlo Nemes Narrates a Scene from 'Son of Saul.'" Movies. *The New York Times*. 21 January 2016. Accessed 15 June 2017. https://www.nytimes.com/2016/01/22/movies/laszlo-nemes-narrates-a-scene-from-son-of-saul.html.

Nemes, László. 2015. DVD. *Son of Saul*. Directed by László Nemes. Sony Classics.

Novick, Peter. 1999. *The Holocaust in American Life*. New York: Houghton Mifflin Co.

Ofer, Dalia, and Lenore J. Weitzman, eds. 1998. *Women in the Holocaust*. Yale University Press.

Oznick, Cynthia. 1990. *The Shawl*. New York: Vintage. Knopf Doubleday Publishing Group.

Parker, Andrew, and Eve Kosofsky Sedgwick. 1995. "Introduction." *Performativity and Performance*. Edited by Andrew Parker and Eve Kosofsky Sedgwick. New York: Routledge. 1–18.

Paterson, Tony. 2010. "Auschwitz 'I Will Survive' Dance Video Is Internet Sensation." *Independent*. 15 July 2010. Accessed 24 August 2015. https://www.independent.co.uk/arts-entertainment/music/news/auschwitz-i-will-survive-dance-video-is-internet-sensation-2027725.html.

Patraka, Vivian. 2001. "Spectacular Suffering: Performing Presence, Absence, and Witness at U.S.Holocaust Museums." *Memory and Representation: Constructed Truths and CompetingRealities*. Edited by Dena Elisabeth Eber and Arthur G. Neal. Bowling Green State University Popular Press 139–166.

———. 1999. *Spectacular Suffering: Theatre, Fascism, and the Holocaust*. Indiana University Press.

Pennebaker, James W., and Becky L. Banasik. 1997. "On the Creation and Maintenance of Collective Memories: History as Social Psychology." *Collective Memory of Political Events: Social Psychological Perspectives*. Edited by James W. Pennebaker, Dario Paez, and Bernard Rimé. Lawrence Erlbaum Associates, Publishers. 3–20.

Peterson, Nancy J. 2002. "Postmodernism and Holocaust Memory: Productive Tensions in the United States Holocaust Memorial Museum." *Productive Postmodernism: Consuming Histories and Cultural Studies*. Edited by John N. Duvall. New York: State University of New York Press. 167–195.

Phelan, Peggy. 1998. "Introduction." *The Ends of Performance*. Edited by Peggy Phelan and Jill Lane. New York: New York University Press. 1–19.

Phillips, Kendall. 2004. "Introduction." *Framing Public Memory*. Edited by Kendall Phillips. University of Alabama Press. E-Book Accessed 15 March 12017.

Plant, Richard. 1988. *The Pink Triangle: The Nazi War Against Homosexuals*. New York: Holt Paperbacks. MacMillan Publishers.

Pollock, Della. 1998. "Performing Writing." *The Ends of Performance*. Edited by Peggy Phelan and Jill Lane. New York: New York University Press. 73–103.

Powell, Lawrence N. 2000. *Troubled Memory: Anne Levy, the Holocaust, and David Duke's Louisiana*. University of North Carolina Press.

———. 2019. "Preface." *Troubled Memory: Anne Levy, the Holocaust, and David Duke's Louisiana*. The University of North Carolina Press. Power, Samantha. 2003. *A Problem from Hell: America and the Age of Genocide*. New York: Perennial.

Reading, Anna. 2002. *The Social Inheritance of the Holocaust: Gender, Culture, and Memory*. New York: Macmillan.

Rensmann, Lars. 2004. "Collective Guilt, National Identity, and Political Processes in Contemporary Germany. *Collective Guilt: International Perspectives*. Edited by Nyla R. Branscombe and Bertjan Doosie. Cambridge University Press. 169–192.

Resnais, Alain. 1955. *Nuit et Broillard*. (*Night and Fog*). Film. Directed by Alain Resnais. France.

Rice, Jenny, and Jeff Rice. 2014. "18 Pop-up Archives." *Rhetoric and the Digital Humanities*. Edited by Jim Ridolfo and William Hart-Davidson, Chicago: University of Chicago Press, 245–254.

Ringelheim, Joan, and Ester Katz. 1983. *Proceedings of the Conference on Women Surviving the Holocaust*. Institute for Research in History.

Rittner, Carol Ann, and John K. Roth, eds. 1993. *Different Voices: Women and the Holocaust*. New York: Paragon House.

Roach, Joseph. 1995. "Culture and Performance in the Circum-Atlantic World." *Performativity and Performance*. Edited by Andrew Parker and Eve Kosofsky Sedgwick. New York: Routledge. 45–63.

Romney, Jonathan. 2015. "Dead Man Walking." *Film Comment*. Vol. 51, no. 6 (November/December): 22–25. https://www.filmcomment.com/article/son-of-saul-lazlo-nemes-pro/.

Rosen, Alan. 2009. "David Boder: Early Postwar Voices: David Boder's Life and Work." *Voices of the Holocaust*. Paul V. Gavin Library. Illinois Institute of Technology. Accessed 15 May 2017. https://voices.iit.edu.

———. 2012. *The Wonder of Their Voices: The 1946 Holocaust Interviews of David Boder*. Oxford: Oxford University Press.

Rosenfeld, Alvin H. 2013. *The End of the Holocaust*. Bloomington: Indiana University Press.

Rotem Shosh, Stephanie. 2013. "The Construct of Memory." *Architectural Narratives of Holocaust Museums*. Berlin: Peter Lang.

Rothberg, Michael. 2009. *Multidirectional Memory: Remembering the Holocaust in the Age of Decolonization*. Stanford: Stanford University Press.

Rothstein, Edward. 2011. "The Memory of the Holocaust, Fortified." *The New York Times*. 22 April 2011. Accessed 31 January 2012. https://www.nytimes.com/2011/04/23/arts/design/illinois-holocaust-museum-education-center-in-skokie-review.html?mtrref=r.search.yahoo.com&gwh=879875EB2E09A7AB986C08291EB2A522&gwt=pay.

Rudoren, Jodi. 2012. "Proudly Bearing Elders' Scars, Their Skin Says 'Never Forget.'" *The New York Times*. www.nytimes.com. 30 September 2012. Accessed 28 March 2014. https://www.nytimes.com/2012/10/01/world/middleeast/with-tattoos-young-israelis-bear-holocaust-scars-of-relatives.html?mtrref=r.search.yahoo.com&gwh=8F8B49477B61020BCF529C1C10B9A563&gwt=pay.

Saint Augustine. 2002. *The Confessions of Saint Augustine*. Translated by E. B. Pusey. Project Gutenberg. Released online June 2002. Accessed 15 July 2017. www.gutenberg.org.

Sanderlin, Elena. Assistant to the Director. 2015. *Florida Holocaust Museum* (Personal Interview). 18 March 2015.

Santora, Marc, and Joanna Berendt. 2018. "Poland's Leader Finds an Ally in Trump even as He Brings Courts to Heel." *The New York Times*. 17 September 2018. www.nytimes.com.

Sarfatti Larson, Magali. 1997. "Reading Architecture in the Holocaust Memorial Museum: A Method and an Empirical Illustration." *From Sociology to Cultural Studies: New Perspectives*. Edited by Elizabeth Long. Blackwell Publishers. 62–91.

Satlin, Alana Horowitz. 2017. "Donald Trump Pays Tribute to Holocaust Victims While Banning Refugees: His Statement also Never Actually Mentions the Jewish People." *Huffington Post online*. www.Huffpost.com. 27 January 2017.

Schechner, Richard. 1998. "What Is Performance Studies Anyway?" *The Ends of Performance*. Edited by Peggy Phelan and Jill Lane. New York: New York University Press. 357–362.

Schultz, Debra. 2016. *Going South: Jewish Women in the Civil Rights Movement*. New York: New York University Press.

"Searching for Meaning After a Jewish Cemetery Is Desecrated." 2017. *Fresh Air Radio Show*. National Public Radio. 1NPR.org. 16 March 2017. Accessed 20 July 2017.

Segal, Lynne. 2012. *Out of Time: The Pleasures and the Perils of Aging*. London: Verso.

Sherwood, Harriet. 2017. "Reports of Antiseimitic Incidents Increase to Record Levels in the UK." *The Guardian*. 1 February 2017. Accessed 26 July 2017. https://www.theguardian.com/world/2017/feb/02/reports-of-antisemitic-incidents-increase-to-record-levels-in-uk.

Sicher, Efraim, Editor. 1998. *Breaking the Crystal: Writing and Memory after Auschwitz*. University of Illinois Press.

Siegal, Nina. 2017. "Anne Frank Who? Museums Combat Ignorance about the Holocaust." *New York Times*. www.nytimes.com. 21 March 2017. Web. Accessed 26 July 2017. https://www.nytimes.com/2017/03/21/arts/design/anne-frank-house-anti-semitism.html

Simon, Scott (host). 2011. "Ben Kingsley on Portraying Holocaust History." Interview. "Weekend Edition." *National Public Radio (NPR)*. 19 March 2011. Accessed 17 July 2017.

Sivlov, C. 1947. *Nuremberg Trials*. Film. Directed by C. Sivlov Soviet Union.

Smith, Stephen D. 2014. "Refinding the Past: The Last of the Unjust." Interview with Claude Lanzmann." *PastForward*. USC Shoah Foundation. Spring (2014): 32–33. Accessed 13 June 2017. http://sfi.usc.edu/pastforward.

Spiegelman, Art. 1986. *Maus: A Survivor's Tale I: My Father Bleeds History*. New York: Pantheon.

———. 1991. *Maus: A Survivor's Tale II: And Here My Troubles Began*. New York: Pantheon.

Stephens, Bret. Book Review. *Antisemitism: Here and Now* by Deborah Lipstadt. NYTimes.com. 30 January 2019. https://www.nytimes.com/2019/01/30/books/review/deborah-e-lipstadt-antisemitism.html?searchResultPosition=1.

Stier, Oren Baruch. 2005. "Different Trains: Holocaust Artifacts and the Ideologies of Remembrance." *Holocaust and Genocide Studies*. Vol. 19, no.1: 81–106.

Striff, Erin. 2003. "Introduction: Locating Performance Studies." *Performance Studies*. Edited by Erin Striff. Houndsmills: Palgrave Macmillan. 1–13.

Taylor, Kate. 2015. "We Wanted to Give Back Dignity to the Dead." *The Globe and Mail (Canada)*. 26 December 2015. R12. Lexis Nexis. Accessed 20 June 2017.

Tec, Nechama. 1987. *When Light Pierced the Darkness: Christian Rescue of Jews in Nazi-Occupied Poland*. Oxford: Oxford University Press.

The Auschwitz-Birkenau museum website. 2015. "The Seventieth Anniversary of the Liberation of Auschwitz." Accessed 18 January 2016. Państwowe Muzeum Auschwitz-Birkenau w Oświęcimiu.

The World at War. 1973. DVD. Imperial War Museum in cooperation with Thames Television. 26 episodes. UK.

Toporek Finder, Esther. 2014. "The Legacy of Testimony: The Next Generation." *PastForward*. USC Shoah Foundation. (Spring): 10–11. Accessed 13 June 2017. http://sfi.usc.edu/pastforward.

Turan, Kenneth. 1993. "Restraint From the Master of Razzmatazz: 'Schindler's List' is a major departure for Steven Spielberg. He and his collaborators have created an indelible picture of the Holocaust." Film Review. *LA Times*. 15 December 1993. Web. Accessed 21 June 2017. http://articles.latimes.com/1993-12-15/entertainment/ca-1949_1_steven-spielberg.

"Twenty years later: The Legacy of *Schindler's List* and the USC Shoah Foundation." 2014. Special Anniversary Feature. *PastForward*. USC Shoah Foundation. (Spring): 19–21. Web. Accessed 13 June 2017. http://sfi.usc.edu/pastforward.

Tydor-Baumel, Judith, and Tova Cohen Editors. 2003. *Gender, Place and Memory in the Modern Jewish Experience: Re-Placing Ourselves.* New York: Vallentine.

United States Holocaust Memorial Museum. 2007. "Excerpts from the President's Commission Report." *Holocaust Encyclopedia*. 6 April 2007. Accessed 15 April 2007. www.ushmm.org.

United States Holocaust Memorial Museum. n.d. *Holocaust Encyclopedia.* Entry: "Writing News." Search Term: 1936 German newspaper. Accessed 25 July 2017. www.ushmm.org.

United States Holocaust Memorial Museum. n.d. *Holocaust Encyclopedia.* Entry: Combating Holocaust Denial: Evidence of the Holocaust Presented at Nuremberg. Search Term: "Nuremberg Testimonies." Accessed 17 March 2017. www.ushmm.org.

United States Holocaust Memorial Museum. n.d. *Holocaust Encyclopedia.* Entry: "International Holocaust Remembrance Day" Accessed 17 March 2017. www.ushmm.org.

United States Holocaust Memorial Museum. n.d. "Memorial Books A-G." Accessed 25 July 2017. www.ushmm.org.

United States Holocaust Memorial Museum. n.d. 'Mission Statement." Accessed 7 April 2007. www.ushmm.org.

United States Holocaust Memorial Museum. 1996. "Shoah Outtakes." *Steven Spielberg Film and Video Archive*. First Accessed 1 June 2012.

United States Holocaust Memorial Museum. n.d. *Traveling Exhibitions.* "Deadly Medicine: Creating the Master Race." Accessed 6 June 2017. www.ushmm.org.

USC Shoah Foundation: The Institute for Visual History and Education. 2007–2017. *Visual History Archive*, "About/Collecting." University of Southern California. 2007–2017. Accessed 13 June 2017. https://sfi.usc.edu/vha/collecting.

USC Shoah Foundation: The Institute for Visual History and Education. 2007–2017. *Visual History Archive*, "Home/About Us." University of Southern California. 2007–2017. Accessed 13 June 2017. https://sfi.usc.edu/vha/home/aboutus.

Vick, Karl. 2005. "Iran's President Calls Holocaust 'Myth' in Latest Assault on Jews." *The Washington Post*, A Section; A01, 15 December 2005. Final Edition. *LexisNexis.* Accessed 2 February 2006.

Vinciguerra, Thomas J., ed. 2001. *Conversations with Elie Wiesel: Elie Wiesel and Richard D. Heffner*, Schocken Books.
Visual Culture and the Holocaust. 2001. Edited by Barbie Zelizer. Newark: Rutgers University Press.
Vivian, Bradford. 2012. "The Paradox of Regret: Remembering and Forgetting the History of Slavery in George W. Bush's Goree Island Address." *History and Memory*. Vol. 24, no. 1 (Spring/Summer): 5–38.
"Voices Project." 2009. *Voices of the Holocaust.* Paul V. Gavin Library. Illinois Institute of Technology. Accessed 15 May 2017. https://voices.iit.edu.
Wachsmann, Nikolaus. 2016. "Nightmare of Crime." *Sight and Sound*. Vol. 26, no. 5 (May): 18–20. Web. Accessed 15 June 2017.
Wagner-Pacifici, Robin, and Barry Schwartz. 1991. "The Vietnam Veterans Memorial: Commemorating a Difficult Past." *American Journal of Sociology*. Vol. 97, no. 2 (September): 376–420.
Wajnryb, Ruth. 2001. *The Silence: How Tragedy Shapes Talk*. Crow's Nest NSW: Allen & Unwin.
Waxman, Zoë. 2004. "Testimony and Representation." *The Historiography of the Holocaust*. Edited by Dan Stone. Palgrave Macmillan. 487–507.
Waxman, Zoë Vania. 2006. *Writing the Holocaust : Identity, Testimony, Representation*. Oxford: Oxford University Press.
Wiesel, Elie. 1999. *And the Sea Is Never Full: Memoirs 1969–*. Translated by Marion Wiesel. New York: Alfred A. Knopf.
———. 1990. *From the Kingdom of Memory: Reminiscences*. New York: Summit Books, Simon & Schuster.
———. 2006. *Night.* Translated by Marion Wiesel. New York: Hill and Wang.
———. 1960. *Night.* Translated by Stella Rodway. New York: Bantam Books.
———. (1960; 2006) *The Dawn Trilogy*. Translated by Frances Frenaye. New York: Hill and Wang.
Wieviorka, Annette. 2006. *The Era of Witness*. Translated by Jared Stark. New York: Cornell University Press.
Wilder, Billy. 1945. *Death Mills*. Film. Directed by Billy Wilder, United States.
Wilkomirski, Binjamin. 1996. *Fragments: Memories of a Wartime Childhood*. Translated by Carol Brown. New York: Janeway Shocken Books.
Wineburg, Sam, Susan Mosborg, Dan Porat, and Ariel Duncan. 2007. "Common Belief and the Cultural Curriculum: An Intergenerational Study of Historical Consciousness." *American Educational Research Journal*. Vol. 44, no. 1 (March): 40–76.
Wodak, Ruth. 1997. Introduction. *Gender and Discourse.* Edited by Ruth Wodak. Sage. 1–20.
Wohl, Michael J. A., and Nyla R. Branscombe. 2004. "Importance of Social Categorization for Forgiveness and Collective Guilt Assignment for the Holocaust." *Collective Guilt: International Perspectives*. Edited by Nyla R. Branscombe and Bertjan Doosie. Cambridge: Cambridge University Press. 284–308.
Young, James E. 2002. *At Memory's Edge: After Images of the Holocaust in Contemporary Art and Achitecture.* Yale University Press.

———. 1993. *The Texture of Memory: Holocaust Memorials and Meaning*. Yale University Press.

———. 2008. "The Texture of Memory: Holocaust Memorials in History." *Cultural Memory Studies: An International and Interdisciplinary Handbook*. Walter de Gruyter, 357–365.

Young, James. 1988. *Writing and Rewriting the Holocaust: Narrative and the Consequences of Interpretation*. Indiana University Press.

Zacharek, Stephanie. 2016. "In the Midst of Atrocity, Son of Saul Seeks Grace." *TIME*. Vol. 187, no. 2 (25 January 2016): 62. Accessed 15 June 2017.

Zelizer, Barbie. 1997. "Every Once in Awhile: Schindler's List and the Shaping of History." *Spielberg's Holocaust: Critical Perspectives on Schindler's List*. Edited by Yosefa Loshitzky. Indiana University Press. 18–40.

———. 2001. "Introduction." *Visual Culture and the Holocaust*. Edited by Barbie Zelizer. Newark: Rutgers University Press. 1–12.

———. 2001. "Gender and Atrocity: Women in Holocaust Photographs." *Visual Culture and the Holocaust*. Newark: Rutgers University Press, 247–272.

Zelizer, Barbie, Editor. 2001. "*Visual Culture and the Holocaust*. Newark: Rutgers University Press.

Zerofsky, Elisabeth. 2018. "Is Poland Retreating from Democracy?" *The New Yorker*. 30 July 2018. 18–24. https://www.newyorker.com/magazine/2018/07/30/is-poland-retreating-from-democracy.

Index

absence, 31, 59; of condemnation, 185; evocative performative and, 99

access, 50n22, 161; archives and, 78; digital media and, 45; films and, 53–54; to outtakes, 87; stories and, 34

action, 113, 115n7, 190; connection and, 182n40; memory performance and, 76–79; present and, 142; responsibility and, 170; voice and, 108–11

activism, 109; women and, 111, 114n1

ADL. *See* Anti Defamation League

affect, 3, 38, 152, 163; audiences and, 137–43; connection and, 53–54, 80; museums and wonder as, 153–54; orientations toward, 69–72

affective anchor, 163, 164–65; FHM and, 170

affective attachments, 153

affective investment, 159

after-affect: *Schindler's List* and, 51–81; *Son of Saul* and, 66–67

agency, 43, 60; performative consequential as, 173; survivors and, 136; voice and, 31

Ahmed, Sara, 10; community of witnesses by, 90; on emotion, 138; on orientations, 28; queering orientations by, 153

ambiguity, 26, 59, 85n35; performative incursion and, 139

Anne Frank: Diary of a Young Girl (Frank), 165

Anti Defamation League (ADL), 79, 128

antisemitism, 14–15, 21n29

anxiety, 70

Anzaldua, Gloria, 11, 26–27

AP. *See* Associated Press

apathy, 101

aperture, 78; rhetoric and, 61

appropriateness, 127

Arbeit Macht Frei gate, 129, 138

archives, 48n12; access and, 78; education and, 79; LAMOTH and, 183n42; online, 80; platform for, 85n39–86n44; testimony, 23–47

art, 60, 82n17; exhibitions and, 108; *Shoah* as, 30, 48n5

artifacts, 7, 138, 148n29; after-affect and, 77; performance of, 13; relationships and, 114; speech acts as, 55

asphyxiation, 99

Associated Press (AP), 140

atrocity, 93, 104, 148n22

audiences, 40, 56; address to, 103; affect in, 137–43; connection and, 45; dialog with, 17; disorientation of, 42; distance and, 71, 83n20; manipulation of, 41; memory performance and, 45–46; museums and, 156; orientations and, 3, 58–61; readiness of, 97; responses from, 178; in United States, 58, 103
Auschwitz camp, 38, 96, 129; tattoos and, 132
auto/biography, 114n2; collaboration and, 100, 107; memoirs and, 88, 93; performative public memory and, 90–92; women and, 94

Baer, Elisabeth, 94
Balog, Katalin, 69; on Nemes, 77
Baumel, Judith Tydor, 20n20
behaviors, 104, 134, 148n30; bystander and, 32; connection to, 113
being moved, 52
Berlin Wall, 100
Bernard-Donals, Michael, 9, 52
Bernstein, Sidney, 126
bias, 109, 117n19
binaries, 13, 83n22; both/and as, 37, 188; breaks with, 58–61; *Dancing in Auschwitz* video and, 129–31; disruption of, 36; emotion and, 152; good/evil as, 58–59; *Shoah* and, 29–33. *See also specific binaries*
binary representations, 30; deconstruction of, 72–76, 103
Biren, Paula, 40
bodies, 72, 74, 178; degradation of, 124, 125, 126; emotions and, 52; films and, 144; reclamation of, 121–46; stories and, 137
Bondy, Ruth, 132
books, 8–9
Bratu-Hansen, Miriam, 68
burials, 72, 74
bystanders, 35, 60, 188; behaviors and, 32

camp sites: film and, 29. *See also specific camps*
Carter, Jimmy, 157
cemeteries, 14, 21n30
de Certeau, Michel, 134
Charlottesville, Virginia, 185
children, 36, 182n36; survivors as, 6, 100
chronos, 7
cinematography, 71, 83n19
Civil Rights movement, 98
collaboration, 48n9, 170, 182n38; auto/biography and, 100, 107; education and, 158; memory work and, 89; Powell in, 99, 109; texts as, 114nn1–2; women and, 49n16
collective memory, 95
commissions, 49n21
commodification, 60
community, 90; connection with, 113; context of museums, 158–62; spaces for memorial and, 151–79; viewing community, 55–56, 81n6
community of witnesses, 90
confrontation, 101, 112
connection, 75, 182n40; action and, 182n40; affect and, 53–54, 80; audiences and, 45; behaviors and, 113; community and, 113; discourse and, 27; generations and, 135; humanity and, 43; importance of, 140; relationship of, 139; reorientation and, 37–40
construction, 11–12, 91; process of, 26
content, 152
context, 95, 118n25, 138; community context, 158–62; re-contextualization and, 167; representations and, 166
conversations, 17
corpses, 39
countermovement, 113
crematoria, 68, 74
Cultural Politics of Emotion (Ahmed), 10, 52
Czechoslovakia, 42–43

Dallas Holocaust Museum (DHM), 159–60, *160*; Frank and, 165–66, *166*
Dancing in Auschwitz (video), 121, *130*; bodies and, 127–28
death, 139; mourning of, 143–44
deconstruction, 47; of binary representations, 72–76, 103
defamiliarization, 126, 129, 137, 147n15
deferred memories, 115n7; women and, 87–114
degradation, 146n2; of bodies, 124, 125, 126; spaces of, 127
dehumanization, 76
Delbo, Charlotte, 92, 118n28
descendents, 1
Deutschkron, Inge, 32
devices, 55
DHM. *See* Dallas Holocaust Museum
dialogic, 112, 115n4; between survivors, 91
diaspora, 130
difference, 9, 101, 105; orientations to, 97; repetition of, 165; settings and, 135
Different Voices (anthology), 9
dignity, 71
discomfort, 42
discourse, 118n32; connection and, 27
discovery, 10
disorientations, 28; audiences and, 42; memory work and, 101
Displacement Camps (DP), 92, 106
disrespect, 104
disruption, 34, 36, 48n9; of gender binaries, 91; reclamation and, 128
distance: audiences and, 71, 83n20; emotions and, 60
distribution, 189
diversity, 68
documentaries, 14, 46, 121; objectivity and, 60; representation and, 125; *Shoah* as, 30; Spielberg on, 59
documents, 114n3
Doron, Dana, 131; encounter by, 133
Doward, Jamie, 16

DP. *See* Displacement Camps
Duke, David, 87, 107–8, 110; business and, 113; embrace by, 185

education, 85n40, 152, 182n32; archives and, 79; benefit of, 88; collaboration and, 158; Frank diary in, 165; LAMOTH and, 177; technology and, 80
effect. *See* impact
Eichengreen, Lucille, 94
Eichmann, Adolph, 97
Elias, Ruth, 32; reproductive choice and, 44; testimony of, *38*, 38–39
emotion, 33, 44, 74, 122; Ahmed on, 138; binaries and, 152; body and, 52; distance and, 60; evocation of, 64–65; facts and, 110; humanity and, 75; as inescapable, 141; movement and, 178; truth and, 38; wonder and, 154
engagement, 29
Erzahi, Sidra, 93; on motives, 94
events, 14, 18n5; art and, 30; as genocide, 126; memorialization and, 17; representations of, 57
exhibitions, 108; imagery and, 167; sound and, 177
expectations, 134
experiences, 99, 131; complexity of, 152; as human, 1; museums and, 153; of *Sonderkommando*, 41–43; writing about, 106

facts, 126; clarification of, 95; emotion and, 110
false binaries, 35
family, 145
Fast, Omar, 61
fear, 111; of judgment, 93
Felman, Shoshana, 55, 82n9, 97
feminism, 20n20; feminist perspectives and, 8, 93; memory work and, 156
FHM. *See* Florida Holocaust Museum
fiction: construction of, 61–63; memory and, 62; truth and, 69

films, 13, 83n18, 126; access and, 53–54; access to outtakes of, 87; after-affect of, 51–81; approach to, 59; bodies and, 144; camp sites and, 29; edit of, 35; Nemes on, 64; *Son of Saul*, 63–66
Finkelstein, Norman, 18n9
Finsi, Maurice, 136–37
Florida Holocaust Museum (FHM), *161*, 161–62; Frank and, 169–70
Foxman, Abraham, 128, 145
Frank, Anne, 48nn3–4, 82n14, 181n30; affective anchor as, 164–65
freedom, 103
function, 65, 132; *kairotic* force and, 78

Gallup Poll, 109
Gaynor, Gloria, 130
gaze, 134, 148n26
Gelles, Ayal, 122, 141–42, *142*
gender, 8, 19nn17–18, 20n20; guards and, 104; museums and, 151–79; norms and, 72–76; performance and, 2, 23–47; rhetoric and, 25–27; spheres and, 91
gender binaries: disruption of, 91; emotions and, 52; representation of, 31, 49n14; subversion of, 44
gender orientation, 33–37
gender performance, 151–79
gender roles, 98; subversion of, 107
generations, 133; interactions between, 135; texts and, 121–46
genocide, 18n5, 21n31, 179n2; events as, 126; testimony and, 80–81
genre, 53, 147n10; adherence to, 126; Holocaust and, 69; museum spaces as, 163
Germany, 88, 111, 128
gestures, 70
Goldberg, Malka, 36
Gorgias, 8, 19n14
grief, 73
Gross, Jon, 57

Halberstam, Jack, 12
Hardman, Anna, 9, 10
Haskins, Ekaterina, 33–34
hate, 17
Hawhee, Debra, 7; on *kairos*, 56
heroism, 170
Hillman, Laura, 96, 118n25
Hirsch, Marianne, 4, 5, 7, 18n2, 147n15; on position, 32; on postmemory, 147n19
historians, 7, 138; truth and, 101–2
historiographic context, 25–26
history, 4, 62; fear and, 111; memory and, 5, 155; museums as, 177–78; of sites, 160
HMH. *See* Holocaust Museum Houston
Holocaust, 1; facts and, 95; genre and, 69; media and, 78; myth of, 60; in public memory, 2; representations and, 4–6; trauma of, 153
Holocaust denial, 4, 50n24, 86n45, 119n40; publicity and, 56; Rockwell and, 107
Holocaust Museum Houston (HMH), *160*, 160–61; Frank and, 166–67, *167*
Holocaust studies, 12–14
homosexuality, 117n20
hope, 140
Hull, Harry, 99
humanity, 164; connection and, 43; emotion and, 75; warning to, 94
Hungarian National Film Fund, 67
Hungary, 15
hyper-nationalism, 47

ideals, 23
identity, 11, 168; fragility of, 91, 101; masculinity and, 60; memory and, 102; national identity, 103, 157, 164
ideology, 50n24; associations with, 21; neo-Nazi, 89
imagery, 65, 166; counterpoints to, 68; exhibitions and, 167; before Nazis, 183n46; replicas of, 135; trauma and, 124

immigrants, 122; immigration bans, 16
impact, 54; culture and, 57; visitors and, 152, 178
indifference, 72, 161; resistance and, 75
information, 18n9, 28, 170; details and, 34; memory and, 102
intergenerational dialogue, 111–13
the Internet, 15
intimacy, 153; affect and, 143; museums and, 159
Isakson, Siegi, 160–61
isolation, 133
"I Will Survive" (Gaynor), 130

kairos, 8; Hawhee on, 56; motive to tell and, 94–97; of public memory, 25–33
kairotic effect, 33–37
kairotic force, 7; function as, 78; meaning of, 113; of sites, 159
kairotic moments, 39
Kanada, 73
Kingsley, Ben, 82n14
KKK. *See* Ku Klux Klan
Klüger, Ruth, 88, 188; performative citational and, 100–105
knowledge, 105, 115n9; absence of, 99; realignment of, 102
Korman, Adolek, *127*
Korman, Jane, 14, 121; *Dancing in Auschwitz* video by, 127
Krekó, Péter, 66
Kremer, Lillian, 20n21
Ku Klux Klan (KKK), 107

labels, 130
LAMOTH. *See* Los Angeles Museum of the Holocaust
Langer, Lawrence, 152
language, 51, 112, 119n35; sensory diversity and, 68
Lanzmann, Claude, 13, 146n6; dedication to, 23–25
Larson, Magali Sarfatti, 155
Laub, Dori, 55, 82n9, 97
letters, 106, 110

Levi, Primo, 18n4, 84, 92, 115n3, 116n14
Levinas, Emmanuel, 52
Levy, Anne, 87; on fear of judgment, 93; memoir by, 89
Levy, Ruth, 89; performative evocative and, 97–100
Lichtman, Ada, 36
lies, 70
life, 74, 103; celebration of, 143–44
Lipstadt, Deborah, 16, 119n40
listening, 92–94; memory performance and, 40–46
locations, 123–24
Los Angeles Museum of the Holocaust (LAMOTH), 162, *162*, 181n28; archives and, 183n42; education and, 177; Frank and, 167–68, *168*

manipulation, 41
Manley, Carol, 160, 181n23
mapping, 58
masculinity, 44; gender norms and, 72–76; identity and, 60; privilege and, 82n8
mastery/domination, 35
material traces, 131
meaning, 62, 141, 146n8; sites of, 134; tattoos and, 136; terminology and, 188
media, 55, *130*; access and, 45; Holocaust and, 78; reactions to, 139; social media and, 47
memoirs, 18n4, 84n24, 117n20, 118n28; autobiography and, 88, 93; as episodic, 93; by Hillman, 96; of Levy, A., and R., 89; women and, 85n36
memorial acts, 132
memorialization, 5; books on, 8–9; events and, 17; mourning and, 140; online, 33–34; perspectives on, 140–41; theoretical framework and, 26
memorial making, 26, 48n6

memorials, 151–79
memory, 2, 17; building and texts, 112; fiction and, 62; history and, 5, 155; identity and, 102; as imagined, 102; metonymy and, 62–63; occlusion of, 145; tools and, 80; value and, 91; writing and, 88. *See also specific types of memory*
memory objects, 126–27; tattoos as, 132
memory performance, 82n14; action and, 76–79; audiences and, 45–46; listening and, 40–46; position and, 129; social responsibility as, 170–75
memory work, 114; collaboration and, 89; disorientation of, 101; feminism and, 156
mestiza consciousness, 11, 26–27
metonymy, 59; memory and, 62–63; performance and, 64; unknown and, 65
Mintz, Alan, 80
Modlinger, Martin, 62
morality, 83n23; privilege of choice, 93
mourning, 85n33, 142; of death, 143–44; memorialization and, 140
Mueller, Filip, 41–43, *42*
multidirectional memory, 5, 16
museums, 85n38, 180nn18–19; audience and, 156; gender performance and, 151–79
myth, 60

Nachshon, Abramo, 122, 141–42, *142*
names, 112
narratives, 39, 133; deferred memory as, 90, 99; national identity and, 103, 157, 164; receptivity of, 97; truth and, 64
nationalism, 4
Nazis, 96, 104; ideology and, 21; imagery before, 183n46; propaganda and, 15
Nemes, László, 63–66; Balog on, 77
Neo-fascism, 14

neo-Nazism, 89; businesses and, 113; in United States, 98
New Orleans States-Item newspaper, 106
Night (Wiesel), 96, 116n14, 117n23
non-binary, 143–44, 155; representations as, 188
Novick, Peter, 18n9
Numbered documentary, 121; body reclamation in, 131–37
Nuremberg trials, 1

objectivity, 60, 61, 162
occlusion, 95, 119n38, 145
orientations, 27–29, 153; affect and, 69–72; Ahmed on, 28; audiences and, 3, 58–61; to difference, 97; shift in, 137–43
other, 146n1; construction of, 65

Palestine, 81n1
passive/active binary, 32
past, 141; subjective affects and, 163–64
patriarchy, 60
performance, 89; artifacts and, 13; construction and, 11–12; gender and, 2, 23–47; metonymy and, 64
performative citational, 100–105
performative consequential, 158–62; agency and, 173; museum outreach and, 175–77
performative counterpressure, 91, 101, 102, 165, 166, 169
performative evocative, 97–100
performative incursion, 139
performative public memory, 90–92
performative subjectivity, 91; reorientation and, 105–8
perspectives, 2, 79; feminist, 8, 93; importance of, 13; on memorialization, 140–41; *Numbered* documentary and, 122; reorientation of, 125–27; on research, 110; on tattoos, 132; texts and, 88
phere, 7, 56, 71
phere of kairos, 90

place, 123; reclamation of, 124–25; USHMM space and, 157–58
point of view, 68
Poland, 51, 81n2; immigrants from, 122
Pollock, Della, 58, 96, 123–24, 144
position, 129
possibility, 153
postmemory, 6, 147n19
Powell, Lawrence, 89, 106; collaboration with, 99; on Levy, A., 109
Preempting the Holocaust (Langer), 152
present, 112; action in, 142
pride, 135
privilege: masculinity and, 82n8; moral choice as, 93
propaganda, 15
public memory, 5, 48n9, 155; choice and, 61–63; gender and performance in, 23–47; Holocaust in, 2; performative public memory, 90–92; progression of, 7; re-opening of, 54–58; reorientation of, 66–67; rhetoric and, 6–11; *Son of Saul* and, 63–66; terminology and, 81n4

queer, 153; terminology as, 3
Queer Phenomenology (Ahmed), 10–11, 58

Rabinowitz, Helen, 135–37, *137*
racism, 14, 98, 107
rationality, 33
reclamation: bodies and, 121–46; place and, 124–25
re-contextualization, 167
reflections, 101; Spielberg and, 77
relationships, 62; artifacts and, 114; of connection, 139
reorientation, 28, 105; connection and, 37–40; performative subjectivity and, 105–8; of perspectives, 125–27; of public memory, 66–67
representability, 155
representations, 20n20; context and, 166; documentaries and, 125; events and, 57; of gender binaries, 31, 49n14; as genderless, 156; Holocaust and, 4–6; as non-binary, 188; tattoos as, 136; Zelizer on, 65
research, 110
resilience, 67; of women, 39
resistance, 10, 31; indifference and, 75; women and, 37–38, 73
Resnais, Alain, 126
respect, 104, 148n32
revisionists, 57, 109. *See also* Holocaust denial
Reynolds, Nedra, 123
rhetoric, 4, 115n9; aperture and, 61; gender and, 25–27; public memory and, 6–11
rhetorical performative, 154–57
rhetorical triangle, 189
Rickey, Beth, 113
Robinson, Norman, 113
Rockwell, George Lincoln, 98; denial and, 107
Rosenfeld, Alvin H., 62
Rosenzweig, Vera, 134–35, *135*
Rothberg, Michael, 5

Schindler, Oskar, 77, 82n15, 96
Schindler's List (film), 51–81
scholars, 12, 20n24
screenshots, *130*
Sedgwick, Kosofsky, 12
Selektions, 102
self-reflection, 101
sex, 34
sexism, 60
Shoah (film), 13, 48n5; testimony archive and, 23–47
Simon Wiesenthal Center, 108
Sinai, Uriel, 131
sites, 123, 161, 179n8; data from, 154; history of, 160; *kairotic* force of, 159; of meaning, 134; of trauma, 128
situs, 123
Smith, Stephen, 58
Sobibor death camp, 36

social responsibility, 170–75
Sonderkommando, 49n20, 69, 75, 83n23, 147n21; experiences of, 41–43
songs, 127; singers and, 35
Son of Saul (film), 63–66, *74*; after-effect of, 66–67
sophism, 19n14
sound, 70, 84n30; exhibits and, 177
speech acts, 55, 148n25
Spielberg, Steven, 51–81
Spitzer, Leo, 4; on position, 32
stereotypes, 57
Still Alive: A Holocaust Girlhood Remembered (Klüger), 88
St. Louis Holocaust Museum and Education Center, 178
stories, 98, 103; access and, 34; activity and, 136; bodies and, 137; deference of, 95; storytelling and, 42; survivors and, 82n13; tattoos and, 133
Streicher, Julius, 15
Stuecke (pieces), 76
Der Sturmer, 15
subjective affects, 163–64
subjectivities, 77; as multiple, 89
survivors, 31, 49n20, 82n8; celebration and, 128, 142; children as, 6, 100; dialogic between, 91; isolation and, 133; stories and, 82n13; tattoos of, 136; testimonies of, 24

Talmud, 94
tattoos, 122; stories and, 133; of survivors, 136; as voluntary, 132
technology, 28, 85n39; education and, 80
terminology, 17n1, 84n29, 146n3, 183n44; Auschwitz as, 129; meaning and, 188; Nazi as, 104; public memory and, 81n4; queer as, 3
testimonies, 85n38, 131, 148n25; Elias and, 38–39; engagement with, 44; genocide and, 80–81; of survivors, 24; of women, 36

texts, 9–10, 109; collaboration as, 114nn1–2; generations and, 121–46; memory building and, 112; perspectives on, 88
theoretical framework, 6–11; memorialization and, 26
Theresienstadt family camp, 32, 48n11
The Times-Picayune, 110
time, 53; conflagration of, 41
tools, 80
touch, 70
trauma, 124, 182n31; Holocaust as, 153; sites of, 128
trials, 97
tropes, 60, 73, 126
Troubled Memory (Levy, A.), 109
truth, 3, 84n29; emotions and, 38; fiction and, 69; historians and, 101–2; narratives and, 64; perception of, 53

United Nations, 15–16
United States, 118n31, 148n22; audiences in, 58, 103; neo-Nazism in, 98; policies of, 16; silence and, 185; USHMM and, 182n37
United States Holocaust Memorial Museum (USHMM), 24, 181n29; archives at, 48n12; outtakes at, 87; place and space of, 157–58; *Shoah* reels at, 33; Silberman Fellowship at, 37; United States and, 182n37
Uris, Leon, 1
USHMM. *See* United States Holocaust Memorial Museum

value, 24, 145; memory and, 91
verisimilitude, 83n19
victims, 71
viewing community, 55–56, 81n6
visibility, 156; women and, 104
voice: absence of, 31; action and, 108–11; agency and, 31; multiplication of, 152; women and, 46

vulnerability, 143

Wachsmann, Nikolaus, 71
Warsaw Ghetto Uprising, 36
Weiter Leben (Klüger), 100
white supremacists, 118n31, 119n37, 140; in Charlottesville, VA., 185; Duke as, 87, 107. *See also* neo-Nazism
Wiesel, Elie, 96, 116n14, 117n18
Wilder, Billy, 126
women, 31, 48n10; activism and, 114n1; auto/biography and, 94; collaboration and, 49n16; deferred memories and, 87–114; exclusion of, 33, 35; memoirs and, 85n36; reproductive rights and, 44; resilience of, 39; resistance and, 37–38, 73; testimonies of, 36; tropes and, 60; visibility and, 104; voices of, 46
World War II, 1
writing, 106, 114, 134, 146n1; act of, 40, 55; memory and, 88

xenophobia, 47

Yad Vashem museum, 151–54
Young, James E., 154
YouTube, 145

Zelizer, Barbie, 10, 20n25, 147n13; on representations, 65
Zitler, Shep, 92, 112
Zyklon B gas, 70

About the Author

Lisa A. Costello, Ph.D. is an interdisciplinary scholar and activist with articles on the Holocaust, rhetoric, writing, feminism, and/or gender. *American Public Memory and the Holocaust: Performing Gender, Shifting Orientations* is her first monograph. She is an Associate Professor in Writing and Linguistics and teaches courses in writing, rhetoric, gender, and the Holocaust and is the Director of the Women's, Gender, and Sexuality Studies Program at Georgia Southern University. She has participated in seminars at the United States Holocaust Memorial Museum and the Holocaust Educational Foundation.

www.ingramcontent.com/pod-product-compliance
Lightning Source LLC
Chambersburg PA
CBHW070829300426
44111CB00014B/2494